HELPING THE SUICIDAL PERSON

Tips and Techniques for Professionals

STACEY FREEDENTHAL

Routledge
Taylor & Francis Group

NEW YORK AND LONDON

First published 2018
by Routledge
711 Third Avenue, New York, NY 10017

and by Routledge
2 Park Square, Milton Park, Abingdon, Oxon, OX14 4RN

Routledge is an imprint of the Taylor & Francis Group, an informa business

© 2018 Stacey Freedenthal

Library of Congress Cataloging-in-Publication Data
A catalog record for this book has been requested

ISBN: 978-1-138-94694-1 (hbk)
ISBN: 978-1-138-94695-8 (pbk)
ISBN: 978-1-315-66582-5 (ebk)

Typeset in Baskerville
by Wearset Ltd, Boldon, Tyne and Wear
Printed and bound by CPI Group (UK) Ltd, Croydon, CR0 4YY

This book is dedicated to all those lost to suicide's campaign, to those who made it out alive, and to those who battle, still.

Contents

Acknowledgments

To my clients, past and present, who taught me more about helping the suicidal person than any books, classes, or training ever could; to my students at the University of Denver Graduate School of Social Work, who enriched my learning with their questions and contributions; to my loving husband Pete and our son Ian, who both provided tremendous support, patience, and good cheer; to my mom, who continued in her role as my lifelong cheerleader; to my dad, who, weeks before he died, told me he was certain I would write this book; to my sisters, who were available for big-sisterly advice; to my friend Tamara Suttle, who gave me much-needed motivational advice, reviewed the book proposal, and gave me feedback on portions of the manuscript; to my colleague Thomas Ellis, who generously shared his expertise in suicidology when reviewing the proposal and manuscript; to my coach Beth Vagle, who helped me sustain focus and momentum during this large project; to my editor Anna Moore, who made publishing this book possible – to all these people, and to others not named here, I give my gratitude for your support. Thank you.

Author's Notes

For the sake of gender neutrality, this book uses the pronouns "they," "them," or "their" when referring generically to an individual.

All of the author's clinical case scenarios are fictional, and any resemblance to a person is coincidental.

About the Author

A licensed clinical social worker, I have more than 20 years of experience in the field of suicide prevention. Beginning with my volunteer work as a suicide hotline counselor in Dallas in 1995, I have worked with hundreds of people who considered suicide, attempted suicide, or experienced the suicide of a family member, friend, or someone else important to them. My work has taken place in psychiatric and medical emergency rooms, counseling centers, and psychotherapy offices.

Almost every facet of my professional life pertains to suicide prevention in some way. As a psychotherapist, my practice specializes in helping people touched by suicide, whether they struggle with suicidal thoughts, tried to die by suicide, or lost someone they love to suicide. As an associate professor at the University of Denver Graduate School of Social Work, I teach a course on suicide assessment and intervention, and I conduct research on suicidal individuals' experiences. I have authored or co-authored dozens of peer-reviewed scholarly articles and conference presentations on suicide-related topics such as the measurement of suicidal intent, help-seeking by suicidal youth, and suicidal individuals' reasons for living. For my website www.speakingofsuicide.com, I have written dozens of articles for suicidal people, their loved ones, and professionals who help them. As of January 2017, the website was receiving more than 80,000 visitors per month.

Even with all my years of experience, research, and knowledge, the mysteries of the suicidal mind continue to humble me. As a result, I pursue as much knowledge as possible about how to help people who are tempted, sometimes tormented, by suicide's call. My pursuit has led me to attend many hours of training and conferences, to read countless articles and books on suicide prevention, and to immerse myself in the mind of suicidal individuals by reading their memoirs, fiction, and poetry.

These endeavors have taught me so much about helping suicidal people that I want to share my knowledge with as many helping professionals as possible. This book is the result. May it broaden your knowledge and skills, and may it positively touch the lives of suicidal people who come to you for help.

Introduction

Every year, tens of thousands of mental health professionals sit face to face with people who reveal a wish to stop living. In the U.S. alone, in a single year, an estimated 10 million adults and 2 million adolescents seriously consider suicide (Substance Abuse and Mental Health Services Administration, 2005; Lipari et al., 2015). Of these, more than 40,000 die by suicide. Suicide's devastation underscores the importance of solid training and skills in suicide risk assessment and intervention. Even so, graduate education in schools of psychology, social work, counseling, and marriage and family therapy include little training on how to help a suicidal person, according to the psychologist William Schmitz and colleagues (2012). They note: "Competence in the assessment of suicidality is an essential clinical skill that has consistently been overlooked and dismissed by the colleges, universities, clinical training sites, and licensing bodies that prepare mental health professionals" (p. 294). Given suicide's profound toll, this omission is stunning.

These gaps in education often leave professionals ill-equipped to answer crucial questions about helping people at risk for suicide:

- What can therapists say and do (and *not* say and do) to learn whether a person is considering suicide?
- What are fruitful and sensitive ways to explore the depths of the person's suicidal wishes?
- How can therapists gain insight into the suicidal person's level of danger, and what can they do to help ensure the person's survival?

- How can therapists help the suicidal person respond constructively to destructive thoughts, rediscover hope, diminish the pain that leads to suicidal thinking, shed the wish to die, and build resilience?

The aim of this book is to answer those questions.

About the Book

This book provides a highly practical toolbox for mental health professionals. Some books on working with suicidal clients focus primarily on suicide risk assessment, not treatment. Those that go beyond risk assessment often are either academic in tone or quasi-treatment manuals focused on a single theory or approach, leaving out the many other techniques that abound. *Helping the Suicidal Person: Tips and Techniques for Professionals* is different. In a conversational style, it gives concrete advice for real-world practice. The techniques described here can be interspersed into any type of therapy, no matter what your theoretical orientation is, and no matter whether it's the client's first, tenth, or one-hundredth session with you. Every tip is followed by a clinical vignette or, less commonly, an elaboration on a technique.

The book covers diverse aspects of helping the suicidal person, starting with examining your own personal experiences and fears, and moving into covering the essential areas of risk assessment, safety planning, and treatment planning, and then providing a rich assortment of tips for reducing the person's suicidal danger and rebuilding the wish to live. The tips generally are ordered according to where in the therapeutic process you would encounter the specific issue with a person. For example, you need to be well-versed in techniques for openly discussing suicide and uncovering suicidal ideation in order to conduct a solid risk assessment, so those tips come first. A section on helping the person after a suicide attempt comes late in the book because it will not apply to all suicidal individuals.

The tips and techniques come from a wide variety of theories and interventions, including cognitive behavior therapy, dialectical behavior therapy, acceptance and commitment therapy, mindfulness-based cognitive therapy, solution-focused therapy, problem-solving therapy, the Collaborative Assessment and Management of Suicidality, and the Attempted Suicide Short Intervention Program. Other tips draw from professionals' years of experience, including my own.

A Note about Empirically Supported Treatments

Mental health professionals are called upon to use techniques that work. With suicidal people, effective treatments truly can make the difference between life and death. Additionally, the scarcity and expense of resources make it important to use interventions with an established record of effectiveness. The use of empirically supported treatments in suicide prevention, however, is tempered by the constraints of real-world practice and research.

Suicide research presents extraordinary challenges. Foremost, the rarity of suicide limits our ability to study it. To detect whether an intervention can reduce suicide by 15% in one year in the general population, researchers would need to give the intervention to 13 million people (Gunnell & Frankel, 1994). Researchers would need a much smaller sample if they used a high-risk sample, such as people who recently attempted suicide. Even so, such a study would still require 45,000 people (Gunnell & Frankel, 1994).

As a result of these logistical challenges, studies tend to look at whether an intervention reduces suicidal ideation and suicide attempts, not suicide itself. Several treatments have demonstrated effectiveness at reducing suicidal ideation or suicide attempts, including cognitive behavior therapy, dialectical behavior therapy, mindfulness-based cognitive therapy, problem-solving therapy, the Collaborative Assessment and Management of Suicidality, and the Attempted Suicide Short Intervention Program. Ideally, you will learn one or more of these empirically supported interventions in depth and adhere to its guidelines. Many of the book's tips and techniques draw from these established interventions.

Helping the Suicidal Person: Tips and Techniques for Professionals also contains tips and techniques that have no research studies documenting their effectiveness in isolation of other techniques, if at all. Many of the suggestions are simply common sense. To name just a few examples: Understand how your own biases can affect your work with suicidal individuals. Frankly explore the person's suicidal thoughts, planning, and intent. Respond with empathy, validation, and a sincere desire to understand. Understand the cultural context of the person's suicidal thoughts. Seek consultation.

A technique's lack of *evidence* of effectiveness is not the same as lack of *effectiveness*. Oftentimes, it simply means that the intervention has not yet been tested. Consider the case of parachutes. As a satirical (but factual) research article cleverly noted, no randomized controlled trial demonstrates that a parachute saves lives when someone jumps out of an airplane (Smith & Pell, 2003). Real-world experience takes precedence over the lack of research when it comes to parachutes. The same context exists for many techniques for reducing suicide risk.

Even when evidence of effectiveness exists, people often do not conform to what research findings predict. It is up to you to monitor whether your interventions help your unique clients. After all, in the research landscape of randomized controlled trials and sophisticated statistical analyses of vast data sets, a lone person's outcomes are considered the least important evidence of effectiveness. To that person, those outcomes are the most important of all.

A Note about the Term "Suicidal"

For the sake of parsimony, I use the term "suicidal" throughout the book to characterize anybody who is thinking of ending their life. Suicidality exists in degrees. At one end of the continuum are people who only occasionally have suicidal thoughts and reject them immediately. At the other end are people so consumed by suicidal urges that they are moments away from ending their life. Every suicidal person needs a safe and nonjudgmental space to discuss suicidal wishes (*Tips 8–18*) and a comprehensive suicide risk assessment (*Tips 19–33*). Beyond that, the tips and techniques to use depend on where the person lies on the continuum of suicidality.

A person who unequivocally intends to die by suicide *today* is not in a place to make a hope kit (*Tip 64*), come up with coping statements (*Tip 69*), or practice mindfulness (*Tip 74*). Instead, you will want to focus on maintaining the person's safety, whether via hospitalization (*Tip 35*), safety planning (*Tip 38*), removal of firearms from the home (*Tip 40*), reducing access to other means for suicide (*Tip 41*), or some combination of those measures. Where extreme risk for suicide is not present, the agenda moves on to planning treatment (*Tips 44–50*), reducing psychological pain (*Tips 51–54*), exploiting the person's ambivalence about suicide (*Tips 55–59*), building hope (*Tips 60–65*), helping the person change or defuse suicidal thoughts (*Tips 66–72*), strengthening coping skills (*Tips 73–76*), and working to prevent another suicidal crisis (*Tips 85–89*).

In short, this book describes tips and techniques for helping anyone who lies anywhere on the suicidal spectrum, but not all techniques are appropriate with everyone. You should use these techniques according to your clients' unique needs and circumstances.

Works Cited

Gunnell, D., & Frankel, S. (1994). Prevention of suicide: Aspirations and evidence. *British Medical Journal, 308*(6938), 1227–1234.

Lipari, R., Piscopo, K., Kroutil, L. A., & Miller, G. K. (2015). Suicidal thoughts and behavior among adults: Results from the 2014 National Survey on Drug Use and Health. *NSDUH Data Review.* Rockville, MD: Substance Abuse and Mental Health Services Administration.

Schmitz, W. M., Allen, M. H., Feldman, B. N., Gutin, N. J., Jahn, D. R., Kleespies, P. M., … & Simpson, S. (2012). Preventing suicide through improved training in suicide risk assessment and care: An American Association of Suicidology task force report addressing serious gaps in US mental health training. *Suicide and Life-Threatening Behavior, 42*(3), 292–304.

Smith, G. C., & Pell, J. P. (2003). Parachute use to prevent death and major trauma related to gravitational challenge: Systematic review of randomised controlled trials. *British Medical Journal, 327*(7429), 1459.

Substance Abuse and Mental Health Services Administration. (2005). Suicidal thoughts among youths aged 12 to 17 with major depressive episode. *The NSDUH Report: National Survey on Drug Use and Health.* Rockville, MD: Author.

one
Understanding Suicide and You

Tip 1: Reflect on Your Biases about Suicide

"Your ethical, moral, and philosophical conceptualization of suicide will have direct and indirect influence on your clinical practice."
Dana Worchel and Robin Gearing
(2010, p. 4)

Mental health professionals need to have a solid understanding of their attitudes toward suicide and suicidal behavior. Whether they consider suicide to be a sin or a right, their stance can negatively influence assessment and treatment, even outside of their awareness. Professionals who view suicide as unequivocally wrong may have difficulty listening nonjudgmentally as a person describes compelling reasons for wanting to die by suicide. Conversely, people who view suicide as permissible might hesitate to thwart an individual's suicide, leading to an avoidable tragedy. In many smaller ways, a professional's stance toward suicide prevention can disrupt treatment.

To examine your attitudes toward suicide prevention, consider the following questions:

- What do you believe about people who attempt or die by suicide?
- Do you believe suicide should always be prevented? Why or why not? And if you do not believe it should always be prevented, under what circumstances should a person be permitted to die by suicide without intervention?

- Do you view suicide as selfish? Why or why not?
- Do you view suicide as cowardly? Why or why not?
- Is suicide a sin? Again, why or why not?
- Under what circumstances would you consider suicide for yourself? (If it seems incomprehensible to want to kill yourself, why?)

The purpose of the questions above is to jump-start your honest examination of your suicide-related beliefs. There are no right or wrong answers. However, myths, biases, and logical inconsistencies shape some people's answers, and they are considered below.

Should Suicide Always Be Prevented?

This question, like the others, contains no right or wrong answer, but inconsistency can be revealing. Examine whether your response differs based on the person's age, physical health, mental health, or life circumstances. Also consider how your views on suicide prevention could affect how you respond to a suicidal person, and what safeguards you take (or neglect to take) to ensure that your views do not interfere with providing the most effective and ethical care possible to the suicidal person.

Is Suicide Selfish?

Many people lament that people who die by suicide hurt loved ones and damage the community as a whole (Hecht, 2013). The man whose suicide leaves behind a young widow to raise four children on her own, the teacher whose suicide profoundly scars her students – these kinds of deaths provoke accusations of selfishness. Almost always, however, people who die by suicide do so under the duress of mental illness, hopelessness, trauma, pain, or some other seemingly inexorable problem. It is questionable whether the person is to blame for actions that stem from forces beyond the person's control.

The psychologist Thomas Joiner (2010) also disputes the notion of selfishness by pointing out that many people who attempt or die by suicide actually want to help the people they love, not hurt them. Falling for the lies of depression, hopelessness, or other mental pain, they often believe, mostly to the astonishment of their family and friends, that their suicide will make life easier for others. However misguided it may be, the wish to spare others is hardly selfish.

Is Suicide Cowardly?

Some people view suicide as "taking the easy way out." Others note that it requires courage to overcome the survival instinct and actually end one's life (Joiner, 2010).

Is Suicide a Sin?

This question summons deeply personal beliefs. Whatever your beliefs, it is worth noting that the major world religions once condemned suicide universally but now make allowances for suicide that occurs as a result of mental illness or impairment (Nelson et al., 2012).

In Closing

It is impossible to be neutral about suicide. Bias is inescapable. To not care one way or the other allows for the possibility that suicide should not always be prevented, which in itself is a bias. Uncover your own biases, and make a plan for how to help someone in spite of them.

The Judgmental Therapist

A clinical social worker for five years, Ashley held negative judgments about suicide. She believed suicide to be a sin, selfish, and cowardly. As a result, when she asked a client if they were thinking of dying by suicide and the person said no, she invariably responded by exclaiming, "Oh, good!" Sometimes she would elaborate: "People who kill themselves are only thinking of themselves. It devastates those left behind." Her clients learned quickly that if indeed one day they did consider suicide, Ashley would judge them negatively. When that day came, some chose not to tell her, and others left treatment altogether. For the sake of her clients, when a client reports that they are not considering suicide, a better response would be: "Would you be willing to tell me in the future if that changes for you?"

Works Cited

Hecht, J. M. (2013). *Stay: A history of suicide and the philosophies against it.* New Haven, CT: Yale University Press.

Joiner, T. (2010). *Myths about suicide.* Cambridge, MA: Harvard University Press.

Nelson, G., Hanna, R., Houri, A., & Klimes-Dougan, B. (2012). Protective functions of religious traditions for suicide risk. *Suicidology Online, 3,* 59–71.

Worchel, D., & Gearing, R. E. (2010). *Suicide assessment and treatment: Empirical and evidence-based practices.* New York, NY: Springer Publishing.

Tip 2: Take Stock of Your Experiences with Suicide (or Lack Thereof)

"Our own histories with suicide, whether that be our own suicidality, the loss of a loved one to suicide, or the death of a former patient to suicide, will greatly impact how we approach and respond to people who actively think about suicide ..."

Nadine Kaslow
(in Pope and Vasquez, 2016, p. 324)

Many mental health professionals have personal experience with suicide or suicidality. In one study of psychiatrists, psychiatric nurses, psychologists, and social workers, 43% reported ever having considered suicide, and 5% had made a suicide attempt (Ramberg & Wasserman, 2000). If mental health professionals are representative of the general population, then we can assume that half have known someone personally who has died by suicide, with almost 40% of those people reporting that the person who died was a family member (Cerel et al., 2016). Suicide also touches professionals in their work. Studies indicate that 23% of professional counselors, 30% of psychologists and social workers, and 50% of psychiatrists have had a client die by suicide (McAdams & Foster, 2000; Jacobson et al., 2004; Ruskin et al., 2004).

These experiences with suicide cannot help but influence one's professional work with suicidal individuals. On the positive side, people with "lived experience" often have keen insight and empathy for others on similar journeys. On the negative side, there is the danger that lived experience with suicidality or suicide loss can give rise to rescue fantasies, overidentification, boundary violations, and even outright impairment. Subtler effects can also occur, such as avoiding asking or talking about suicide.

Professionals who lost someone to suicide or experienced suicidality themselves need to explore how their experiences positively and negatively affect the ways that they talk about suicide with clients and the actions that they take (or do not take) as a result. If your self-examination reveals areas of concern, then awareness is not enough. You also need a strategy to manage your reactions to avoid doing harm. In general, personal psychotherapy, supervision, and consultation can help prevent past troubles from intruding on your present effectiveness.

Can Suicidal Professionals Help Suicidal People?

Many people with suicidal thoughts manage to observe the thoughts dispassionately, easily resist any urges to act on them, and recognize them as a symptom, not a powerful force or fact. This is a goal for our clients and a reality for many mental health professionals afflicted with a chronic mental disorder such as major depression or bipolar disorder. In such cases, when the professional is detached from their suicidal thoughts and lacks any intent to act on them, then it usually is appropriate to continue seeing clients.

If the suicidal thoughts gain strength and become seductive, then the professional must take extra measures to ensure fitness for practice. Therapists caught up in suicidal thinking can do harm to the people they are there to help. For example, a client's articulation of suicidal thoughts can draw the helping professional into an internal debate about whether to die by suicide, making it impossible for the professional to devote their full attention to the client. The psychiatrist Shawn Shea (2011) recommends that mental health professionals who are experiencing suicidal thoughts receive mental health treatment and, separately, consultation or supervision. The treatment provider and the supervisor or consultant should communicate with each other and work collaboratively with the suicidal professional to assess whether the person can continue seeing clients without doing harm.

Can Professionals Without Lived Experience Help Suicidal People?

A person's lived experience with suicidality need not be harmful, and it can actually be helpful. People who have survived a suicidal crisis may have insights into the experience that others lack. Jack Gorman, a former psychiatrist, writes of the awakening he had when, after decades of treating suicidal patients, he became dangerously suicidal. "I now realize that I never really understood what it means to want to die," he wrote in 2013. Gorman goes on to state that he had believed that suicidal individuals were frightened and confused by their self-destructive urges. Then he learned firsthand that suicide could seem perfectly rational, ethical, and even necessary to the suicidal person.

A suicidal history is certainly not a requirement for effectively and empathically helping suicidal individuals, just as someone without a history of addiction can be a good addictions counselor. But some people who have never personally experienced suicidal thoughts struggle to understand how someone could want to end their life. If that applies to you, I recommend reading memoirs by people who have survived a suicidal crisis. Here are just a few examples in which the author does a superb job portraying suicidal experiences:

- *Cracked, Not Broken: Surviving and Thriving after a Suicide Attempt*, by Kevin Hines (Rowman & Littlefield Publishers);
- *An Unquiet Mind: A Memoir of Moods and Madness*, by Kay Redfield Jamison (Vintage Books);
- *This Is How It Feels: A Memoir: Attempting Suicide and Finding Life*, by Craig Miller (CreateSpace Independent Publishing);

- *Darkness Visible: A Memoir of Madness*, by William Styron (Random House);
- *Waking Up: Climbing through the Darkness*, by Terry L. Wise (Missing Peace, LLC).

"Now I React with Intention and Awareness"

"Mama, where's Daddy?" Family lore has it that those were the first words Daquan ever spoke, when he was almost two years old, just a few weeks after his father died by suicide. In adolescence, Daquan faced his own suicidal thoughts. He attempted suicide twice, once at the age of 16 and again at 22, before he was diagnosed with bipolar disorder and stabilized with medication. Now 36 and a school psychologist, Daquan works at a high school for at-risk students. Students often disclose to Daquan that they are thinking about suicide or have made an attempt.

At first, when Daquan started working at the school five years earlier, talking with suicidal students triggered painful memories and grief. A few times, he had to lock himself in his office and cry at his desk. Then he found himself avoiding the topic of suicide or changing the subject when students brought it up. Eventually, he resumed therapy and explored the open wounds from his father's suicide and his own suicide attempts, as well as the gifts of insight and empathy that his experiences provided.

Daquan says the most valuable aspect of therapy was learning to ground himself in the present moment so that he could focus on the needs of the student sitting in front of him, instead of getting lost in his past trauma. "I'm no longer on auto-pilot," he says. "Now I react with intention and awareness. That wasn't always the case."

Works Cited

Cerel, J., Maple, M., De Venne, J. V., Moore, M., Flaherty, C., & Brown, M. (2016). Exposure to suicide in the community: Prevalence and correlates in one U.S. state. *Public Health Reports, 131*(1), 100–107.

Gorman, J. (2013). *I never really understood what it means to want to die.* Retrieved 31 January, 2017, from http://attemptsurvivors.com/2013/04/01/i-never-really-understood-what-it-means-to-want-to-die/.

Jacobson, J. M., Ting, L., Sanders, S., & Harrington, D. (2004). Prevalence of and reactions to fatal and nonfatal client suicidal behavior: A national study of mental health social workers. *Omega: Journal of Death and Dying, 49*(3), 237–248.

McAdams III, C. R., & Foster, V. A. (2000). Client suicide: Its frequency and impact on counselors. *Journal of Mental Health Counseling, 22*(2), 107–121.

Pope, K. S., & Vasquez, M. J. T. (2016). Responding to suicidal risk. In *Ethics in psychotherapy and counseling: A practical guide* (6th ed., pp. 314–334). Hoboken, NJ: John Wiley & Sons.

Ramberg, I. L., & Wasserman, D. (2000). Prevalence of reported suicidal behaviour in the general population and mental health-care staff. *Psychological Medicine, 30*(5), 1189–1196.

Ruskin, R., Sakinofsky, I., Bagby, R. M., Dickens, S., & Sousa, M. G. (2004). Impact of patient suicide on psychiatrists and psychiatric trainees. *Academic Psychiatry, 28*(2), 104–110.

Shea, S. C. (2011). *The practical art of suicide assessment: A guide for mental health professionals and substance abuse counselors.* Stoddard, NH: Mental Health Presses.

Tip 3: Confront "Suicide Anxiety"

"The treater who is held emotionally hostage by terror of the patient's suicide cannot respond empathically and helpfully."
Thomas Gutheil
(in Koekkoek et al. 2008, p. 203)

Almost every mental health professional fears the loss of a client to suicide (Pope & Tabachnick, 1993). It is a devastating outcome. In many cases, the professional feels overwhelming grief at the death of someone they cared about and tried to help. Feelings of incompetence, guilt, or inadequacy often emerge. Accusations of wrongdoing, a lawsuit, and a licensing board complaint may follow the suicide. Colleagues sometimes react judgmentally and insensitively. Many professionals experience post-traumatic stress symptoms, such as intrusive thoughts, images, and dreams about the suicide, as well as avoidance of the topic of suicide (Gutin et al., 2011). The prospect of losing a client to suicide creates "suicide anxiety" – a feeling of unease so potent that some professionals refuse to accept suicidal clients or they avoid the topic of suicide altogether.

Some degree of anxiety when helping suicidal individuals is healthy. A life is at stake. Healthy fear keeps people careful and attentive to danger. The psychotherapist Andrew Reeves (2010) notes, "I would be concerned about any counselor who claimed never to have felt anxiety or apprehension when working with suicidal potential, and would further wonder whether they are sufficiently present in their work to practice safely and ethically" (p. 143). Especially in cases of high suicide risk, to never have any fear could suggest a degree of callousness or burnout that inhibits empathy.

The challenge is to not be immobilized by fear or, on the other hand, to overreact. Fearful professionals may avoid the topic of suicide, conduct only a cursory suicide risk assessment, and provide superficial interventions (Jahn et al., 2016). On top of that, unacknowledged fear can lead professionals to take actions primarily, even if unconsciously, for their own benefit. These actions, such as unnecessary hospitalization, can help relieve the professional's anxiety but hurt the suicidal person in the process (*Tip 36*).

Work to understand your own anxiety and fears. It can help to ask yourself these questions:

- *"What scares me about trying to help a suicidal person?"*
- *"What might I do differently if I were not so afraid?"*

Uncovering and challenging your suicide anxiety will help you to remain attentive when a client describes, often in painful ways that are difficult to hear, how desperately they want to end their life.

Self-awareness helps, and so does taking action. Become as educated and skilled as you can about effectively helping suicidal people. Talk through your fears with others, such as colleagues, a supervisor, a consultant (*Tip 43*), or a psychotherapist. Cognitive-behavioral therapy, for example, can help you to evaluate the validity and helpfulness of your anxious thoughts, to catch yourself in cognitive distortions, and to not let your anxiety overtake you at the suicidal person's expense.

As I noted earlier, some people fear losing a client to suicide so much that they refuse to treat suicidal individuals. This is regrettable. Mental health professionals have an ethical obligation to achieve and maintain competence in their area of practice. The need for suicide assessment and intervention skills spans *all* areas of practice. So if you are haunted by the prospect of a client's suicide, rather than hide, seek out the training, knowledge, and support that you need to work effectively with suicidal individuals, even when you are afraid.

"I Dodged a Bullet"

"I really need to see someone," a stranger on the line said. "Do you have any openings?"

Gabriel, a mental health counselor, invited the man to tell him more about his situation. The caller described a bleak period of depression. He felt worthless. He had insomnia. Nothing gave him joy or pleasure. And he found himself occasionally thinking of suicide.

Fear swept through Gabriel. When suicide was on the table, he thought only of the possible tragic endings, not the possibilities for helping someone to heal, grow, and thrive. What if he accepted this suicidal stranger as his client, and the man died? Others might blame him. Worse, he thought, he might never forgive himself.

"I don't think I'm the person to help you," he told the man. "If you're having suicidal thoughts, you should go to an emergency room right away for an evaluation."

"But I'm not in an emergency. I mean, yeah, I'm thinking of suicide. But I'm not really going to do it. Can't you do the evaluation?"

Gabriel said it was not his area of expertise and again referred him to an emergency room. The man felt alone and rejected. If a mental health professional could not bear to hear him talk about suicide without "freaking out," he thought, then who could?

Meanwhile, Gabriel felt relieved. "I dodged a bullet," he thought, without giving any thought to the effects that his avoidance had on the young man who had called out to him for help.

Works Cited

Gutin, N., McGann, V. L., & Jordan, J. R. (2011). The impact of suicide on professional caregivers. In J. R. Jordan & J. L. McIntosh (Eds.), *Grief after suicide: Understanding the consequences and caring for the survivors* (pp. 93–111). New York, NY: Routledge.

Jahn, D. R., Quinnett, P., & Ries, R. (2016). The influence of training and experience on mental health practitioners' comfort working with suicidal individuals. *Professional Psychology: Research and Practice, 47*(2), 130–138.

Koekkoek, B., Gunderson, J. G., Kaasenbrood, A., & Gutheil, T. G. (2008). Chronic suicidality in a physician: An alliance yet to become therapeutic. *Harvard Review of Psychiatry, 16*(3), 195–204.

Pope, K. S., & Tabachnick, B. G. (1993). Therapists' anger, hate, fear, and sexual feelings: National survey of therapist responses, client characteristics, critical events, formal complaints, and training. *Professional Psychology: Research and Practice, 24*(2), 142.

Reeves, A. (2010). *Counselling suicidal clients.* London: Sage Publications.

Tip 4: Be Alert to Negative Feelings Toward the Suicidal Person

"Whether it be unresolved issues from the clinician's past being triggered or realistic reactions to the patient's behaviors, the reactions of clinicians towards patients may result in feelings of incompetence, hopelessness, demoralization, hostility, and/or withdrawal from emotional involvement with the client."

Noel Hunter
(2015, p. 38)

Negative reactions to suicidal individuals are so common that a classic article focuses solely on "countertransference hate" (Maltsberger & Buie, 1996). A suicidal person may provoke negative reactions in various ways. The person might criticize you or become angry that you are not helping them to feel better. The person might do things that seem to undermine your work together, such as arrive late for appointments or miss them altogether, reject reasonable recommendations, and hide that they feel suicidal. And sometimes the suicidal person, despite working hard at getting better, might still get worse. This lack of progress itself can inspire feelings of impotence, anger, and resentment, whether rational or not, in the helping professional.

Pay attention to any negative judgments and emotions that arise when you work with a suicidal person. Unchecked aversion or malice can result in your withholding concern and empathy, making injudicious comments, reacting with impatience, or even abandoning the suicidal person (Maltsberger & Buie, 1996). If you find yourself having a negative reaction to a suicidal client, consider discussing your situation with a consultant (*Tip 43*) or your own therapist. Also, these questions can help you critically examine your reactions:

- "Am I angry that this person is not improving despite my hard work? If so, am I blaming the person for this lack of improvement when it would be more appropriate (and compassionate) to blame their illness, stress, or pain?"
- "Am I taking it personally that this person is not improving? Do I view it as an insult when they complain that I am not helping? Are there genuinely areas where my clinical approach could be improved? If so, how can I better help this person?"
- "Do I resent that the suicidal person has power over me, because they can die by suicide regardless of my efforts and wishes? If so, how can I accept that reality without taking out my resentment on the person?"
- "Do I feel manipulated, blackmailed, or coerced by the suicidal person? If so, how am I responding in ways that might reinforce such behaviors? Am I maintaining proper boundaries and resisting a sense of obligation to rescue the person?"

Beware of personalizing. The suicidal person is not intentionally trying to hurt you by remaining suicidal or getting worse. Suicidal people typically experience painful emotions, distorted thoughts, and in a great many cases mental illness or post-traumatic responses. To view their lack of recovery as malevolent is akin to blaming a person with epilepsy for spilling coffee on your carpet while they are having a seizure.

Viewing the suicidal process as something that happens to the person, rather than something that the person orchestrates, can help you cultivate compassion and patience. Any perceived advantage that may come to the suicidal person, whether that advantage is increased attention, support, or power, typically is an accidental byproduct, not an explicit objective, of the suicidal person's actions. As the psychologist Alec Miller and colleagues (2007) state, "The fact that the therapist feels manipulated does not mean that manipulation was the client's intent" (p. 81).

Where the suicidal person does seem to use suicidal behavior as a means to curry attention, love, or support, remember that the person engages in such actions *because they work* (Linehan, 1993). The prospect of suicide is often a potent motivator for others to rally around the hurting person, to show they care, and to do whatever they can to help. For people who seldom experience such support, others' concern can impart a sad message: *Nobody cares about me unless they think I am going to die.* The person might not even be consciously aware of this dynamic.

The psychologist Marsha Linehan (1993), who developed dialectical behavior therapy, emphasizes the need for *phenomenological empathy* – that is, an empathic stance that recognizes these fundamental assumptions: The suicidal person is doing the best they can. The person wants to improve. It is unfair to blame the person for not using skills that they do not yet have. The therapist needs to regard with equal compassion their own responses, even when they experience feelings of anger and impatience. Such feelings are to be experienced with curiosity, not suppressed or condemned.

"Is She Dead?"

The psychiatrist checked the waiting room for the fifth time in 15 minutes. His patient, Amber, still was not there. "She's late again," he thought. "Or did she do it this time? *Is she dead?*"

Amber, 25, had been his patient for four months. During that time, there was seldom a session in which she did not report having vivid suicidal thoughts. Each time, she did not meet criteria to be hospitalized. She lacked intent, or she had a half-hearted plan to travel across the country and jump off the Golden Gate Bridge, and she could not afford the airfare. That sort of thing. But still, when she was late for sessions – which was more often than not – the psychiatrist's thoughts returned to the same question: *Is she dead?*

Five more minutes, he thought. *Five more minutes, and then I call her.* Just as those five minutes were almost up, Amber bounded into the room, a cup from Starbucks in one hand, her cell phone in the other. She sat down with a smile, apologized for being late, and, without pausing, launched into an update about her week.

In a flash, the psychiatrist's concern gave way to anger. *How could she be so inconsiderate? Couldn't she at least have the courtesy to call?* If Amber had been a friend and not a patient, he might have spoken those thoughts aloud. Instead, he took a deep breath, silently acknowledged his anger, and focused on the person sitting in front of him. As he did so, he remained curious about his anger. He knew he needed to say something, but it needed to be for her benefit, not his. He could get his own needs met later, in consultation with a colleague.

After Amber breathlessly gave her update, he brought up her habitual lateness. He explored with her what it might mean, in terms of her prioritization of therapy and her motivation to work on her issues. He expressed empathy about her struggles and recognized that she was doing the best she could.

He also told her of his concern when she did not come on time. "I worry," he said. "I worry that you might have acted on your suicidal thoughts."

When he said this, Amber's eyes welled with tears. "It didn't occur to me that you'd care," she said. "It always feels like nobody cares if I live or die."

The psychiatrist's anger dissipated as he took in what it must feel like to be Amber, in all of her pain. Yet it was his anger that had gotten him to this deeper level of empathy. He was grateful that he had greeted his anger with a stance of acceptance, curiosity, and restraint.

Works Cited

Hunter, N. (2015). Clinical trainees' personal history of suicidality and the effects on attitudes towards suicidal patients. *The New School Psychology Bulletin, 13*(1), 38–46.

Linehan, M. M. (1993). *Cognitive-behavioral treatment of borderline personality disorder.* New York, NY: Guilford Press.

Maltsberger, J. T., & Buie, D. H., Jr. (1996). Countertransference hate in the treatment of suicidal patients. In J. T. Maltsberger & M. J. Goldblatt (Eds.), *Essential papers on suicide* (pp. 269–289). New York, NY: New York University Press.

Miller, A. L., Rathus, J. H., & Linehan, M. M. (2007). *Dialectical behavior therapy with suicidal adolescents.* New York, NY: Guilford Press.

Tip 5: Reject the Savior Role

"Therapeutic concern cannot extend to an assumption of total responsibility for the patient's life. In short, the psychotherapist must avoid the trap of the omnipotent rescuer and instead convey to the patient a sense of enlightened caring and concern."
Bruce Bongar and Glenn Sullivan
(2013, p. 180)

Some mental health professionals relax their boundaries in their efforts to stop a person from dying by suicide. This can include significantly extending sessions or offering extra sessions at no charge, having long and frequent phone conversations between sessions, and forgiving no-shows despite having an otherwise firm cancellation policy. In extreme cases, professionals have actually welcomed a suicidal client into their home for visits, invited the person on family vacations, gone shopping or to dinner with the person, and visited the person's home (Gabbard, 2003). Professionals who cross boundaries, whether insidiously or egregiously, very often are driven by fear: *If I don't do this, the person might die.*

The problem with playing the role of rescuer is three-fold: It exhausts the mental health professional. It builds dependency in the client. And it does not necessarily succeed at preventing suicide. To the contrary, the psychiatrist Herbert Hendin (1996) notes that "a therapist's own inclination to see himself as the savior or rescuer of the suicidal patient" can perpetuate the person's suicidal behavior (p. 431). Hendin gives the example of a young woman who attempted suicide multiple times. Each time, she called her therapist immediately afterward. Each time, he rushed to wherever she was. Although the therapist might have felt he was keeping his client alive, he was not helping her to gain the skills she needed to live.

Even seemingly heroic measures may not save a life. Hendin tells of a different therapist who felt coerced by a client to call her every morning for a year, out of fear that she would die otherwise. Still, the client killed herself. Hendin concludes: "Had more effort been spent in challenging and understanding the patient's attempt to structure how and in what manner the therapist was to show interest, rather than gratifying the patient's demands, the therapy would have had more chance of success" (Hendin, 1996, p. 430).

For those reasons, it is necessary to be firm yet compassionate when you feel compelled to make exceptions for a client. There are times when late-night phone calls are necessary (*Tip 45*), when sessions must be extended in order to arrange a client's safe transport to a hospital, when you will forgive your cancellation fee because the client missed a session for an unavoidable reason. The trick is to know when you are relaxing boundaries out of therapeutic considerations, rather than out of fear, coercion, or the belief that no one else but you can help the suicidal person. The distinction between therapeutic considerations and your own self-interests sometimes is not clear. If in doubt, it's always best to seek consultation (*Tip 43*).

"Wow, Even My Shrink Doesn't Care About Me"

Tony, 34, called his psychologist on a Sunday afternoon. "I'm so lonely," he told her. "I'd be better off dead." The psychologist did a quick assessment and judged that Tony was not at high risk for suicide. She reviewed his safety plan with him and then moved to end the call. Tony said, "Wow, even my shrink doesn't care about me. Now I damn well want to kill myself."

At an earlier time in her career, that sort of comment would have moved the psychologist to stay on the phone longer. There were times she spent hours on the phone with a client in an effort to defuse the person's suicidal urges. But she learned the hard way that such a response can engender dependency and reinforce the suicidal communications. So she said: "I'm sorry that my needing to go causes you to feel rejected. This sounds like something we definitely need to talk about more in your next session. In the meantime, do you need to go to an emergency room to stay safe?"

Tony was silent for a few moments. "No," he said. "I'm not really going to kill myself." He paused again and then said softly, "I was angry."

Tony said he would follow his safety plan, starting with a jog to get his mind off of things. And he agreed to call his psychologist to set up an emergency appointment if the need arose before his next scheduled session.

Works Cited

Bongar, B., & Sullivan, G. (2013). *The suicidal patient: Clinical and legal standards of care.* Washington, DC: American Psychological Association.

Gabbard, G. O. (2003). Miscarriages of psychoanalytic treatment with suicidal patients. *The International Journal of Psychoanalysis, 84*(2), 249–261.

Hendin, H. (1996). Psychotherapy and suicide. In J. T. Maltsberger & M. J. Goldblatt (Eds.) *Essential papers on suicide* (pp. 427–441). New York, NY: New York University Press.

Tip 6: Maintain Hope

"The ongoing experience of bearing a patient's intense despair and hopelessness is extraordinarily difficult, and can erode one's own sense of hope."

Mark Schechter and colleagues
(2013, p. 319)

The suicidal mind tries to persuade the person it inhabits that there is no hope, that death is the only solution. The suicidal mind will try to persuade you, too. And you might even become persuaded. You might come to view the person's pain, paralysis, or despair as so unbearable that you become convinced that the person will die by suicide, or even that they should. Be careful. It is hard to lend a person hope if you yourself have none.

Elsewhere in this book, I discuss ways to help inspire hope in the suicidal person (*Tips 60–65*). Here, I provide some tips for *you* to maintain hope:

Embrace the opportunity for empathy. The hopelessness that you feel is probably a microcosm of the suicidal person's hopelessness. Look at what your feelings can teach you about the person's pain and needs.

Use consultation or psychotherapy. Another professional can help you to examine your sense of despair, to identify steps to take in the treatment that you might have overlooked, and to reconcile your sense of futility with the person's needs for change (*Tip 43*).

Find hope in the person's still being alive. Something has stopped the person from dying so far. Even better, they are coming to you for help. The person has some ambivalence, even if they profess not to, or else they would not still be talking with you (*Tip 56*). These simple facts, though often taken for granted, are reasons for hope.

Recognize the potential of treatment. The psychologist Edwin Shneidman (1996) notes, "The happy fact is that there are thousands of people who have been helped, their lives saved, by the intervention of therapy by psychologists, psychiatrists, physicians, suicide prevention workers, and others" (pp. 164–165). It's true: Psychotherapy and some medications can help reduce suicidal thoughts and suicide attempts (Erlangsen et al., 2015; Calati & Courtet, 2016; Zalsman et al., 2016).

Remember situations that seemed hopeless, but proved otherwise. The world is full of people who were moments away from suicide, or who actually did attempt suicide and survived, and whose lives turned around dramatically. Hope can be found in the simple fact that more than 90% of people who survive a suicide attempt do not go on to die by suicide, even many years after the attempt (Owens et al., 2002).

Read memoirs by suicidal individuals. Many people have written personal accounts of their own transformation from suicidal despair to healing and hope. Reading these accounts can infuse you with hope. *Tip 2* lists some memoirs that are both exquisitely painful yet ultimately inspiring.

In Closing

No matter how challenging and painful a suicidal person's situation is, as long as the person is alive, change is possible. Even if the person's mental illness, physical pain, or other circumstances cannot change, their experience of it can change. People can learn new coping skills, improve their quality of life, find meaning in their experiences, work toward goals, and develop a sense of acceptance about what they cannot change.

Sometimes, you will need to carry hope for a suicidal person. Sometimes, you will need to rediscover hope within yourself. Whatever you do, however you do it, try not to let your sense of hopelessness masquerade as truth, and avail yourself of therapy or consultation if it does.

Searching for Hope

She kept looking at the dog. Wrapped in a leather harness, sitting at her client's feet, the German shepherd was a bleak reminder of the toll that mental illness had taken on her client, Horacio, and of the obstacles that lay before him. Five years earlier, at the age of 17, Horacio had gouged his eyes out, obeying the disembodied voices that commanded him to do so. Thereafter, his depression and auditory hallucinations relented only rarely. He attempted suicide three more times, with each attempt coming progressively closer to ending his life.

Now, his clinical social worker, Alexa, found herself staring at the dog, questioning whether anything but more pain and suffering lay ahead for Horacio. Alexa came to believe that Horacio would die by suicide no matter her efforts. She found herself wishing for some sort of psychiatric hospice care, where nurses could keep him comfortable as he worked his way up to ending his life.

At her next session with her psychotherapist, Alexa discussed her sense of despair. Then it hit her. The hopelessness she felt was a mere window into Horacio's own experience of hopelessness, fear, and despair. With the help of her therapist, Alexa came to see that there was hope for Horacio. She could help him to suffer less, cope more, and find meaning in his life, even with his disabilities. These realizations invigorated Alexa, and she greeted Horacio at his next session with a renewed focus on possibilities and options.

A year later, Horacio was still alive. His auditory hallucinations remained, but with Alexa's help Horacio had learned to regard the voices in his head as thoughts to observe instead of orders to obey. He had rediscovered hope and developed goals. With funding from his local vocational rehabilitation agency, he was taking college courses. He hoped to become a rehabilitation counselor, so that he could help others afflicted with both mental illness and blindness. Horacio still experienced symptoms of depression and suicidal thoughts from time to time. He had learned to cope with them and to find value in his life regardless.

Works Cited

Calati, R., & Courtet, P. (2016). Is psychotherapy effective for reducing suicide attempt and non-suicidal self-injury rates? Meta-analysis and meta-regression of literature data. *Journal of Psychiatric Research, 79,* 8–20.

Erlangsen, A., Lind, B. D., Stuart, E. A., Qin, P., Stenager, E., Larsen, K. J., ... & Winsløv, J. H. (2015). Short-term and long-term effects of psychosocial therapy for people after deliberate self-harm: A register-based, nationwide multicentre study using propensity score matching. *The Lancet Psychiatry, 2*(1), 49–58.

Owens, D., Horrocks, J., & House, A. (2002). Fatal and non-fatal repetition of self-harm. *British Journal of Psychiatry, 181*(3), 193–199.

Schechter, M., Goldblatt, M., & Maltsberger, J. T. (2013). The therapeutic alliance and suicide: When words are not enough. *British Journal of Psychotherapy, 29*(3), 315–328.

Shneidman, E. S. (1996). *The suicidal mind.* New York, NY: Oxford University Press.

Zalsman, G., Hawton, K., Wasserman, D., van Heeringen, K., Arensman, E., Sarchiapone, M., ... & Zohar, J. (2016). Suicide prevention strategies revisited: 10-year systematic review. *The Lancet Psychiatry, 3*(7), 646–659.

two
Overcoming
the Taboo

Tip 7: Face Your Fears

"The clinician's ability to calmly and matter-of-factly explore suicidal thought often provides a platform from which the patient's long endured silence about suicide can be broken."

Shawn Shea
(2011, p. 110)

Many people, even professionals with extensive experience, avoid raising the topic of suicide with their clients. For example, in a study of psychotherapists working with actors pretending to be clients, researchers found that the psychotherapists rarely uttered the word "suicide" or explicitly asked about suicidal thoughts, even though the actors intentionally portrayed clients at elevated risk for suicide (Reeves et al., 2004). The authors noted that both the therapist and client seemed "to collude in not specifically naming suicide as an active possibility" (p. 64). At a time when many suicidal individuals need help speaking what seems unspeakable, this collusion can have tragic consequences.

One of the biggest obstacles to directly asking a person about suicidal thoughts is fear. Many fears, in fact. Over the years, in my work as a teacher and consultant, I have observed these common themes: fears of putting the idea in the person's head, fear of making suicidal ideation worse, fear of angering the person, and, finally, fear of the person saying yes when asked if they are thinking of suicide.

Fear of Putting the Idea in the Person's Head

A frequent fear is that asking about suicidal thoughts will plant the idea. Studies of both adolescents and adults have examined this possibility and found that asking about suicide does not make people want to die by suicide (Harris & Goh, 2017). (And if you're skeptical, ask yourself now if reading this material has made you want to kill yourself. If the research is any indication, your answer is no.) Leaving aside the research findings, the fear of giving somebody the idea of suicide presumes that people could not come up with the idea on their own. In reality, it is impossible for anyone but a very young child to not already know about suicide. People learned about suicide many years before they ever set foot in a therapist's office.

Fear of Exacerbating Suicidal Thoughts

Even though asking about suicidal thoughts does not give someone the idea, could the question make existing suicidal thoughts worse? Quite a few researchers have investigated that question in recent years. Overwhelmingly, asking about suicidal ideation did not have a positive or negative effect. For very small proportions of people, suicidal thoughts did briefly increase, and they decreased in others (Dazzi et al., 2014). Even if suicidal ideation does worsen, that is not a reason to stop assessing suicide risk. Medicine is rife with diagnostic tests, from blood draws to colonoscopies, that cause physical pain. The potential for negative effects is justified by the information that these tests obtain.

Fear of Offending or Angering the Person

Stigma wraps itself so tightly around suicide that simply to ask someone if they are thinking of suicide feels, to some people, like delivering an insult. Professionals need to not perpetuate that stigma. People who consider suicide are not doing something morally wrong. Meanwhile, techniques such as shame attenuation, normalization, and gentle assumption (*Tip 9*) can help soften the inquiry for clients who themselves stigmatize suicide (Shea, 2011).

Over the years, I have asked hundreds of people in clinical settings if they were considering suicide. Most have answered matter-of-factly "no" or "yes." Some visibly have experienced relief on unburdening their secret. Nobody has ever become angry with me for asking about suicidal thoughts. If they did get angry, that would be okay. Anger is an emotion to be explored, not a toxin to be avoided. And, as with the discomfort of medical tests, it is a small price to pay to get at information as important as suicidal ideation.

Fear of the Person Saying "Yes"

For many professionals, a prospect even more frightening than asking about suicidal thoughts is hearing the answer. They fear the person will say "yes." The possibility of the person dying by suicide is deeply unsettling. Some professionals doubt their competence. On a smaller scale, the answer "yes" can create a logistical headache if the session needs to go longer than planned or hospitalization occurs. These fears must be overcome, or at least tolerated (*Tip 3*). It is far better to know when a person is contemplating suicide than to not know, even if the knowledge is frightening. This book gives many tips and techniques for what to do when you ask a person about thoughts of suicide and the answer is "yes."

"Do You Ask?"

Early in my career, I worked at a telephone counseling hotline where staff were required to rate each call on a scale of 0 to 4, based on the severity of the caller's suicidal ideation. A "0" meant that the person had expressed no suicidal ideation at all or had said "no" when explicitly asked if they were considering suicide. A "4" was reserved for callers who were either in the midst of a suicide attempt or had attempted suicide shortly before the call. Almost none of my calls rated a "0." Most were a "1" (mild suicidal ideation) or a "2" (moderate suicidal ideation).

One day I was speaking with another counselor there, and she said she almost never had a suicidal caller. "Why do you think you have so many callers who are suicidal, and I don't?" she asked.

Without really thinking, I said, "Do you ask?"

I instantly felt regretful. Of course she asked! She had a master's degree in a counseling field and years of clinical experience. I felt certain I had offended her, as if I were questioning her skills.

Indeed, she was aghast at my question, but not for the reason I expected. "No, I would never ask that!" she said animatedly. She explained that she did not want to give anybody the idea. Moreover, she said, if someone is thinking of suicide, they would volunteer the information. (As *Tip 8* explains, she was wrong.)

Over the years, in trainings, classes, and consultations, I have met many other experienced mental health professionals who hold these views. It no longer surprises me when an experienced professional tells me they avoid asking people if they are considering suicide, but it does worry me. Avoiding this crucial question can contribute to a tragedy.

Works Cited

Dazzi, T., Gribble, R., Wessely, S., & Fear, N. T. (2014). Does asking about suicide and related behaviours induce suicidal ideation? What is the evidence? *Psychological Medicine, 44*(16), 3361–3363.

Harris, K. M., & Goh, M. T. (2017). Is suicide assessment harmful to participants? Findings from a randomized controlled trial. *International Journal of Mental Health Nursing, 26*(2), 181–190.

Reeves, A., Bowl, R., Wheeler, S., & Guthrie, E. (2004). The hardest words: Exploring the dialogue of suicide in the counselling process: A discourse analysis. *Counselling and Psychotherapy Research, 4*(1), 62–71.

Shea, S. C. (2011). *The practical art of suicide assessment: A guide for mental health professionals and substance abuse counselors.* Stoddard, NH: Mental Health Presses.

Tip 8: Directly Ask about Suicidal Thoughts

"Nobody ever asked me if I was experiencing suicidal thoughts, so I didn't feel able to disclose them to anyone."
Kevin Hines, who jumped off the Golden Gate Bridge and survived
(Hines et al., 2013)

There is a common belief that people who are considering suicide will readily volunteer the information to a mental health professional. To withhold such thoughts, the thinking goes, would be akin to a person who is suffering a heart attack going to the emergency room and never mentioning that their chest hurts. In fact, numerous research studies have documented that many people do *not* spontaneously disclose their suicidal thoughts to a psychotherapist, psychiatrist or other professional. One study looked at 100 people who died by suicide (Isometsä et al., 1995). At their final appointment, 80% did not tell the professional that they were having suicidal thoughts. Within 24 hours, they were dead.

Contradictory advice exists on how direct to be when asking about suicide. One school of thought (e.g., Joiner et al., 2009) advocates tackling the question directly, and then asking questions more generally about any wish to be dead:

- *"Do you have thoughts of killing yourself?"*
- *"Do you ever wish you were dead?"*
- *"Do you sometimes wish you could go to sleep and never wake up?"*

Others argue against directly asking about suicidal ideation without first some buildup to the question. Sadly, suicide is still a heavily stigmatized topic. The psychiatrist Yoshimoto Takahashi (1997) notes, for example, that he would never recommend directly asking a Japanese client about suicidal thoughts. Instead, he would first ask more generally about the person's troubles, feelings of hope and despair about the future, relationships with others, and sense of personal value.

Along the same lines, psychologists Craig Bryan and David Rudd (2006) recommend a "hierarchical approach to questioning." They note, "By gradually progressing in the intensity of the interview, the clinician can potentially reduce anxiety or agitation in the patient while improving rapport" (p. 188). Bryan and Rudd's questions start broadly by addressing the troubles the person is facing, then the person's symptoms, then hopelessness, and then suicidal thinking (p. 188):

- *"How have things been going for you recently? Can you tell me about anything in particular that has been stressful for you?"*
- *"Have you been feeling anxious, nervous, or panicky lately?"*
- *"It's not uncommon when depressed to feel that things won't improve and won't get any better; do you ever feel this way?"*

- *"People feeling depressed and hopeless sometimes think about death and dying; do you ever have thoughts about death and dying?"*
- *"Have you ever thought about killing yourself?"*

No research addresses whether a direct or gradual approach to suicide questioning is better. In the absence of such knowledge, it is up to you to decide which route to take, based on the client's needs, preferences, cultural background, and overall situation. Personally, I try to be direct wherever possible, to avoid giving the impression that I am afraid to discuss the topic of suicide openly, or that it is embarrassing or shameful to contemplate suicide. At the same time, for some people – clients and professionals alike – the topic of suicide is so difficult to discuss that starting small is better than never starting at all.

"Are You Thinking of Hurting Yourself?"*

Siobhan, a counseling intern, was so afraid of talking about suicide that she dared not speak the word. It was almost a superstition: "If I say the word, it makes it more likely to happen," she said. So she was ill-equipped to respond well when Jamar, a 14-year-old teenager, told her, "Sometimes I just don't care about anything. Nothing seems to matter anymore."

"That sounds so difficult," she said. She wondered if he wanted to kill himself, but her anxiety intruded. So she used a euphemism favored by many people: "Are you thinking of hurting yourself?"

"No way!" he said emphatically. "I'm already hurting enough."

Soon after the session, Jamar wrote a suicide note to his parents and took a bottle of ibuprofen. His younger sister found him unconscious in his bed, and he was taken by ambulance to the hospital.

At his next session, Siobhan said to Jamar, "I'm confused. Please help me to understand so I can do better. I asked you if you wanted to hurt yourself, and you said no."

"I didn't want to hurt myself," he said. "That's why I took pain pills, so that I wouldn't feel any pain."

Siobhan had learned an important, almost fatal, lesson about the need to speak frankly about suicide.

* This example was inspired by a vignette in Shea, 2011, p. 120.

Works Cited

Bryan, C. J., & Rudd, M. D. (2006). Advances in the assessment of suicide risk. *Journal of Clinical Psychology, 62*(2), 185–200.

Hines, K., Cole-King, A., & Blaustein, M. (2013). Hey kid, are you OK? A story of suicide survived. *Advances in Psychiatric Treatment, 19*(4), 292–294.

Isometsä, E. T., Heikkinen, M. E., Marttunen, M. J., Henriksson, M. M., Aro, H. M., & Lonnqvist, J. K. (1995). The last appointment before suicide: Is suicide intent communicated? *American Journal of Psychiatry, 152*(6), 919–922.

Joiner, T. E., Jr., Van Orden, K. A., Witte, T. K., & Rudd, M. D. (2009). *The interpersonal theory of suicide: Guidance for working with suicidal clients.* Washington, DC: American Psychological Association.

Shea, S. C. (2011). *The practical art of suicide assessment: A guide for mental health professionals and substance abuse counselors.* Stoddard, NH: Mental Health Presses.

Takahashi, Y. (1997). Culture and suicide: From a Japanese psychiatrist's perspective. *Suicide and Life-Threatening Behavior, 27*(1), 137–146.

Tip 9: Turn to Techniques for Eliciting Sensitive Information

"Undertaking a suicide risk assessment is potentially life-saving, but the clinical encounter is utterly dependent on what the patient chooses to reveal or keep hidden."

Alys Cole-King and colleagues
(2013, p. 276)

People lie, often by omission. Not everyone, of course, but many suicidal people deny or understate their self-destructive thoughts. They might fear hospitalization, stigma, or negative judgment (*Tip 12*). Worse, they might fear being thwarted from carrying out their suicide plans. To help overcome these obstacles to disclosure, the psychiatrist Shawn Shea (2011) describes excellent techniques for eliciting sensitive information. Some of these techniques were developed in other fields, such as substance use counseling and sex research. These "validity techniques," as Shea calls them, include normalization, shame attenuation, symptom amplification, gentle assumption, denial of the specific, and behavioral incident.

Normalization

Normalization involves asking about suicidal ideation only after making clear that it is normal to think of suicide at one time or another, especially in painful or difficult circumstances. And it's true: In the U.S., almost 10 million adults per year seriously consider suicide (Lipari et al., 2015). Among adolescents, almost one in five high school students report that they seriously considered suicide in the prior 12 months (Kann et al., 2016).

It's not necessary to go into statistics in order to normalize suicidal ideation. You can allude generally to other people who have experienced similar pain, hopelessness, or difficult situations, and thought of suicide as a result.

> "Many people with depression like yours can feel so bad that they think of suicide. Have you had suicidal thoughts?"

Shame Attenuation

Many people feel ashamed of their suicidal thoughts or behaviors (*Tip 84*). They blame themselves. The technique of shame attenuation blames the person's pain, illness, or situation instead. It is similar to normalization, except that you do not invoke others who have the same experiences.

"With all the pain and hopelessness you feel, do you think of killing yourself?"

Gentle Assumption

If someone feels any shame, embarrassment, or fear about disclosing suicidal ideation, then "yes–no" questions can deter the person from answering honestly. Saying "yes" can feel like an admission of guilt. To avoid that problem, the technique of gentle assumption calls for you to act as if the person already answered "yes." If the gentle assumption is incorrect, there is no harm done; the format of the question allows for a response of "none" or "never." If the question seems like too much of an assumption for you, you can add "if at all" to the end.

"What are some ways you have thought of killing yourself?" (vs. "Have you thought of ways to kill yourself?")

"How many times in your life have you attempted suicide, if at all?" (vs. "Have you attempted suicide?")

The technique of gentle assumption has been used extensively in sex research. As an example, the Kinsey Institute discovered that more people were willing to disclose that they masturbated if the researchers asked "How old were you when you first started masturbating?" instead of "Do you masturbate?" (Gebhard & Johnson, 1979). Asking about the age when a person started masturbating implicitly conveys that yes, of course people masturbate. It really does matter how you ask questions.

Symptom Amplification

You need to know not only if the person is thinking of suicide, but also how often and how intensely. A person might be embarrassed to answer these questions honestly, out of fear that they are thinking of suicide "too much." Symptom amplification calls for you to exaggerate the possibilities, though not to an absurd degree. This gives room for the person to answer honestly without necessarily feeling that they are thinking of suicide excessively.

"How many times a day do you think of suicide? 20? 30?" (to which the person responds, "Oh gosh no, not that much. Only 5–10 times, I'd say.")

Denial of the Specific

Instead of asking a single overarching question that covers many possibilities, the "denial of the specific" technique requires you to ask separately about each possibility. As Shea notes, it is easier to disingenuously say "no" to a single generic question than it is to numerous specific questions. So, ask separately about each specific possibility rather than stringing together multiple options in one question.

> With each of these possibilities, the professional waits for the person's response before moving on to the next possibility: "Have you ever thought of jumping off a high place, like a bridge or a building? ... Have you thought of taking an overdose? ... Hanging yourself? ... Shooting yourself? ...Cutting yourself?"

Behavioral Incident

For this technique, you ask questions about each step in the person's thoughts and behaviors in response to stress, pain, hopelessness, or other difficult emotions or situations that might trigger suicidal thoughts. This method is similar to a behavioral chain analysis (*Tip 79*), but with a different aim: to gather accurate information about suicidal thoughts and behavior, rather than to analyze the triggers, functions, and consequences of a behavior. By breaking the client's experience down into very concrete details, you help strip away any vagueness or distortions that might obscure the person's true experience.

> "When you took out the bottle of pills, what happened next? ... What did you do next? ... Then what did you do? ... What were you feeling when you did that?"

Summing Up

No assessment technique is perfect. Some people who want to die by suicide simply will not reveal their thoughts and plans. Still, these validity techniques can convey to a person that suicidal ideation does not deserve their embarrassment, shame, or fear of your negative judgment.

Works Cited

Cole-King, A., Green, G., Gask, L., Hines, K., & Platt, S. (2013). Suicide mitigation: A compassionate approach to suicide prevention. *Advances in Psychiatric Treatment, 19,* 276–283.

Gebhard, H., & Johnson, A. B. (1979). *The Kinsey data: Marginal tabulations of the 1938–1963 interviews conducted by the Institute for Sex Research.* Bloomington, IN: Indiana University Press.

Kann, L., McManus, T., Harris, W. A., Shanklin, S. L., Flint, K. H., Hawkins, J., … & Zaza, S. (2016). Youth risk behavior surveillance: United States, 2015. *Morbidity and Mortality Weekly Report Surveillance Summaries, 65*(6), 1–180.

Lipari, R., Piscopo, K., Kroutil, L. A., & Miller, G. K. (2015). Suicidal thoughts and behavior among adults: Results from the 2014 National Survey on Drug Use and Health. NSDUH Data Review. Rockville, MD: Substance Abuse and Mental Health Services Administration.

Shea, S. C. (2011). *The practical art of suicide assessment: A guide for mental health professionals and substance abuse counselors.* Stoddard, NH: Mental Health Presses.

Tip 10: Embrace a Narrative Approach: "Suicidal Storytelling"

"The lethality and risk assessment process tends to create a focus on the needs of the clinician ... as opposed to paying attention to the contextually-grounded story of the client."

James Rogers and Karen Soyka
(2004, p. 12)

To understand the person's suicidal thoughts, it often feels necessary to ask a litany of questions: *"How often do you think of suicide?" "How intensely?" "Do you have a plan?" "Do you have the means?" "Do you intend to act on your plan?"* Often, these questions better serve the clinician's needs for data about suicide risk than the suicidal person's needs to feel heard, understood, and less alone in their pain. Before barraging the person with your questions, invite the person to share their story, using a narrative approach that psychiatrist Konrad Michel and psychologist Ladislav Valach (2011) call "suicidal storytelling."

Michel and Valach offer these examples of questions that invite the suicidal person to share their suicidal story (pp. 71–72):

- *"Could you tell me how you got to the point that you wanted to put an end to your life?"*
- *"I would like you to tell me the story of what led to the suicidal crisis. Just let me listen to you."*
- *"I would like you to tell me in your own words how it came about that you harmed yourself."*

The person might ask where to begin. An encouraging, welcoming response would be to say something along the lines of, *"Feel free to start wherever you want. There is no right or wrong way to tell your story."* Some suicidal individuals briefly and cursorily summarize their story, depriving it of the richness that helps facilitate connection and healing. To encourage more disclosure, Michel and his colleague, psychologist Anja Gysin-Maillart (2015), ask the following: *"Okay, you have now given me a short account of what happened. Now, let's look at it in more detail. In my experience there is always a personal story behind [suicidal thoughts or] a suicide attempt"* (p. 72).

You should avoid interrupting the person's narrative except for times you want to clarify points or gain more depth. You can help the person fill in the gaps with brief, open-ended questions: *"Can you tell me more about...?" "Can you help me understand...?" "What happened next?"*

The narrative interview is a core piece of an evidence-based intervention for people who have attempted suicide, called the Attempted Suicide Short Intervention Program (ASSIP) (Gysin-Maillart et al., 2016). Using the narrative approach, you can succeed not only at gaining the person's story, but also at meeting their story with empathy, curiosity, and respect. Once you have developed a detailed understanding of the suicidal person's experiences from their perspective, the need to do a comprehensive suicide risk assessment remains (*Tips 19–34*). First, connect with the person around their uniquely personal and painful story.

"Nobody Has Ever Asked Me to Tell My Story Before"

With his arms crossed against his chest, Arjun waited for the questions. He had just told his new therapist, a licensed professional counselor, that he had thoughts of suicide. And Arjun knew from experience what was to come: the interrogation about his plans, motives, and intent.

The counselor surprised him. Instead of asking a series of questions, she said, "I'd like to hear how you came to think of suicide. Please tell me your story."

Arjun, 54, told her of the feelings of failure and worthlessness, the long nights as his mind churned with regrets until the sun came up and, exhausted, he went to work. He explained that his work as an accountant distracted him from his ruminations, until he returned home again to endure the same cycle.

"I'd like to hear more," the counselor said. "How did you get from feeling so low to thinking of suicide?"

This question took Arjun back to his first years of life, nearly five decades earlier, when he was first sexually abused by his father. The abuse continued for 10 years, until a neighbor, a fellow victim, made an outcry and Arjun's father was arrested. Ever since, depressed moods overwhelmed Arjun with intermittent fury, unleashing condemnations about his failure to protect himself or the neighbor. Even this many years later, for months at a time, the regret consumes him until, inexplicably, it grants him a reprieve for a year, maybe two, before returning again. Each time, the onslaught is so searing that he yearns to kill himself.

"You've suffered so much," the counselor said. "Your father hurt you for so many years. And now your mind is hurting you."

She and Arjun spoke a bit more about the pain he had endured, and the counselor responded with empathy and a sincere desire to understand. Although Arjun's narrative covered many decades, it took him only 10 minutes to tell it.

"Right now I feel very strange," Arjun said. "A little lighter. This is rather astounding to consider, but nobody has ever asked me to tell my story before."

"No?" the counselor asked.

"Truly no," he said. "I've seen many psychiatrists over the years. They often have asked if I was suicidal. Some even asked why. But not in the way you did. Instead, they wanted to know all about my suicidal thoughts, but not really about me. And when I'd say no, do not worry yourself, I'm not going to do anything, they basically changed the topic. Almost as if they were covering themselves, do you know what I mean?"

"Do you mean they wanted to make sure you're not going to kill yourself?" the counselor asked.

"Yes, and then when I assure them I'm not, they are satisfied because I will not die and they will not get sued. They are satisfied, but I am not."

"Well," the counselor said. "I do also have those questions. I care about you and want to be sure you're safe."

"I understand that," Arjun said. "But you also wanted to hear my story when nobody else has. And you did hear me, really hear me. I can't tell you how much that means to me. This may sound odd, but it gives me a bit of hope."

Works Cited

Gysin-Maillart, A., Schwab, S., Soravia, L., Megert, M., & Michel, K. (2016). A novel brief therapy for patients who attempt suicide: A 24-months follow-up randomized controlled study of the Attempted Suicide Short Intervention Program (ASSIP). *PLoS Medicine, 13*(3), e1001968.

Michel, K., & Gysin-Maillart, A. (Eds.). (2015). *ASSIP: Attempted Suicide Short Intervention Program – A manual for clinicians.* Boston, MA: Hogrefe Publishing.

Michel, K., & Valach, L. (2011). The narrative interview and the suicidal patient. In K. Michel & D. A. Jobes (Eds.), *Building a therapeutic alliance with the suicidal patient* (pp. 63–80). Washington, DC: American Psychological Association.

Rogers, J. R., & Soyka, K. M. (2004). "One size fits all": An existential-constructivist perspective on the crisis intervention approach with suicidal individuals. *Journal of Contemporary Psychotherapy, 34*(1), 7–22.

Tip 11: Ask about Suicidal Imagery, Too

"If therapists do not ask about images, they tend not to get reports of them."

Ann Hackmann and colleagues
(2011, p. 62)

Many people report that they have no suicidal thoughts but then, on further exploration, it turns out they do picture themselves in the act of suicide or its aftermath (Crane et al., 2012). These images of a future act are called "flash-forwards," in contrast to "flashbacks" of past events (Holmes, et al., 2007). Imagery evokes stronger emotional responses than verbal material (Di Simplicio et al., 2012), so these flash-forwards are especially important to uncover.

As with inquiries about suicidal thoughts (*Tip 8*), it is important to ask directly about imagery:

- *"Do you have daydreams or other mental pictures about suicide? … About death?"*
- *"When you think about suicide, what do you see?"*
- *"Have you rehearsed suicide in your imagination?"*

Also ask about any images indirectly related to suicide: *"Do you get pictures in your mind's eye of anything else about death or suicide, like your funeral or people's reactions?"*

Determine whether the images are voluntary or intrusive, and uncover the person's reaction to the mental pictures they imagine:

- *"How do these images make you feel? For example, do they comfort you, or do they disturb you?"*
- *"Do you feel like you can control whether you have these mental pictures? … Do you want to stop having them?"*
- *"Do these images make you want even more strongly to kill yourself? Do they make you want to stay alive?"*

Imagery of suicidal acts reveals how intensely the person considers suicide, but it is important to assess imagery for another reason, too. Mentally rehearsing killing oneself can make the image – and the act of suicide – less distressing over time. The person gets used to the idea, maybe even more drawn to it. This is consistent with the psychologist Thomas Joiner's theory (2005) that people must become desensitized to the horror of suicide to overcome the survival instinct. So, suicidal images do not only need to be assessed. The images also need to be addressed, which is covered in *Tip 70*.

Examples: Different Images, Different Results

In her mind's eye, Clarissa saw her funeral – her parents weeping by the closed mahogany coffin; her ex-husband grim-faced and alone; her co-workers dumbfounded; the black leather sign-in book by the door; even the floral wreath adorned with white carnations, white mums, and snap-dragons placed beside the coffin. The picture comforted her. In her present world, it felt like nobody cared about her. She was alone. Knowing how people would grieve her death helped her recognize that they appreciated her life.

Geraldo, on the other hand, had an image so compelling that it felt more like a waking dream than mere thoughts. He saw himself stepping in front of a bus. He envisioned the specific, tree-lined street, the glass and brick storefronts behind the trees, the yellow and green coloring of the bus, even the clear blue sky above. For several weeks now, this image came to him at random times throughout the day. He both dreaded his mind's torment and felt moved to heed its call.

Works Cited

Crane, C., Shah, D., Barnhofer, T., & Holmes, E. A. (2012). Suicidal imagery in a previously depressed community sample. *Clinical Psychology & Psychotherapy, 19*(1), 57–69.

Di Simplicio, M., McInerney, J. E., Goodwin, G. M., Attenburrow, M. J., & Holmes, E. A. (2012). Revealing the mind's eye: Bringing (mental) images into psychiatry. *The American Journal of Psychiatry, 169*(12), 1245–1246.

Hackmann, A., Bennett-Levy, J., & Holmes, E. A. (2011). *Oxford guide to imagery in cognitive therapy.* New York, NY: Oxford University Press.

Holmes, E. A., Crane, C., Fennell, M. J., & Williams, J. M. G. (2007). Imagery about suicide in depression: "Flash-forwards"? *Journal of Behavior Therapy and Experimental Psychiatry, 38*(4), 423–434.

Joiner, T. (2005). *Why people die by suicide.* Cambridge, MA: Harvard University Press.

Tip 12: Uncover Fears of Hospitalization and Other Obstacles to Disclosure

"I am consistently amazed at how many people flatly deny suicidal ideation when first asked, despite the presence of such ideation. The clinician should seldom, if ever, leave the topic after a single denial."

Shawn Shea
(2011, p. 122)

Many people conceal their suicidal thoughts (*Tips 8–9*). They might feel embarrassed, dread your judgment, treat suicide as a taboo topic, or fear being committed to a psychiatric hospital. For these reasons, even when a person adamantly says they are not thinking of suicide, it is wise to maintain healthy skepticism. Ask follow-up questions, and explore reasons the person might have for withholding information.

Tip 9 describes ways to ask about suicidal ideation that go beyond a single question. You can move from the specific (e.g., *"Do you have thoughts of suicide?"*) to the general (e.g., *"Do you ever wish you could go to sleep and never wake up?"*), or, conversely, from the general to the specific. When a person says they are not having thoughts of suicide, the psychiatrist Shawn Shea (2009) recommends asking again, but "softening" the question. For example, Shea offers this follow-up question: *"Have you had fleeting thoughts of suicide, even for a moment or two?"*

Another technique is to explore the person's willingness to disclose suicidal thoughts in the future. The person's response can reveal hesitancies to disclose suicidal thoughts in the present:

- *"In the future, if you were thinking of killing yourself, would you feel comfortable telling me?"*
- *"What would make it hard to tell me you were thinking of suicide? What are you afraid could happen?"*

In my experience, people commonly fear that if they disclose suicidal thoughts, they will be committed to a psychiatric hospital where they will languish indefinitely. The fear of hospitalization is one reason why, as part of the informed-consent process, you should explain the very narrow circumstances that call for hospitalization. In addition to openly discussing this with my clients, I state in my written policies:

If you are at extremely high risk of acting on suicidal thoughts, I may need to take steps to protect your safety without your consent. Disclosing suicidal thoughts or plans does *not* constitute extremely high risk if you do

not intend to act on them very soon. Please let me know if you have concerns about what you can share without my being required to intervene. I
am committed to your being fully informed about the limits of confidentiality when extreme risk for suicide exists.

It never hurts to reiterate your policy as needed. Once a person hears that even
people with serious suicidal thoughts usually do not need to be hospitalized (*Tips
35–36*), they might feel more inclined to share.

"You'd Lock Me Up in a Padded Room"

Melody shook her head when the psychologist asked her if she had
thoughts of killing herself. The psychologist instantly had his doubts.
Melody, 40, had described symptoms of depression and anxiety, two conditions that often stimulate suicidal thoughts. And there seemed to be hesitation, if brief, between his question and Melody's shake of the head.

"I'm wondering about something," the psychologist said. "In the future,
or even now, if you were having thoughts of suicide, would you feel that
you could tell me?"

"I don't think so," Melody said softly. "I'd be too afraid."

"Oh? Do you feel comfortable telling me what you'd be afraid of?"

"Well to be honest, I'm afraid you'd lock me up in a padded room,"
Melody said.

"I see. You're scared you'd be committed to a hospital?" the psychologist asked. Melody nodded, and the psychologist continued, "I'm glad you
brought that up so that I can clarify this. A lot of people think that they will
be hospitalized against their will if they are just thinking of suicide. But
that's not true. I view hospitalization as a last resort. You have to be on the
verge of suicide for me to recommend it, and even then I would want to
look into whether there are other ways to keep you safe."

"What would that look like ... being on the verge of suicide?" Melody
asked.

"It would have to be a very extreme situation," the psychologist said.
"Like, if you told me, 'Look, I have a loaded gun at home and I'm going
to shoot myself tonight,' and you wouldn't agree for someone to come
and take the gun, and you wouldn't or couldn't go along with your safety
plan, I'd need to take measures to keep you from shooting yourself. On
the other hand, even if you tell me that you're thinking of suicide many
times a day, if you don't intend to kill yourself in the near future, not
only would I not recommend hospitalization, but most hospitals
wouldn't admit you."

"That makes me feel better," Melody said. "I'm not on the verge of
killing myself, but I do think about it."

"I'm grateful that you felt you could tell me, and I want to hear more about that," the psychologist said. "But first I want to say a couple more things about hospitals. I wonder if you know that most people are hospitalized only for several days. And a lot of hospitals aren't bad places to be. I just wanted to say that, in case you do get to a point where there's no way to keep you safe besides hospitalization. I wouldn't want you to have a horror-show picture in your head of what would happen."

"I really don't think it would ever come to that," Melody said. "I think about suicide a lot but it's not something I'd ever really do."

"OK, let's talk about that," he said. "I'd like to hear your story of how you came to think about suicide..."

Works Cited

Shea, S. C. (2009). Suicide assessment: Part 2: Uncovering suicidal intent using the Chronological Assessment of Suicide Events (CASE approach). *Psychiatric Times, 26*(12), 17.

Shea, S. C. (2011). *The practical art of suicide assessment: A guide for mental health professionals and substance abuse counselors.* Stoddard, NH: Mental Health Presses.

three
Joining with the Suicidal Person

Tip 13: Recognize that, for Some People, You are an Enemy

"At a fundamental level, the life-and-death nature of suicidality can potentially pit patients (who may see suicide as a personal right) against their clinician (who may understand that preventing suicide, using whatever means necessary, is both a statutory and professional obligation)."

M. David Rudd and colleagues
(2001, p. 113)

You and the suicidal person may have two different agendas. The suicidal person wants to stop suffering. You want the suicidal person to stay alive. These agendas can converge, if you and your client work together on ways to reduce suffering that do not involve suicide. But sometimes the person clings to suicide so tenaciously that your agendas clash, and you risk becoming the suicidal person's adversary. This is especially true if you move to involuntarily hospitalize the person, involve significant others against their wishes, or take other unwelcome measures to keep the person safe. In less extreme circumstances, the person might perceive you as trying to take suicidal thoughts away from them before they are ready, like a parent wresting a security blanket from a child (*Tip 55*).

Acknowledging and exploring the differing agendas is important. When an adversarial stance exists, the suicidal person might feel compelled to hide important facts and emotions from you. Even worse, they might stop seeing you altogether, further withdrawing from the realm of possibilities and hope.

The key to avoiding an adversarial role is to forge an alliance with the suicidal person, find common ground in your goals, and collaborate with them in all aspects of treatment (*Tip 14*). Address your potentially opposing agendas, and openly explore with the person how much – or how little – they view you as someone who can help them. Also explore their fears that you can hurt them in some way, such as having them hospitalized against their will (*Tip 12*). Above all, wherever possible, avoid trying to coerce or control the person, which is discussed in the next tip.

"I Wish I'd Never Met You"

Jack, 74, did not want to be in this doctor's office. The baby blue box of tissues, the soft lighting, the doctor looking at him from her brown leather chair – all of these reeked of weakness. He was a Vietnam Veteran. A third-generation Army man. He was not weak.

The psychiatrist, Dr. Weinstein, asked the customary intake questions. Jack disclosed vague, fleeting suicidal thoughts. He told her he did not have any intent to act on them. But Dr. Weinstein knew that over the weekend, Jack had retreated to his workroom in the basement and put a gun to his head. His wife Misty walked in before he pulled the trigger. Misty called the police, an ambulance took him to the emergency department, and he was cleared for discharge on the condition that their adult son remove the gun from Jack and Misty's home before they returned home, and Jack would follow up with a psychiatrist on Monday.

"I'm wondering about something," Dr. Weinstein said. "We're strangers to each other. I know it can feel uncomfortable to tell a stranger very private information about yourself. Do you want to be here talking with me?"

Jack laughed softly as he fiddled with his cap. "No ma'am," he said. "To be completely honest, I wish I'd never met you."

"OK, so you don't want to be here. Can you tell me more?" she asked.

"I don't think you can help me. You're just here to keep me from doing what I might want to do and what is my God-given right to do – to end my life on my terms."

"I see, I'm an obstacle in your path if you want to kill yourself," Dr. Weinstein said. "Obviously, as a medical professional who cares about you, I don't want you to take your life. And yet, based on how you answered my questions earlier, you still want to die to a degree. So we have different agendas. What's that like for you?"

"Honestly, I don't mean any offense, but it pretty much makes you the enemy. I'm only here because my wife and the ER doc insisted on it. I didn't have any rights in this matter. I feel like a child."

"It makes sense that you feel like I am the enemy," the psychiatrist said. "I like to think that I am an enemy of suicide, but an ally of the part of you that wants to live. As long as you're here, is there something we can work on together that might help you to want to live again?"

Jack was silent for a minute. Then he said, "If you could give me something to help me sleep, that'd be a start. I haven't had a full night's sleep for two months. And maybe if there's something you could do to help me quiet down all the noise in my head, that would be good, too."

Now the two had a common goal. Together, they could form an alliance around helping Jack to sleep and calm his thoughts. Dr. Weinstein had averted a power struggle with an openly antagonistic patient, in the service of his survival.

Work Cited

Rudd, M. D., Joiner, T., & Rajab, M. H. (2001). *Treating suicidal behavior: An effective, time-limited approach.* New York, NY: Guilford Press.

Tip 14: Avoid Coercion and Control Whenever Possible

"From beginning, to middle, to end – collaboration is the key."

David Jobes

(2016, p. 4)

In their understandable desire to prevent the suicidal person from dying, many mental health professionals resort to coercive and controlling actions. This stance can intensify the adversarial nature of the relationship between professional and client (*Tip 13*), create power struggles, and alienate the suicidal person. The counterpart to coercion and control is collaboration. Instead of fueling an adversarial relationship, collaboration calls for you and the suicidal person to join together against the forces that drive the suicidal wish.

Coercion is extracting a promise, sometimes in the form of a written contract, from the suicidal person not to attempt suicide (*Tip 37*). Collaboration is working together with the suicidal person to devise a plan that identifies tools and resources for staying safe (*Tip 38*).

Coercion is issuing an ultimatum to the suicidal person: Give up suicide as an option, or find another therapist. Collaboration is nonjudgmentally exploring the person's attachment to suicide (*Tip 55*), while striving to help the person find alternative solutions (*Tips 60–62*).

Coercion is turning to psychiatric hospitalization – even, in some cases, threatening the person with hospitalization – for suicidal ideation that does not rise to the level of imminent danger, often as a means to soothe your anxiety about working with someone at risk for suicide (*Tip 36*). Collaboration is working together to keep the person out of the hospital, unless hospitalization becomes unavoidable to save the person's life in the face of extreme danger (*Tip 35*).

There are times when some level of coercion and control is necessary to keep the person safe. In the context of imminent suicide risk, you may need to coerce a person to consent to hospitalization, or even to take control and pursue involuntarily hospitalization (*Tip 35*). When coercive measures are necessary to preserve safety or set limits, the objective is to help the suicidal person. When coercive measures are used unnecessarily, the objective typically is to help allay the anxiety that often comes with trying to help a suicidal person.

An Elaboration: Collaborative Assessment and Management of Suicidality

A key framework for developing a collaborative partnership with the suicidal person is the Collaborative Assessment and Management of Suicidality (CAMS), developed by psychologist David Jobes (2016). The CAMS approach acknowledges that "the clinical alliance is *the* essential vehicle for delivering a potentially life-saving series of clinical interventions" (Jobes, 2009, p. 3). To nurture this alliance, CAMS take a stance of working *with* the suicidal person to help resolve the problems and pain that drive the suicidal wish, rather than working *against* the person's plans for suicide. CAMS' collaborative stance is consistent with many tips and techniques in this book. CAMS calls for helping the person develop a safety plan (*Tip 38*) and avoiding hospitalization whenever possible (*Tip 36*). The CAMS therapist validates that the wish to die makes sense (*Tip 17*), acknowledges that suicide is always an option (*Tip 18*), maintains a focus on suicidality and the problems that move people to consider suicide (*Tip 44*), and generates hope by exploring plans, dreams, and goals for the future (*Tip 63*). Notably, CAMS can be used in concert with any theoretical orientation or clinical approach.

The collaborative spirit of CAMS is demonstrated physically. During the risk assessment interview, the clinician sits next to the person, if the person consents, so that the two can complete the risk assessment side by side as partners, handing the form back and forth to each other. In a similar fashion, the suicidal person becomes a "co-author" of the treatment plan. Be sure to get the person's permission beforehand to sit alongside them. As Jobes (2016) notes, "Taking a seat next to a patient is never to be done lightly; the request to do so must be sincere, with exquisite sensitivity to personal space, perceived status, trauma history, gender, and cultural dynamics" (p. 55).

Research findings about CAMS are promising. CAMS has been linked to reductions in suicidal ideation in seven correlational studies (Jobes et al., 2015) and in two randomized controlled trials, considered the gold standard in intervention research. In one randomized controlled trial, suicidal outpatients who received CAMS care had greater reductions in suicidal ideation, hopelessness, and overall distress, compared to those in the control group (Comtois et al., 2011). In the other randomized controlled trial, participants with borderline personality disorder and a recent suicide attempt received CAMS or dialectical behavior therapy (DBT), also an evidence-based treatment for reducing suicidal behavior (Andreasson et al., 2016). Fewer people in the CAMS group attempted suicide or engaged in non-suicidal self-injury. Although the differences were not statistically significant, it is notable that the results defied the study authors' expectations; they thought that DBT would be superior. A naturalistic comparison study in an inpatient setting also showed that CAMS care reduced suicidal ideation and suicide cognitions significantly more than treatment as usual did (Ellis et al., 2015).

For more information about CAMS, the book *Managing Suicidal Risk: A Collaborative Approach* (Jobes, 2016) describes in extensive detail the CAMS procedures and philosophy, assessment measures, related quantitative and qualitative research findings, a lengthy case history that spans the book, and adaptations of CAMS for diverse groups and settings.

Works Cited

Andreasson, K., Krogh, J., Wenneberg, C., Jessen, H. K., Krakauer, K., Gluud, C., ... & Nordentoft, M. (2016). Effectiveness of dialectical behavior therapy versus collaborative assessment and management of suicidality treatment for reduction of self-harm in adults with borderline personality traits and disorder: A randomized observer-blinded clinical trial. *Depression and Anxiety, 33*(6), 520–530.

Comtois, K. A., Jobes, D. A., O'Connor, S., Atkins, D. C., Janis, K., Chessen, C. E., ... & Yuodelis-Flores, C. (2011). Collaborative assessment and management of suicidality (CAMS): Feasibility trial for next-day appointment services. *Depression and Anxiety, 28*(11), 963–972.

Ellis, T. E., Rufino, K. A., Allen, J. G., Fowler, J. C., & Jobes, D. A. (2015). Impact of a suicide-specific intervention within inpatient psychiatric care: The Collaborative Assessment and Management of Suicidality. *Suicide and Life-Threatening Behavior, 45*(5), 556–566.

Jobes, D. A. (2009). The CAMS approach to suicide risk: Philosophy and clinical procedures. *Suicidologi, 14*(1), 3–7.

Jobes, D. A. (2016). *Managing suicidal risk: A collaborative approach* (2nd ed.). New York, NY: Guilford Press.

Jobes, D. A., Au, J. S., & Siegelman, A. (2015). Psychological approaches to suicide treatment and prevention. *Current Treatment Options in Psychiatry, 2*(4), 363–370.

Tip 15: Resist the Urge to Persuade or Offer Advice

"Being empathic with the suicidal wish means assuming the suicidal person's perspective and 'seeing' how this person has reached a dead end without trying to interfere, stop, or correct the suicidal wishes."

Israel Orbach
(2001b, p. 173)

It can be exceptionally challenging to listen to someone who wants to die. You understandably might feel tempted to give advice or reassurance, to convince the person that their suicidal thinking is wrong, or to otherwise talk the person out of suicide. However, premature efforts to challenge the person's suicidal stance can leave the person feeling alienated, which can then intensify feelings of hopelessness. As the psychologist David Jobes and psychiatrist John Maltsberger note, the suicidal person needs "neither lectures nor pep talks" (1995, p. 209). To feel heard, understood, and less alone, the person needs empathy.

An empathic stance does not call for you to condone suicide. Rather, empathy means seeing things the way the other person sees things *as if* you were that person, while never losing sight of the fact that you are not (Rogers, 1959). Not only do you understand how much the person is hurting, but you also can see why the person views suicide as a reasonable and tempting option. The psychologist Israel Orbach (2001a) calls this "extreme empathy on the verge of total identification" (p. 141).

Consider the scenario of a crisis counselor called out to the scene where a young man is sitting on the roof of a tall building. He plans to jump. The counselor tells the suicidal person, "I am going to try to convince you not to kill yourself." Arguing that suicide would be a "terrible mistake," the counselor tries to assure the person that "the worst is already behind you." The pain is temporary, the counselor says, before urging the young man to consider the agony of friends and family members who would grieve his death.

The counselor is following a suicide prevention script set forth by psychologist Haim Omer and philosopher Avshalom Elitzur (2001). The pleas are compelling, but also problematic. The suicidal person has almost certainly considered all these points already and, for whatever reason, rejected them. Your efforts at persuasion can shut the door to further exploration of the person's thoughts and feelings. Worse still, the anti-suicide argument can place the counselor and suicidal person in opposite corners, each intent on defending their own point of view.

The article describing this script was challenged by another one. The title of the first article asked, "What would you say to a person on the roof?" The second article's title asked, "How would you *listen* to a person on the roof?" (Orbach, 2001a). Empathically listening to the suicidal person requires not trying to talk the person out of suicide, not offering superficial reassurance that things will get better (how can anyone truly know?), not warning the person about suicide's effects on others, and not prematurely rushing in to help solve the person's problems or fix their situation.

There is a time for questioning the suicidal person's assertions of worthlessness, of hopelessness, and so on. By all means, do not accept the person's feelings as facts (*Tips 66–70*). First, listen. Listen without immediately trying to change what you are hearing, no matter how hard it is to hear.

"I'm a Bad Person, and I Don't Deserve to Live"

It was 3 a.m. and Joseph, 17, was still awake, unwillingly. Thoughts raced through his head, creating a ruminative stew of self-hate and despair. He called a crisis hotline. "I can't get to sleep," he told the counselor on the other end of the line. "I can't stop thinking that I'm a bad person, and I don't deserve to live."

The hotline counselor instinctively wanted to say, "You're a good person, and you absolutely deserve to live." But she knew that those words would be hollow. She was a stranger. If she countered his harsh words with reassurance, it was not likely that he would suddenly experience an epiphany and realize he was a good person. Instead, he would probably feel alone and misunderstood. He might decide that the counselor did not want to know how he felt, perhaps even that she was incapable of helping, further entrenching his feelings of brokenness.

So the counselor resisted her urges to talk him out of his self-hatred. Instead, she said, "It must be so painful to feel that you're bad and don't deserve to live. Tell me more …"

Works Cited

Jobes, D. A., & Maltsberger, J. T. (1995). The hazards of treating suicidal patients. In M. B. Sussman (Ed.), *A perilous calling: The hazards of psychotherapy practice* (pp. 200–214). Oxford: John Wiley & Sons.

Omer, H., & Elitzur, A. C. (2001). What would you say to the person on the roof? A suicide prevention text. *Suicide and Life-Threatening Behavior, 31*(2), 129–139.

Orbach, I. (2001a). How would you listen to the person on the roof? A response to H. Omer and A. Elitzur. *Suicide and Life-Threatening Behavior, 31*(2), 140–143.

Orbach, I. (2001b). Therapeutic empathy with the suicidal wish: Principles of therapy with suicidal individuals. *American Journal of Psychotherapy, 55*(2), 166–184.

Rogers, C. (1959). A theory of therapy, personality and interpersonal relationships, as developed in the client-centered framework. In S. Koch (Ed.), *Psychology: A study of science* (Vol. 3, pp. 184–256). New York, NY: McGraw-Hill.

Tip 16: Understand the Person's Reasons for Dying

"It is critical that helpers both tolerate and invite the ... expression of reasons for dying."

John Draper and colleagues
(2015, p. 264)

It is axiomatic that in order to understand a person's suicidal wishes, you must understand why the person wants to die. If you take a narrative approach (*Tip 10*), then the reasons why suicide tempts the person usually emerge naturally. You still need to make sure you truly understand what drives the person's suicidal desire.

A valuable technique is to invite the person to persuade you why suicide is the best option. The psychologist Israel Orbach (2001) states, "As a tactic, I ask the suicidal person to actually 'convince' me that suicide is the only solution left and communicate with him or her from that empathic focus" (p. 173). To ensure that you fully understand why the person considers suicide, summarize the person's reasons and ask if you have understood correctly. Ideally, the person will say something along the lines of, "Yes, that's it." Be mindful of the person's *"yes, but…"* responses. Although *"yes, but…"* sometimes signals a person's resistance to change, more often it is a sign that the therapist has not fully understood. If the suicidal person says *"yes, but…"* when you summarize their reasons for considering suicide, or if the person otherwise indicates that you have not fully understood, this is an opportunity to ask clarifying questions. You might say something like, *"I think I'm not fully understanding the pain that you're in. What pieces am I missing?"*

Another helpful technique is to ask the person to list their reasons for wanting to die. Then invite the person to rank order the importance of each reason, from most important to least. This list is a component of the Suicide Status Form (*Tip 21*) (Jobes, 2016). The list will come in handy later, too, when exploring ambivalence and comparing reasons to die to reasons to stay alive (*Tip 57*).

These simple acts of reflection, empathy, and curiosity have the added benefit of ensuring that you bear witness to the person's pain without trying to fix, change, or talk the person out of it (*Tip 15*). By exploring the person's reasons for wanting to die, you signal a willingness to join them in a place where many others in the person's life refuse to go.

"Yes, But That's Not It Entirely"

It started only days after she had her baby girl. Ayshah, 33, stopped being able to sleep more than a couple hours a night, even at times when her baby slumbered in silence. Bouts of inexplicable crying came next, born from a sense of despair that had no rational explanation. Ayshah's husband was helpful and supportive, but she felt isolated from those who loved her. And her baby gave her no joy. Now, as her baby reached her six-month birthday, Ayshah believed she was not a good mother. "She'd be better off without me," Ayshah said. "I can't meet her love with love."

As she spoke, the licensed professional counselor, Zikri, experienced many temptations to correct her distortions. *How could a baby be better off with a dead mother?* he thought. *The trauma would haunt her daughter for the rest of her life. Post-partum depression is temporary. Her daughter's loss would be permanent.* He kept his thoughts silent. He needed to understand, not persuade.

Zikri summarized his understanding of Ayshah's reasons for dying, with no editorializing on his part. "It sounds like you want to end your life because you are in so much emotional pain," he said, "and you are convinced that things cannot get better for you."

"Yes, but that's not it entirely," she said.

"I'd like to understand better. What have I left off?" Zikri asked.

She lowered her head and wept. "I'm a failure," she said. "I'm a failure as a mother."

"How painful it must be to feel that way," he said. "I bet you expected this to be a joyous time."

"I did," she said. "I thought I would be happy, not miserable."

Zikri had a better understanding of his client's reasons for wanting to die. This knowledge would help foster a therapeutic stance of connection and empathy, while also guiding him in planning interventions to help Ayshah restore the wish to live.

Works Cited

Draper, J., Murphy, G., Vega, E., Covington, D. W., & McKeon, R. (2015). Helping callers to the National Suicide Prevention Lifeline who are at imminent risk of suicide: The importance of active engagement, active rescue, and collaboration between crisis and emergency services. *Suicide and Life-Threatening Behavior, 45*(3), 261–270.

Jobes, D. A. (2016). *Managing suicidal risk: A collaborative approach* (2nd ed.). New York, NY: Guilford Press.

Orbach, I. (2001). Therapeutic empathy with the suicidal wish: Principles of therapy with suicidal individuals. *American Journal of Psychotherapy, 55*(2), 166–184.

Tip 17: Validate the Wish to Die

"Feeling suicidal is a valid, understandable response to emotional pain."

John Chiles and Kirk Strosahl
(2005, p. 97)

The word "validation" has many meanings. In the context of psychotherapy, validation occurs when you convey that a person's emotions, behaviors, wishes, and fears are understandable in the context of the person's experience. The psychologist Marsha Linehan (1997) notes that there is always *something* to validate, no matter how small, in what a person thinks, feels, or does. In the case of suicidal wishes, your challenge is to find the part that makes sense – "the grain of wisdom," as Linehan calls it (p. 359) – and acknowledge that it is a logical response to what the person is going through.

In validating the person's desire to die, you are not affirming that suicide is the right (that is, valid) choice. As Linehan notes, "Validation has nothing to do with social desirability and is not a synonym for praise" (p. 358). Validation is evidence of empathy, not agreement. So, with the person who is certain that they will never get better and should die by suicide as a result, you can agree that their pain and hopelessness feel impossible to endure much longer. You can validate that feelings of unrelenting pain lead to suicidal desire in many cases. You can note that many people would feel suicidal, too, in the same situation. In other words, you understand why the person thinks suicide is the solution to their pain, even if you do not agree.

"I Just Want This Pain to Stop"

Traumatic memories relentlessly torment Lupe, a Marine veteran who served three tours of duty in Iraq between 2002 and 2007. Five years after she returned to civilian life in the U.S., she still experiences flashbacks and panic attacks when confronted with reminders of the traumas she experienced and witnessed.

"I'm never going to get better, and I'm just bringing down my parents and brothers," Lupe, 39, tells the clinical social worker completing her intake interview. "They worry about me all the time. If I kill myself, they can move on with their lives."

"That's so painful," her social worker said. "What you went through in Iraq was traumatic. You feel you will never get better, and you hate the effect that your trauma has on the people you love. With all of that, I can understand why you are thinking of suicide."

"Really? You don't think I'm bat-shit crazy for thinking of doing myself in?" Lupe said.

"No," the social worker said, "if you don't feel any hope that things can get better, it makes sense that one thing you would consider is suicide. You're in pain, and dying seems to be a way to end your pain."

"That's exactly it," Lupe said. "I just want this pain to stop."

"Of course you do," the social worker said. "You've been through hell. And one of the things we can discuss as we get to know each other better is other ways you can get out of that hell without ending your life."

Works Cited

Chiles, J. A., & Strosahl, K. D. (2005). *Clinical manual for assessment and treatment of suicidal patients.* Washington, DC: American Psychiatric Publishing.

Linehan, M. M. (1997). Validation and psychotherapy. In A. C. Bohart & L. Greenberg (Eds.), *Empathy reconsidered: New directions in psychotherapy* (pp. 353–392). Washington, DC: American Psychological Association.

Tip 18: Acknowledge that Suicide is an Option

"Avoid directly suggesting that suicide is not an option – the client knows that it is always an option, and direct opposition by the therapist will serve only to damage rapport."

Wayne Froggatt and Stephen Palmer
(2014, p. 157)

Suicidal people often face pleas to reject suicide. Loved ones and societal messages in general spell out all the reasons why suicide is wrong. These arguments against suicide can push a person into a corner where they feel compelled to defend suicide as an option. If you join those who insist that suicide is not an option, you risk a power struggle that erodes the therapeutic alliance and distracts you and the suicidal person from focusing on constructive solutions.

As someone tasked with helping the person stay alive, you might worry that you are conveying approval of suicide by accepting that it is an option. To the contrary, this acceptance simply reflects the truth of the matter. Except in extreme cases where a person lacks the physical capacity to make a suicide attempt, people have the power to end their life. If you do not know that the person sitting in front of you is intent on dying by suicide, there is little you can do to stop the suicide from happening. By refusing to argue that suicide is not an option, you free up the person to explore with you whether suicide is the *best* option, given other alternatives.

"You Can't Make Me Stay Alive"

Stefan, a nurse at a psychiatric hospital, looked at the blue-haired teenager sitting across from him as he conducted the intake interview. As he asked questions about her suicidal thoughts, she seemed to grow agitated.

"You can't make me stay alive," the teenager, Izzy, said. "I mean, everybody wants me to stop thinking of killing myself. But it's my choice. And it's not like they can be with me every second of every day for the rest of my life to make sure I don't do anything."

"You're really feeling pressured to give up suicide as an option," Stefan said.

"Sometimes it makes me want to kill myself just to prove that no one can stop me from killing myself," Izzy said.

"Well, I agree with you that nobody can make you stay alive," Stefan said.

"You do?" Izzy was visibly surprised. She didn't actually expect the nurse to agree with her.

"Sure," Stefan said. "I certainly want you to stay alive and will do what I can to help you stay alive. But I also know that if you decide you are going to kill yourself and don't tell anybody or drop any clues, then there really is nothing anyone can do to stop you, is there?"

"That's what I keep saying," Izzy said. "But everyone fights me on it."

"Well," Stefan said, "since you can always decide to kill yourself later, would you be willing to try some other things first? I've done this work for 20 years, and there are so many different things out there for you to try that I truly believe you can feel better."

"What kinds of things?" Izzy asked. The nurse explained, and Izzy did something she hadn't done in earlier conversations with other people about alternatives to suicide: She listened.

Work Cited

Froggatt, W., & Palmer, S. (2014). Cognitive behavioural and rational emotive management of suicide. In S. Palmer (Ed.), *Suicide: Strategies and interventions for reduction and prevention* (pp. 139–172). New York, NY: Routledge.

four
Assessing Danger

Tip 19: Gather Remaining Essentials about Suicidal Thoughts and Behavior

"An accurate understanding of suicide risk starts with a thorough and detailed understanding of the patient's suicidal thinking."
M. David Rudd
(2014, p. 332)

Suicidal thoughts, by themselves, are not necessarily a sign of danger. In the U.S., roughly 10 million adults seriously considered suicide in 2014 (Lipari et al., 2015). During that same time, just over 40,000 adults in the U.S. died by suicide. That means that fewer than half of 1% of adults with suicidal ideation die by suicide. Clearly, to gain a better picture of risk, it is necessary to go beyond the mere presence of suicidal thoughts and undertake a comprehensive suicide risk assessment.

Earlier, *Tip 10* discussed the value of listening to the suicidal person's story, without overwhelming the person with questions. The risk assessment interview should not be an interrogation. Yet there are essential areas to cover, and the person seldom addresses all of them in their narrative. You typically need to ask follow-up questions to fill in the gaps.

What follows are topics that, in combination with a good psychosocial assessment and diagnostic interview, are necessary to make a well-reasoned estimate of acute and chronic suicide risk (*Tips 32–33*). A psychosocial assessment should cover the person's psychiatric symptoms and diagnosis, trauma history, substance use, family history of suicide, and other risk factors for suicide. The topics below are specific to the person's suicidal thoughts and actions. Sample questions are provided for the purpose of illustration, but it is recommended that you tailor the questions to each individual client, using the validity techniques described in *Tip 9*.

Suicidal Thoughts and Images

Tips 8–12 describe various ways to uncover suicidal thoughts and images. Although it is ideal to use techniques designed to encourage disclosure, these questions capture the fundamentals:

"Do you wish you were dead?"
"Are you thinking of killing yourself?"
"Do you see mental pictures or images related to suicide? … To death more generally?"

Precipitants and Reasons for Wanting to Die

As *Tip 16* discusses, it is necessary to explore why the person wants to die. This information will usually spontaneously come out in the narrative interview (*Tip 10*). Often, people will give a reason that has lasted a while (e.g., "I've had depression for six months" or "My wife left me last month"). In such cases, ask what happened that transformed the person's pain into suicidal despair.

"What are your reasons for considering suicide?"
"What has changed *recently* that has made you think of suicide (or think of suicide more)?"

Frequency of Suicidal Thoughts or Images

Learn how many times a day or week the person thinks of suicide. As discussed in *Tip 9*, symptom amplification (Shea, 2011) can help reduce shame and invite an honest response:

"How many times a day would you say you think of suicide? 20? 30?"
"How often do you think of suicide? Every hour? Every day?"

Intensity

One way to get at intensity of suicidal desire is to ask the person to rate it on a scale:

> "On a scale of 0 to 10, with 0 being not at all and 10 being completely, how strongly do you want to kill yourself?"

Be careful not to confuse "intensity" with "intent." Somebody can intensely want to die yet lack any intent to actually act on that desire.

Duration

Several time elements need to be assessed: when suicidal thoughts first appeared, when the most recent episode of suicidal thoughts began, and how long suicidal thoughts last when they occur on any given day.

> "When was the first time ever that you had thoughts of killing yourself?" *(Age of onset)*
> "This time around, when did you first start thinking of suicide?" *(Most recent onset, if this is not the first episode)*
> "On a typical day when you have suicidal thoughts, how long do they last each time?" *(Duration)*

Duration is especially relevant because some people have only fleeting thoughts of suicide that they reject immediately, whereas others dwell on their suicidal thoughts for hours. Obviously, the longer the suicidal thoughts last, the more worrisome they are from a clinical standpoint.

Method and Means

Learn what methods the person has considered to end their life and whether the person has the means to carry out any of these methods. The information obviously is essential for safety planning (*Tip 38*), and it also informs your judgment of risk (*Tips 32–33*). If the person specifies a method, ask what other methods they are considering, too. *Always* ask the person if they own or otherwise have access to a gun, whether or not the person discloses that a firearm is a possible method (*Tip 23*).

> "What ways have you thought of killing yourself?" … "What other ways have you thought of?" … "What else?"
>
> "How many guns do you own?"

Preparations and Planning

The more detailed a person's plans and preparations for suicide are, the more severe the danger (Joiner et al., 2003). Preparations can include purchasing a firearm or other means for suicide, writing a will or suicide note, putting one's financial affairs in order, giving away belongings, deciding on a time and place for suicide, or "rehearsing" the act.

> "What actions, if any, have you taken to prepare for killing yourself?"
>
> "Have you taken measures to put your affairs in order, like organizing your belongings, wrapping up financial details, or writing a suicide note?"
>
> "Have you 'rehearsed' suicide in any way?"
>
> "Where would you kill yourself? … When? … How?"

Suicidal Intent and Timing

It is essential to learn how much the person intends to act on their suicidal thoughts or images, and when. Even intense suicidal thoughts may pose little immediate danger if the person has no intention of ever acting on them. Scaling questions are good here, too:

> "How much do you intend to act on your suicidal thoughts, on a scale of 0 to 10, with 0 being you have no intention at all and 10 being you completely intend to kill yourself?"

Timing is equally important. Someone might say with 100% certainty that they are going to die by suicide but, upon further questioning, reveal that they plan to die by suicide decades from now when they are too physically infirm to live independently.

> "If you act on your suicidal thoughts or images, when do you think you would do it?" (*Probe if necessary:* "In a few hours? … A few days? … A few weeks?")

A question that blends intent and timing concerns the person's safety once they walk out the door:

> "How likely do you think you are to act on your suicidal thoughts after you leave here? ... Over the next day or two? ... How about the next couple of weeks?"

Controllability

The person's ability (both perceived and actual) to resist suicidal impulses is an important marker of risk. Of particular concern are individuals who experience command hallucinations telling them to die by suicide (Shea, 2011).

> "How well can you control whether you will act on your suicidal thoughts?"

History of Suicide Attempts

Although most people who survive a suicide attempt do not eventually die by suicide, a previous attempt still places someone at markedly higher risk for suicide (Runeson et al., 2016). Gather information about how many times the person attempted suicide, when, the reasons for attempting suicide, the method (or methods) used, the injuries incurred, the treatment received, and the things that have kept them alive since then.

> "How many times have you attempted suicide?"
> "Tell me the story of what led you to attempt suicide..."

Worst Suicidal Ideation Ever

Research indicates that the intensity of the person's suicidal thoughts and planning during their *worst* suicidal episode is a better predictor of eventual suicide than their *current* level of suicidal ideation (Beck et al., 1999; Joiner et al., 2003).

> "When in your life have you *most* wanted to die by suicide? ... Please tell me about that..."

Follow up with questions about suicidal desire, planning, intent, preparations, and suicidal behavior during this worst-ever episode. Ask, too, how it is that the person survived.

History of Non-Suicidal Self-Injury

Although, by definition, non-suicidal self-injury is not a suicidal behavior, it is a marker of increased risk for suicide (Wilkinson, 2011). Gather information about how often the person has engaged in self-injury, when, what they did, what injuries they experienced, and what positive effects the self-injury has (e.g., distraction from anxiety). *Tip 77* explains non-suicidal self-injury in more depth.

"Have you ever hurt yourself without intending to kill yourself?" ... "What did you do?" ... "How often?"
"In what ways does hurting yourself help you?"

In Closing

This tip has addressed ways to understand more fully the nature of the person's suicidal thoughts and behavior. If the person has a long history of suicidality, then the breadth of information to gather can be overwhelming. *Tip 20* describes an approach for gaining that information in a systematic and manageable fashion, the Chronological Assessment of Suicide Events (Shea, 2011).

Works Cited

Beck, A. T., Brown, G. K., Steer, R. A., Dahlsgaard, K. K., & Grisham, J. R. (1999). Suicide ideation at its worst point: A predictor of eventual suicide in psychiatric outpatients. *Suicide and Life-Threatening Behavior, 29*(1), 1–9.

Joiner, T. E. Jr., Steer, R. A., Brown, G., Beck, A. T., Pettit, J. W., & Rudd, M. D. (2003). Worst-point suicidal plans: A dimension of suicidality predictive of past suicide attempts and eventual death by suicide. *Behaviour Research and Therapy, 41*(12), 1469–1480.

Lipari, R., Piscopo, K., Kroutil, L. A., & Miller, G. K. (2015). Suicidal thoughts and behavior among adults: Results from the 2014 National Survey on Drug Use and Health. NSDUH Data Review. Rockville, MD: Substance Abuse and Mental Health Services Administration.

Rudd, M. D. (2014). Core competencies, warning signs, and a framework for suicide risk assessment in clinical practice. In M. K. Nock (Ed.), *The Oxford handbook of suicide and self-injury* (pp. 323–326). Oxford: Oxford University Press.

Runeson, B., Haglund, A., Lichtenstein, P., & Tidemalm, D. (2016). Suicide risk after non-fatal self-harm: A national cohort study, 2000–2008. *The Journal of Clinical Psychiatry, 77*(2), 240–246.

Shea, S. C. (2011). *The practical art of suicide assessment: A guide for mental health professionals and substance abuse counselors.* Stoddard, NH: Mental Health Presses.

Wilkinson, P. O. (2011). Nonsuicidal self-injury: A clear marker for suicide risk. *Journal of the American Academy of Child & Adolescent Psychiatry, 50*(8), 741–743.

Tip 20: Learn About Prior Suicidal Crises: The CASE Approach

"In my experience, most errors in suicide assessment do not result from a poor clinical decision. They result from a good clinical decision being made from a poor or incomplete database."
Shawn Shea
(2011, p. 150)

Often, it is a daunting task to take a history of a person's suicidal thoughts and behaviors. Especially when a person has thought about or attempted suicide across many months or years, the information to gather can be overwhelming. The CASE approach – short for Chronological Assessment of Suicide Events – is designed to make the task more manageable. Instead of collecting all the facts, feelings, and thoughts about a person's suicidal processes in one free-flowing process, the CASE approach breaks down the information into four sections (Shea, 2011):

1. presenting suicidal thoughts and behaviors (within the prior 48 hours);
2. recent suicidal thoughts and behaviors (within the previous two months);
3. more distant thoughts and behaviors (more than two months ago);
4. suicidal thoughts in the present moment.

This sequence lends itself to a natural conversation (Shea, 2009). Typically, the person wants first to discuss their most recent suicidal thoughts. The CASE approach saves the present moment for last for a couple of reasons. One, the intervening discussion about past suicidality allows time for comfort and trust to build up, making it easier for the person to disclose current suicidal thoughts. Two, suicidal thoughts and intent can shift in the course of the interview. Even if the person starts off the interview by talking about their suicidal thoughts in the present moment, you need to revisit the topic near the end of the interview.

The CASE approach was developed by the psychiatrist Shawn Shea (2011). He recognized that the more suicidal history a person has, the more opportunities there are to miss important information. By dividing the vast areas to cover into smaller, well-defined segments, there is less opportunity for errors of omission.

Reconciling the Narrative and CASE Approaches

The narrative approach (*Tip 10*) and the CASE approach contradict each other. The narrative approach calls for inviting the suicidal person to tell their story in their own way, without form or structure. The CASE approach, on the other hand, prescribes specific regions of time to investigate and the order in which to do so. The two different approaches can be integrated to a degree. For example, instead of saying up front, as you would with a narrative interview, "I'd like to hear the story of how you came to see suicide as an option," the interviewer might break this down into an invitation for the specified time period: "I'd like to hear the story of your suicidal thoughts over the last couple days." The common strength of both the narrative and CASE approaches is the depth of information that they elicit, unlike some common risk assessment approaches that rely on cursory and formulaic questions about key areas of suicide risk.

Works Cited

Shea, S. C. (2009). Suicide assessment: Part 2 – Uncovering suicidal intent using the Chronological Assessment of Suicide Events (CASE Approach). *Psychiatric Times, 26*(12), 17.

Shea, S. C. (2011). *The practical art of suicide assessment: A guide for mental health professionals and substance abuse counselors.* Stoddard, NH: Mental Health Presses.

Tip 21: Cautiously Use Standardized Questionnaires

"No scale, or portion thereof, can substitute for thorough clinical assessment of suicidal ideation."

Robert Simon
(2011, p. 166)

A wide array of scales and questionnaires has been developed to assist in estimating a person's risk for suicide. The use of these standardized questionnaires has advantages and disadvantages. One advantage: Many people more readily will disclose suicidal thoughts in a written questionnaire than in an actual face-to-face interview (Kaplan et al., 1994; Yigletu et al., 2004). Another advantage: Quantifying a person's suicidal ideation with a score provides a way to assess progress and make comparisons over time. (To a degree, simply asking the person to rate their suicidal ideation on a scale of 0 to 10 can serve the same purpose.) In general, suicide assessment questionnaires can help open the door to a rich discussion about different aspects of suicidal thinking.

There are also important disadvantages to using suicide risk scales. Most notably, they have little predictive value (Brown, 2002). Some scales have high rates of false positives, in which they incorrectly label someone as being at high risk for suicide, while others have the opposite problem and miss large numbers of people who are at genuine risk (Quinlivan et al., 2016). An example of false positives and poor predictive value occurred in a study in which researchers assessed levels of hopelessness in psychiatric outpatients and then kept track of who died by suicide over an eight-year period (Beck et al., 1990). Researchers found that almost everyone who died by suicide had scored 9 or above on the Beck Hopelessness Scale. One might assume, then, that a score of at least 9 would be a marker of high suicide risk. However, almost two-thirds of people who did not die by suicide also scored 9 or above on the hopelessness scale.

Standardized scales have other limitations, too. None of the established suicide risk assessment scales has been studied extensively with minority populations. Also, professionals who use standardized suicide risk questionnaires run the risk of relying on them excessively and missing opportunities for a thoughtful discussion with the person about their desires and plans for suicide.

With those caveats in mind, several suicide-related questionnaires are described below.

The Columbia Suicide Severity Rating Scale (C-SSRS)

Used extensively for research, the C-SSRS covers various aspects of suicidal ideation and behavior. It is rather lengthy. If used as a structured interview, its successive battery of questions can seem like an interrogation, which runs counter to the narrative approach (*Tip 10*). As a means to be aware of and to track the person's suicidal ideation, the C-SSRS is also available as a brief screener for the person to fill out. The screener asks about various degrees of suicidal ideation, planning, and behavior. One version of the screener covers lifetime and recent suicidality; another covers suicidality since the last interview.

Many different versions of C-SSRS are available for no charge at http://cssrs. columbia.edu/the-columbia-scale-c-ssrs/cssrs-for-communities-and-healthcare. Training in using the scales is recommended, and information about free online training is available at http://cssrs.columbia.edu/training/training-options.

Suicide Status Form (SSF)

A core piece of the Collaborative Assessment and Management of Suicidality (CAMS), the SSF provides a map for covering most of the key components of a suicide risk assessment. The first part of the SSF is completed together by the suicidal person and therapist, usually sitting side by side to reinforce the collaborative nature of CAMS (*Tip 14*). The SSF calls for the suicidal person to elaborate on their psychological pain, stress, agitation, hopelessness, self-hate, wish to live, wish to die, reasons for living, reasons for dying, and overall risk for suicide.

The remaining portions of the SSF are completed by the clinician. Key areas covered in these portions are different components of suicide risk, such as a suicide plan, history of suicidality, and various warning signs; an outpatient treatment plan; a mental status exam; diagnosis; the person's level of suicide risk; and case notes.

The SSF is included in the book *Managing Suicidal Risk: A Collaborative Approach* (Jobes, 2016).

Scale for Suicidal Ideation

The Scale for Suicidal Ideation contains multiple-choice items that directly relate to the intensity of a person's suicidal desire and intent. Roughly half of the scale items tap into subjective aspects of the person's suicidal intent, such as the degree of their wish to live, wish to die, and desire to make a suicide attempt. The other half of the scale assesses the circumstantial, or objective, indicators of intent. Examples include whether the person has made preparations to attempt suicide, written a suicide note, or made arrangements for others after their death (e.g., drawn up a will).

The scale is available for purchase through Pearson (www.pearsonclinical. com). Only health and mental health professionals may purchase the scale.

Beck Hopelessness Scale

The Beck Hopelessness Scale does not directly address suicidal ideation, but, as noted earlier, its scores correlate with suicide risk in various studies (McMillan et al., 2007). The scale contains 20 true–false items that tap into a person's positive and negative beliefs about the future (e.g., "I never get what I want, so it's foolish to want anything"). Mental health and other health professionals may purchase the scale from Pearson (www.pearsonclinical.com).

Works Cited

Beck, A. T., Brown, G., Berchick, R. J., Stewart, B. L., & Steer, R. A. (1990). Relationship between hopelessness and ultimate suicide: A replication with psychiatric outpatients. *American Journal of Psychiatry, 147*(2), 190–195.

Brown, G. K. (2002). A review of suicide assessment measures for intervention research with adults and older adults. Retrieved on January 30, 2017, from the Suicide Prevention Resource Center website: www.sprc.org/sites/default/files/migrate/library/Brown-ReviewAssessmentMeasuresAdultsOlderAdults.pdf.

Jobes, D. A. (2016). *Managing suicidal risk: A collaborative approach* (2nd ed.). New York, NY: Guilford Press.

Kaplan, M., Asnis, G. M., Sanderson, W. C., Keswani, L., De Lecuona, J. M., & Joseph, S. (1994). Suicide assessment: Clinical interview vs. self-report. *Journal of Clinical Psychology, 50*(2), 294–298.

McMillan, D., Gilbody, S., Beresford, E., & Neilly, L. I. Z. (2007). Can we predict suicide and non-fatal self-harm with the Beck Hopelessness Scale? A meta-analysis. *Psychological Medicine, 37*(6), 769–778.

Quinlivan, L., Cooper, J., Davies, L., Hawton, K., Gunnell, D., & Kapur, N. (2016). Which are the most useful scales for predicting repeat self-harm? A systematic review evaluating risk scales using measures of diagnostic accuracy. *BMJ Open, 6*(2), e009297.

Simon, R. I. (2011). *Preventing patient suicide: Clinical assessment and management.* Arlington, VA: American Psychiatric Publishing.

Yigletu, H., Tucker, S., Harris, M., & Hatlevig, J. (2004). Assessing suicide ideation: Comparing self-report versus clinician report. *Journal of the American Psychiatric Nurses Association, 10,* 9–15.

Tip 22: Privilege Warning Signs Over Risk Factors

"When managing a patient at risk for suicide, clinicians are worried about decisions over the course of the next few minutes, hours, or days, not years."

M. David Rudd
(2008, p. 87)

Researchers have identified hundreds, if not thousands, of suicide risk factors. These are characteristics that, from a statistical perspective, increase the probability that a person could die by suicide. Generally speaking, the most frequently cited psychosocial risk factors for suicide are prior suicide attempts, psychiatric illness, substance abuse, prior psychiatric hospitalization, trauma, grief and loss, social isolation, health problems, and a family history of suicide. Common demographic characteristics linked to increased risk for suicide include male gender, American Indian/Alaska Native or White race (in the U.S.), older age (for White men in the U.S.), homelessness, poverty, unemployment, and firearm ownership. A well-known risk factor for suicide attempts is being gay, lesbian, bisexual, or transgender.

Suicide prevention texts typically emphasize the importance of assessing risk factors for suicide. The person's risk factors certainly are important to explore, especially because they can alert you to the need to probe further about suicidal thoughts. But most people with even the gravest risk factors for suicide (e.g., multiple prior suicide attempts; recent psychiatric hospitalization) do not die by suicide.

Far more salient to the assessment of current risk for suicide are *warning signs*. One of the key distinctions between a suicide warning sign and a risk factor is time (Rudd, 2014). Risk factors typically are static, longstanding, and speak to suicide risk in the long term. In contrast, warning signs usually are dynamic, temporary, and indicate acute escalation of suicide risk now or in the very near future.

Warning Signs for Suicide

Recent research has identified numerous warning signs for suicide (Rudd, 2014):

- frequent, intense suicidal thoughts;
- talking or writing about suicide;
- making preparations for suicide;
- suicide attempt or rehearsal;
- hopelessness;
- agitation;
- anxiety;

- increased anger;
- recklessness or impulsivity;
- dramatic mood changes;
- feeling trapped;
- sense of having no purpose or reasons for living;
- increased use of alcohol or other drugs;
- sleep disturbance; and
- withdrawal from others.

Based on the interpersonal psychological theory of suicide (Joiner, 2005), additional warning signs may include:

- feeling like a burden to others;
- a sense of disconnection from others; and
- an increase in high-risk activities and exposure to violence.

Taken in isolation, no warning sign for suicide is especially meaningful. Even thinking about suicide is not a good warning sign by itself, because so many millions of people who seriously consider suicide do not die by suicide. The more warning signs that are present, the more concerned you should be. On the other hand, someone can have an abundance of warning signs but lack the most important one of all: suicidal intent. Warning signs essentially alert you to the need to carefully assess whether a person might be on the verge of ending their life.

Risk Factors vs. Warning Signs

As a young, heterosexual White woman, Rochelle, 29, didn't have evident risk factors for suicide. She had never been diagnosed with a mental illness, attempted suicide, or even considered suicide in the past. She drank alcohol only occasionally and never used drugs. She was employed, in good health, and free of a trauma history. And nobody in her family had been suicidal, to her knowledge.

When asked, Rochelle professed not to have any suicidal thoughts. Fortunately, the intake therapist at the community mental health center remained alert for warning signs and occasionally asked specific questions to ferret them out. He also spoke with Rochelle's boyfriend, who had brought her to the appointment.

It turned out that for the last four days, Rochelle had hardly slept, falling asleep only for minutes at a time. Her boyfriend reported that she paced the house, going up and down the stairs repetitively, trying to tire herself out so that sleep would come. She was prone to weeping spells, a stark shift from her normally optimistic, positive demeanor.

The therapist asked again about suicidal thoughts in light of this new information. This time, Rochelle described incessant thoughts of taking a bottle of sleeping pills, combined with all the remaining narcotic painkillers that she had for migraine headaches. "Everyone would be better off if I were gone," she said, and she broke into tears. "I'm worthless, bitchy, and broken." When asked, she could not identify any reasons to live.

If the intake therapist had judged Rochelle's suicide risk based solely on her initial denial of suicidal thoughts and on the absence of risk factors, he would have missed the danger that Rochelle was in. Rochelle had few risk factors for suicide but many warning signs. The converse can also be true. Someone might have a tremendous number of risk factors but no suicidal thoughts or other warning signs for suicide, now or in the past. The chances that a person will attempt suicide immediately or in the near future are far more concerning than elevated risk for suicide over many years to come.

Works Cited

Joiner, T. (2005). *Why people die by suicide*. Cambridge, MA: Harvard University Press.

Rudd, M. D. (2008). Suicide warning signs in clinical practice. *Current Psychiatry Reports*, *10*(1), 87–90.

Rudd, M. D. (2014). Core competencies, warning signs, and a framework for suicide risk assessment in clinical practice. In M. K. Nock (Ed.), *The Oxford handbook of suicide and self-injury* (pp. 323–326). Oxford: Oxford University Press.

Tip 23: Screen for Access to Firearms

"The evidence is unequivocal: assessment of firearm ownership and access is an essential component of standardized suicide risk assessment and management."

Barbara Stanley and colleagues
(2017)

People who have access to a firearm are at much higher risk for suicide than those without (Dahlberg et al., 2004), and gun ownership is common in the U.S. (Smith & Son, 2015). So, a suicide risk assessment should always contain this key question: *"How many firearms do you own?"* Even if the person does not own any firearms, more questions need to be asked: *"Do you have plans to get a gun, rifle, or other firearm?"* *"Do you have access to a firearm even though you don't own one?"* If you are interviewing a child or adolescent, ask the youth's parents or guardians these questions, as well.

Never assume that someone does not own a gun, or that the person would volunteer the information without being asked. This point might seem obvious, yet researchers in one study found that mental health professionals asked only 6% of psychiatric patients if they owned a firearm (Carney et al., 2002). The question of whether a suicidal person owns a firearm is too important to be left unspoken. For people who do own or otherwise have access to a gun, *Tip 40* discusses different ways to reduce the danger of the person using the weapon to die by suicide.

"It Feels So Intrusive to Ask"

Just barely more than nine years old, Allie came to her mother with an unsettling announcement: "I want to make myself dead." Her older brother had died in a car accident six months earlier. Allie said she wanted to be with him. Her parents took her to a psychiatrist the next day. The doctor asked Allie how she would end her life. She said she would either hold her breath until she died or shoot herself in the head. Her parents looked at each other and visibly relaxed. She couldn't die from holding her breath, and they didn't own a gun. She was safe. But then the psychiatrist asked if any of the friends or relatives their daughter visited owned a firearm. Allie's parents didn't know.

"I recommend you investigate that," the psychiatrist said.

"It feels so intrusive to ask," the father protested.

"I can understand that," the psychiatrist said. "Yet it's so very important for the safety of your daughter."

The next week, Allie's parents told the psychiatrist that, to their surprise, her best friend's father kept several guns in the house. The friend's father had explained that he kept the ammunition separate and hid the weapons on a high shelf in the closet. They confided in him their concerns about Allie's safety and asked if he could put the firearms where curious children absolutely could not reach them. He readily agreed and did something he had been meaning to do for some time: He bought a gun safe, and hid the key.

Works Cited

Carney, C. P., Allen, J., & Doebbeling, B. N. (2002). Receipt of clinical preventive medical services among psychiatric patients. *Psychiatric Services, 53*(8), 1028–1030.

Dahlberg, L. L., Ikeda, R., & Kresnow, M. (2004). Guns in the home and risk of a violent death in the home: Findings from a national survey. *American Journal of Epidemiology, 160*(10), 929–936.

Smith, T. W., & Son, J. (2015). *General Social Survey final report: Trends in gun ownership in the United States, 1972–2014.* Chicago, IL: National Opinion Research Center at the University of Chicago.

Stanley, I. H., Hom, M. A., Rogers, M. L., Anestis, M. D., & Joiner, T. E. (2017). Discussing firearm ownership and access as part of suicide risk assessment and prevention: "Means safety" versus "means restriction." *Archives of Suicide Research, 21*(2), 237–253.

Tip 24: Inquire about Internet Use

"'Have you been googling suicide lately?' has become a requisite question in the thorough suicide evaluation."

Elias Aboujaoude
(2016, p. 226)

The Internet plays a huge role in people's lives, with untold numbers of people going online to play video games, connect with friends, read up on the news – and learn how to kill themselves. Pro-suicide sites provide information on the "best" suicide methods, give strategies for avoiding rescue, and argue that suicide is justified and should not be prevented. The effects can be devastating. In addition to providing dangerous how-to information, pro-suicide sites normalize suicide and even, in some cases, glorify it (Westerlund, 2013).

Amid these dire developments is some good news. Of the 100 most popular suicide-related sites on the Internet, most are constructive (Westerlund et al., 2012). The constructive sites argue against suicide or neutrally report information about research, policy, and prevention efforts. It is important, then, to ask suicidal individuals not only if they have sought information about suicide online, but also what types of information they have sought.

"I Looked Up How to Tie a Noose"

Miriam listened intently as Isiah recounted his story of how he came to consider suicide. Isiah, 54, had revealed that he thought of suicide about a half-dozen times each day for a few minutes at a time. He did not have a method in mind, and he had no intention of acting on his suicidal thoughts. Or so he said. A clinical social worker with years of experience, Miriam had a needling fear that something was missing.

On a hunch, she asked him, "Do you ever use the Internet to learn more about suicide?"

"A little," Isiah said.

"I know that a lot of people who are thinking of suicide go online to learn about suicide. Some are looking for information that will help them stay alive, and some want information about how to die. And some people just want both kinds of information, really. What kinds of things do you look up?"

Isiah looked down and fell silent. Miriam wondered if she had angered him. After a minute or so of silence, still looking down, he said, "I looked up how to tie a noose."

"That's good for me to know," Miriam said. "It helps me to understand better just how hopeless you must be feeling."

With further discussion, Miriam learned that Isiah had looked up how to tie a noose only two nights ago. And he had rummaged through his basement looking for a rope. And he had found one and set it aside. Needless to say, these new pieces of information led Miriam to realize that Isiah was at much higher risk of suicide than she had initially thought. She was grateful for the discovery.

Works Cited

Aboujaoude, E. (2016). Rising suicide rates: An under-recognized role for the Internet? *World Psychiatry, 15*(3), 225–227.

Westerlund, M. (2013). Talking suicide: Online conversations about a taboo subject. *Nordicom Review, 34*(2), 35–46.

Westerlund, M., Hadlaczky, G., & Wasserman, D. (2012). The representation of suicide on the Internet: Implications for clinicians. *Journal of Medical Internet Research, 14*(5), e122.

Tip 25: Probe for Homicidal Ideation

"Because many murder-suicides result in the death or injury of family members and sometimes mass murder, they cause countless additional morbidity, family trauma, and disruption of communities."
Peter Marzuk and colleagues
(1992, p. 3179)

As challenging as some people find it to ask a person about suicidal thoughts (*Tip 7*), asking about thoughts of killing another person can be even harder. The same fears are stirred up: *Will I anger the person? Will they feel insulted?* And the same fact remains: Despite your discomfort, the question often needs to be asked.

Homicide-suicide is a rare but devastating phenomenon. In the U.S., only 13–55 people out of 10 million perpetrate homicide-suicide (Knoll & Hatters-Friedman, 2015). In comparison, the suicide rate in the U.S. is roughly 100–400 times larger. Even so, about 10 homicide-suicide events happen every week in the U.S., with an estimated 1,200 victims annually (Violence Policy Center, 2015).

A good assessment of homicide risk covers the same information as a suicide risk assessment, but directed at thoughts of harming or killing others. As with suicidal ideation, it's good to take a narrative approach and elicit the person's story of how they came to think of killing another person (*Tip 10*). Then follow up with questions about the frequency, intensity, and duration of homicidal thoughts; any plans and preparations; degree of intent to follow through with homicide-suicide plan; expected timing, if the person does foresee acting on their thoughts; sense of control over homicidal impulses; and any prior violence, including domestic violence. It is also important to assess for factors that might make the person vulnerable to losing control, such as impulsivity, substance use, and command hallucinations.

Questions about homicidal ideation can be uncomfortable to ask, but they are profoundly important. Whatever discomfort you experience in directly asking about homicidal ideation is a small price to pay to potentially save lives.

"It's Too Terrible to Even Consider"

Depression first blanketed Zahra, 27, shortly after she gave birth to her daughter three months ago. At her first appointment with a psychologist, she disclosed that she is ruminating about killing herself. Her psychologist needed to ask Zahra about another worrisome possibility: Is she thinking of harming or killing anyone else, such as her baby?

He drew from the psychiatrist Shawn Shea's (2011) writings about validity techniques to ask this sensitive question (*Tip 9*). "Some people who think of suicide tell me they have thoughts of ending someone else's life, too," the psychologist said. And then, calling upon the technique of gentle assumption, he asked, "What thoughts like that have you had, if any?"

Zahra put her hand over her face. "I'm so ashamed," she said. She sobbed for a couple minutes before getting out the words: "I sometimes think of taking my little girl with me."

"I can see how much it pains you to have those thoughts," the psychologist said. "It must be very frightening. Can you tell me more?"

Zahra explained that at least once a day, the thought of killing her daughter before she kills herself would "pop" into her head. "I think, my life is so miserable, and I don't want her to be miserable, too. And if I kill myself, wouldn't it be an act of mercy to take her with me? That's what I think. But I don't really believe it. It's too terrible to even consider."

The psychologist assessed other elements of risk. Per Zahra's report, she had not given thought to how, when, or where she would kill her daughter, had made no preparations to do so, did not own a firearm, and wanted help in not acting on either her suicidal or homicidal thoughts. She described these thoughts as fleeting and uninvited. Although the psychologist eventually judged Zahra's risk of harming or killing her daughter to be low, his questioning revealed a crucial area for education, intervention, and safety planning. Zahra told him she felt relieved to have shared her "shameful secret." "I wasn't going to say anything about it," she said, "but then you asked."

Works Cited

Knoll, J. L., & Hatters-Friedman, S. (2015). The homicide–suicide phenomenon: Findings of psychological autopsies. *Journal of Forensic Sciences, 60*(5), 1253–1257.

Marzuk, P. M., Tardiff, K., & Hirsch, C. S. (1992). The epidemiology of murder-suicide. *JAMA, 267*(23), 3179–3183.

Shea, S. C. (2011). *The practical art of suicide assessment: A guide for mental health professionals and substance abuse counselors.* Stoddard, NH: Mental Health Presses.

Violence Policy Center. (2015). *American roulette: Murder-suicide in the United States.* Washington, DC: Author.

Tip 26: Collect Information from Family, Professionals, and Others

"It cannot be overemphasized that collaborative sources, such as family members, therapists, and police, may play a defining role in gathering the pieces of the risk assessment puzzle."

Shawn Shea
(2009, p. 5)

Friends, family, and others in the person's life see and hear things that you do not. The offhand remarks about suicide, the stashed pills, the crying jags every morning – these are only some of the things that significant others might observe. In fact, among people who died by suicide, many had disclosed their suicidal thoughts to a close family member or friend but not to their therapist or psychiatrist (Robins, 1981). Assuming there is not a reason that contacting friends or family would injure the suicidal person in some way, you should gather information from loved ones when formulating the suicidal person's level of risk, if possible.

The following questions are useful for obtaining information from significant others:

- *Do you have any concerns about the person? Why or why not?*
- *Has the person recently talked about death or suicide? ... What did they say?*
- *How many times has the person attempted suicide? ... When? ... What happened?*
- *Has the person otherwise engaged in self-injury? ... When? ... What happened?*
- *Is the person doing anything out of the ordinary lately, such as giving things away, not sleeping much, isolating from others, or using more drugs or alcohol than usual?*
- *Does the person own or have access to a firearm?*
- *What other lethal methods does the person have access to, such as prescription painkillers?*
- *Is there anything else you think I should know?*

Except in the case of a life-threatening emergency, you need adults' written permission to reach out to others. You can *receive* information from a concerned third party without your adult clients' consent. In the U.S., the Health Insurance Portability and Authorization Act (HIPAA) sets forth policies for sharing and receiving information without the client's consent. According to the U.S. governmental agency that governs HIPAA, the HIPAA Privacy Rule in no way prevents health care providers from listening to family members or other caregivers who may have concerns about the health and well-being of the patient, so the health care provider can factor that information into the patient's care" (U.S. Dept. of Human Services, 2014).

Some experts recommend contacting family, friends, or other informants even when the suicidal person does not consent and no life-threatening emergency exists to justify the breach in confidentiality. For example, the psychologist Megan Petrik and colleagues (2015) suggest undertaking a risk–benefit analysis of obtaining collateral information without the person's consent. Risks would include damaging the therapeutic relationship and violating ethical and legal codes. Yet risks also may come with *not* obtaining collateral information and support. Whatever route you decide to take, be sure to document both the suicidal person's choice and your own decision-making process (*Tip 34*).

If an adult is ambivalent about providing consent or outright averse to your reaching out to others, try to gain an understanding of their reasons. Elicit from the person the pros and cons of giving you permission to talk with one or more loved ones. This can help reveal cognitive distortions along with realistic fears that might impede the suicidal person from involving others.

The rules of confidentiality are different with children and adolescents. In the U.S., until youth are a certain age, which varies by state, the child's parents or guardians are legally entitled to know – and almost always need to know – if their child is considering suicide.

Beyond friends and family, medical and mental health professionals who have treated the person for depression, substance misuse, or other mental health problems also can help you flesh out your picture of the person's suicide risk. So can teachers or school counselors for youth, probation officers, and so on. If possible, talk to them. It is especially important to ask medical and mental health professionals about any prior suicidal episodes, mental health problems, diagnoses, treatments and their outcomes, and prescribed medications. Also, review treatment records from other professionals, if available.

"We Can All Work as a Team to Help Keep You Safe"

Samantha was concerned. A licensed professional counselor, she listened as Salvatore, 19, described thinking every day of killing himself. Just as she was about to ask him for permission to talk with a family member, he disclosed that fears of rejection by his family fueled his suicidal thoughts. A devout Catholic from a family of devout Catholics, he had been brought up to believe that it was a sin to love someone of the same sex. "And you see," he told her, his head bowed, "I'm gay."

Later in the session, after Samantha had listened to his story, explored his feelings, and assessed suicide risk, she told him, "Whenever I work with someone who has suicidal thoughts, I think it's a good idea to talk to someone in their family. It helps me to learn more about you, and we can all work as a team to help keep you safe in case your suicidal thoughts become dangerous. But your situation is different. Your parents are one of the reasons you feel so scared and confused that you have thoughts of suicide. I still would like to talk to them, but I'd only give them information about things that are essential for your safety. And your sexual orientation isn't one of them. Do you have an objection to my talking to them?"

"I don't know about that," Salvatore said. "What kinds of things would you tell them?"

"Well, I'd like to discuss with them that you're having suicidal thoughts and hear from them what they're seeing, especially since you still live at home. Also I'd like to talk with them about ways to help you stay safe, and ask them to call me if they see anything that concerns them."

"What if they ask you why I want to kill myself?" he asked.

"If they ask, I'll tell them that I can't disclose your reasons for feeling suicidal. It's your private information."

"I guess it's OK, then," Salvatore said. "Later can I change my mind if I don't want them up in my business?"

"Absolutely. It's up to you whether I talk with them. I mean, if there were a true medical emergency – like, if you told me you were going to kill yourself and then left the office before I could say or do anything – then I could call them without your permission. But even then, I couldn't just tell them everything about you, only what I needed to disclose to help you be safe."

"All right, then. It's fine," Salvatore said. "I know that you're just trying to help."

Works Cited

Petrik, M. L., Billera, M., Kaplan, Y., Matarazzo, B., & Wortzel, H. (2015). Balancing patient care and confidentiality: Considerations in obtaining collateral information. *Journal of Psychiatric Practice, 21*(3), 220–224.

Robins, E. (1981). *The final months: Study of the lives of 134 persons who committed suicide.* New York, NY: Oxford University Press.

Shea, S. C. (2009). Suicide assessment: Part 1. Uncovering suicidal intent: A sophisticated art. *Psychiatric Times, 26*(12), 17.

U.S. Department of Health & Human Services. (2014). HIPAA privacy rule and sharing information related to mental health. Retrieved January 23, 2017, from www.hhs.gov/sites/default/files/ocr/privacy/hipaa/understanding/special/mhguidancepdf.pdf.

five
Assessing Protective and Cultural Factors

Tip 27: Examine Reasons for Living

"A seldom-posed but important question is not why depressed patients want to commit suicide, but why they want to live."
Kevin Malone and colleagues
(2000, p. 1084)

As powerful as the person's urges to die may be, often the person's reasons for living provide an even more powerful defense. Strong, heartfelt deterrents to suicide can buffer risk, create ambivalence about dying, and provide a pathway to rebuilding hope. To find out what these deterrents are, it helps to ask an obvious but oft-neglected question: *"What are your reasons for staying alive?"*

Guide the person to be as specific as possible. People who are suicidal tend to overgeneralize, masking an abundance of reasons for living with one word, such as "family." The psychologist Craig Bryan (2007) gives the example of a veteran who came up with "God and family" as his reasons for living. Two is a small number. The apparent dearth of reasons for living left the veteran feeling "deficient and incompetent" (Bryan, 2007, p. 18). So Bryan asked him to list every family member who motivated him to stay alive, and within five minutes the man had 30 reasons to live on his list.

Some people have difficulty providing any reasons at all for living. Hopelessness and tunnel vision almost always accompany suicidal thinking (*Tip 66*). Like the sun hidden behind thick gray clouds, the person's reasons for living might be obscured by darkness. In such cases, ask the person to recall what their reasons were before their suicidal feelings hit:

- *"What used to be your reasons for living?"*
- *"What made life worth living for you before you felt so bad?"*
- *"What would be your reasons for living if you felt better?"*

A useful tool is the Reasons for Living Inventory. Individuals rate the strength of various reasons for living, which fall into six categories on the inventory: survival and coping beliefs; responsibility to family; child-related concerns; fear of suicide/death; fear of social disapproval; and moral objections to suicide (Linehan et al., 1983). The Reasons for Living Inventory, both in a 48- and 72-item version, is available for free at http://depts.washington.edu/uwbrtc/resources/assessment-instruments/.

Generally speaking, a discussion about reasons for living should not occur until you have already gained an understanding of the reasons why the person wants to die (*Tip 16*). Otherwise, the person could feel unheard and invalidated. An added benefit of first discussing reasons for dying is that the person may be moved to spontaneously rebut those points with reasons to stay alive.

Be careful not to impose on the person what you believe should be important reasons for staying alive. For example, some people will entreat the person to consider how suicide would hurt the person's friends and family (e.g., Omer & Elitzur, 2001). This sort of entreaty can provoke feelings of guilt, shame, and inadequacy, which in turn can worsen suicidal desire. Alternatively, the person might believe that dying by suicide would actually help loved ones by relieving them of a burden. In any case, trying to convince the person of reasons to stay alive situates you on opposite sides of a debate, which can alienate the person (*Tip 15*).

What If There Are No Reasons For Living?

When asked their reasons for staying alive, some suicidal people can't think of any. This signals profound hopelessness and potentially high risk for suicide. In these cases, it is important to call upon active listening and empathy, rather than persuasion or advice. Empathize with how awful it must feel for the person to lack any reasons, in their mind, to stay alive. Once you have truly listened and joined with the person in their hopelessness, gently offer hope that you can work together to uncover or build reasons for living.

Some students and professionals have told me they fear asking about reasons for living, in case the person says there are none. "*I don't want to make them feel bad*" is a common sentiment. The reality is that the person already feels bad. They already are aware that they cannot think of any reasons to stay alive. It is far better for you to know of this hopelessness than for the person to keep it private, depriving you of important information about the person's safety and emotional pain. As with other topics in suicide risk assessment, ask the question even if you are afraid of the answer.

"Dogs!"

Tanisha loves dogs. She has three, all mixed breeds rescued from a nearby shelter. Before depression immobilized her, she volunteered every Saturday at the shelter, walking the dogs and interviewing prospective adopters to help the pups get a good home. So when her clinical social worker asked what keeps her going in spite of her suicidal thoughts, Tanisha didn't hesitate: "Dogs!" she said.

"You really love dogs, don't you!" the social worker said. "What else keeps you going?"

"Well, it would kill my mother if I died," said Tanisha, 33. "And also my little sister. But I have to be honest. I'm far more worried about my dogs. I'm terrified about what would happen to them if I died. I would never want them to have to go to a shelter."

"Do you think your suicidal thoughts could ever get so strong that they override your fear for your dogs?" the social worker asked.

Tanisha's answer was almost a whisper. "Yes," she said.

"What would have to happen to overpower your love for dogs?"

"I don't get better," Tanisha said. "If I don't get better, I'll lose my job. My house. My dogs. Then what would there be to live for?"

"That's important for us to know," the social worker said. "Your dogs are a big reason to stay alive, and they could become a reason to die, in your mind, if you were ever to lose them."

"That's why I'm here," Tanisha said. "To prevent that from ever, ever happening."

Works Cited

Bryan, C. J. (2007). Empirically-based outpatient treatment for a patient at risk for suicide: The case of "John." *Pragmatic Case Studies in Psychotherapy, 3* (Module 2), 1–40.

Linehan, M. M., Goodstein, J. L., Nielsen, S. L., & Chiles, J. A. (1983). Reasons for staying alive when you are thinking of killing yourself: The Reasons for Living Inventory. *Journal of Consulting and Clinical Psychology, 51*(2), 276–286.

Malone, K. M., Oquendo, M. A., Haas, G. L., Ellis, S. P., Li, S., & Mann, J. J. (2000). Protective factors against suicidal acts in major depression: Reasons for living. *American Journal of Psychiatry, 157*(7), 1084–1088.

Omer, H., & Elitzur, A. C. (2001). What would you say to the person on the roof? A suicide prevention text. *Suicide and Life-Threatening Behavior, 31*(2), 129–139.

Tip 28: Identify Other Protective Factors

"Most established assessment tools (e.g., self-report measures, structured clinical interviews) focus solely on risk factors, which I believe leaves the clinician with only half the picture."

Peter Gutierrez
(2006, p. 130)

Just as risk factors are those characteristics that increase a person's risk for suicide, protective factors are those that lessen risk. Fundamentally, the absence of a risk factor is in itself protective. Yet protective factors should be assessed in their own right. This moves the assessment away from a solely deficit- and pathology-oriented conversation, a shift that can reconnect suicidal people to personal strengths and resources that they have lost sight of.

The previous tip addressed the need to identify the person's reasons for living. These reasons, when present, are an obvious protective factor. Based on numerous research studies (e.g., Doyle, 2015), other key protective factors to look for include:

- hopefulness and optimism;
- social support and connectedness;
- problem-solving skills;
- coping skills;
- reality-testing skills;
- positive self-esteem;
- a sense of competence and effectiveness;
- marriage;
- cultural sanctions against suicide;
- religious beliefs and commitment; and
- fear of suicide or death.

Although protective factors are important, they also can lose their strength in the face of severe suicide risk (Berman & Silverman, 2014). If a person appears to be at high risk for suicide, do not exaggerate the ability of protective factors to win out. On the other hand, where suicide risk is not high, the presence of protective factors can help the person follow their safety plan, rally social support and other resources, and resist acting on suicidal thoughts.

The Power of Relationships

At first, as the initial interview with Solomon unfolded, the psychologist was concerned about his client's level of suicide risk. At 33, Solomon had several worrisome characteristics. His father had died by suicide when Solomon was a young child. A close friend killed himself five years ago. Diagnosed with depression the previous month, Solomon now had thoughts of suicide every day, lasting a few minutes each time.

Then the psychologist began looking at potential protective factors. He learned that Solomon had a close relationship with his husband, considered their marriage to be strong, and adored their two young sons. Solomon also was close to his mother and sisters. He texted them every day. A couple times a month, everyone got together for a family dinner. Solomon also enjoyed his job as an elementary school teacher, and he and his husband were involved in their community.

Solomon emphatically stated that he did not intend to act on his suicidal thoughts. He felt hopeful that his depression would lift with therapy and time, and he was committed to following his safety plan. He explained that he felt a sense of obligation to his two young sons to resist suicide. "I would never want them to go through what I did when my father killed himself," he said. His religious beliefs helped, too. Solomon believed that life was sacred, to be ended only by God.

Based on these protective factors, combined with Solomon's lack of suicidal planning or intent, the psychologist did not judge Solomon to be at high risk for suicide. The psychologist would continue to assess suicide risk as treatment progressed, in case the intensity of Solomon's suicidal thoughts overtook the power of his relationships and religious beliefs to buffer him from suicidal urges.

Works Cited

Berman, A. L., & Silverman, M. M. (2014). Suicide risk assessment and risk formulation part II: Suicide risk formulation and the determination of levels of risk. *Suicide and Life-Threatening Behavior, 44*(4), 432–443.

Doyle, L. (2015). Risk and protective factors for self-harm and suicide. In L. Doyle, B. Keogh, & J. Morrissey (Eds.), *Working with self harm and suicidal behaviour* (pp. 29–42). London: Palgrave.

Gutierrez, P. M. (2006). Integratively assessing risk and protective factors for adolescent suicide. *Suicide and Life-Threatening Behavior, 36*(2), 129–135.

Tip 29: Pay Attention to Culture

"Without particular attention to cultural variation in suicide risk expression, suicide risk may be underdetected and managed improperly."

Joyce Chu and colleagues
(2013, p. 424)

"Culture-blindness" occurs when a person ignores the influence of culture on human behavior (Berry, 2013). In the context of suicide prevention, this is a significant omission. Ample evidence demonstrates that suicidal behaviors differ based on race, religion, gender, sexual orientation, gender identity, and other aspects of an individual's culture and context:

- Black women in the U.S. die by suicide so rarely that their rate is 70% lower than that of White women (Centers for Disease Control & Prevention, 2016).
- Suicide attempts are less common in individuals who have a religious affiliation, compared to individuals who identify as unaffiliated (Lawrence et al., 2015).
- With rare exceptions, men's suicide rates around the world greatly exceed those of women (Värnik, 2012).
- Lesbian, gay, bisexual, and transgender people have far higher rates of suicide attempts than the general population (Haas et al., 2010).
- Suicide rates are higher than average, sometimes dramatically so, among indigenous groups in diverse regions and countries, including American Indians, Alaska Natives, and Native Hawaiians (Wendler et al., 2012).

The Cultural Theory of Suicide

The cultural theory of suicide, developed by the psychologist Joyce Chu and colleagues (2010), specifies four cultural constructs that influence suicide risk, whether positively or negatively: cultural sanctions, idioms of distress, minority stress, and social discord. *Cultural sanctions* hinge on how much a person's family, religion, or cultural group condemn suicide – or not. In some cultures, suicide is seen as an acceptable, sometimes even normal, response to painful events, such as bringing shame to one's family. In other cultures, suicide itself is seen as shameful. Religion especially can affect the views that people have on suicide (*Tip 30*). When exploring the acceptability of suicide, useful questions include:

- *"How do the people you know view suicide, in terms of whether it's acceptable or not?"*
- *"How acceptable do you think suicide is?"*

- *"Thinking of the cultural group (or groups) that you belong to, how do they tend to view suicide?"*

Idioms of distress concern mainly the different ways that suicidality manifests in diverse cultural groups. This includes differences in symptoms of suicide risk, rates of disclosure of suicidal ideation and behavior, and choice of suicide method. For example, a small U.S. study found that African American and Asian American college students were less likely than White students to disclose their suicidal thoughts on an intake questionnaire at a university counseling center (Morrison & Downey, 2000). The authors note that if counselors had not directly asked study participants about suicidal thoughts, then only 1 of the 36 minority students with suicidal ideation would have been identified.

Minority stress is salient because discrimination, marginalization, and mistreatment stemming from an aspect of one's cultural identity have been linked to increased suicide risk (Chu et al., 2010). *Social discord* also relates to minority stress, especially isolation and family conflict stemming from one's marginalized status. As an example, young people who are lesbian, gay, bisexual, or transgender may experience rejection and even abuse by their parents. For these reasons, it is helpful to explore the suicidal person's experiences of discrimination and isolation in relation to their cultural group, and the person's sense that these experiences are part of the reason they consider suicide.

The Cultural Formulation Interview

Another way to incorporate culture into your suicide risk assessment is to use the Cultural Formulation Interview (American Psychiatric Association, 2013). This interview addresses several major areas in relation to a person's cultural identity and mental health problem (specified here, for the sake of example, as suicidal thoughts and behavior):

- cultural definition of suicidal thoughts and behavior;
- cultural perceptions of the cause of suicidal thoughts and behavior;
- role of cultural identity in increasing or decreasing suicide risk;
- cultural factors influencing coping and help-seeking for suicidal thoughts or behavior;
- cultural factors affecting the therapeutic relationship, such as different cultural backgrounds of the professional helper and suicidal individual, perceived racism of the professional, and language barriers.

A core piece of the Cultural Formulation Interview is to learn how the person views the role of their cultural background or identity in relation to their symptoms. The Cultural Formulation Interview specifies that "cultural background or identity" can mean "the communities you belong to, the languages you speak, where you or your family are from, your race or ethnic background, your gender or sexual orientation, or your faith or religion" (American Psychiatric Association, 2013, p. 753). Other groups with which the person identifies can also affect the person's perceptions of suicide and help-seeking, including veterans, people of specific age groups (e.g., older adults), immigrants, and so on.

The interview calls for asking the person to reflect on the most important aspects of their cultural background or identity. From there, an overarching question to capture cultural aspects of a person's suicidal experience could be: "*Is there anything about your cultural background or identity that makes you more likely to think about suicide or to die by suicide?*" Protective aspects of one's cultural background should also be explored: "*What about your cultural background or identity makes you* less *likely to have suicidal thoughts, or to act on them?*"

The Cultural Formulation Interview is available for free at www.psychiatry. org/File%20Library/Psychiatrists/Practice/DSM/APA_DSM5_Cultural-Formulation-Interview.pdf. It also is available in the *DSM* (American Psychiatric Association, 2013).

"I'm Letting My People Down"

The daughter of a Haitian mother and a Nigerian father, Esperanza identified as Black. Originally named Emmanuel at birth and raised as a boy until she was seven years old, she also identified as a trans woman. Her psychiatrist wondered how Esperanza's cultural identities might affect her suicide risk, for better or for worse.

"Esperanza," the psychiatrist said, "you've said you identify as a Black, trans woman. Are there other pieces of your culture that are important to you?"

Esperanza, 27, smiled. "Nope, Doc. That's me in a nutshell."

The psychiatrist continued. "I'm wondering, which parts of your cultural background do you think affect your suicidal thoughts, if any?"

"Not any, really," Esperanza said. "I mean, you read a lot about trans people being bullied and harassed. Luckily, that just doesn't happen to me, I think because I knew so young that I was a girl. Everyone except my family has always known me as a girl, and my family's always been supportive. So it's a total non-issue for me."

"Good to know," the psychiatrist said. "How about being a person of color? Does that play into your suicidal thoughts at all?"

"Not at all," Esperanza said. "If anything, being a Black woman makes me want to *not* do anything. Black people don't really kill themselves. I mean, not a lot, anyway."

"That's true," the psychiatrist said. "Black women have really low suicide rates. There's even a research article that says suicide is 'a White thing.'" (He was referring to a 1993 article by Kevin Early and Ronald Akers.)

Esperanza laughed slightly. "True, it is a White thing. My people, we don't do that."

"And yet," the psychiatrist said, "you do have thoughts of killing yourself. So there's this cultural expectation that you wouldn't think of it, right?"

Esperanza's eyes welled up. "Yes, I feel like I'm doing something wrong," she said. "I'm letting my people down. Not just other Black people, but also trans people who look to me to be strong. So that's why I have to not do anything. I have to stay alive, not just for me, but for others."

This brief exchange gave her psychiatrist insight into how Esperanza's cultural background affected her suicide risk. And it revealed cultural sources of strength and vulnerability that needed more attention in the sessions to come.

Works Cited

American Psychiatric Association. (2013). *Diagnostic and statistical manual of mental disorders (DSM-5)*. Washington, DC: American Psychiatric Publishing.

Berry, J. W. (2013). Achieving a global psychology. *Canadian Psychology/Psychologie Canadienne, 54*(1), 55–61.

Centers for Disease Control & Prevention. (2016). Injury prevention and control: Data and statistics (WISQARS). Retrieved December 12, 2016, from www.cdc.gov/injury/wisqars/fatal.html.

Chu, J. P., Goldblum, P., Floyd, R., & Bongar, B. (2010). The cultural theory and model of suicide. *Applied and Preventive Psychology, 14*(1), 25–40.

Chu, J., Floyd, R., Diep, H., Pardo, S., Goldblum, P., & Bongar, B. (2013). A tool for the culturally competent assessment of suicide: The Cultural Assessment of Risk for Suicide (CARS) Measure. *Psychological Assessment, 25*(2), 424–434.

Early, K. E., & Akers, R. L. (1993). "It's a white thing": An exploration of beliefs about suicide in the African-American community. *Deviant Behavior, 14*(4), 277–296.

Haas, A. P., Eliason, M., Mays, V. M., Mathy, R. M., Cochran, S. D., D'Augelli, A. R., ... & Clayton, P. J. (2010). Suicide and suicide risk in lesbian, gay, bisexual, and transgender populations: Review and recommendations. *Journal of Homosexuality, 58*(1), 10–51.

Lawrence, R. E., Oquendo, M. A., & Stanley, B. (2015). Religion and suicide risk: A systematic review. *Archives of Suicide Research, 20*(1), 1–21.

Morrison, L. L., & Downey, D. L. (2000). Racial differences in self-disclosure of suicidal ideation and reasons for living: Implications for training. *Cultural Diversity and Ethnic Minority Psychology, 6*(4), 374–386.

Värnik, P. (2012). Suicide in the world. *International Journal of Environmental Research and Public Health, 9*(3), 760–771.

Wendler, S., Matthews, D., & Morelli, P. T. (2012). Cultural competence in suicide risk assessment. In R. I. Simon & R. E. Hales (Eds.), *The American Psychiatric Publishing textbook of suicide assessment and management* (2nd ed., pp. 75–88). Arlington, VA: American Psychiatric Publishing.

Tip 30: Investigate Religious and Spiritual Views of Suicide

"The relationship between an individual's religiosity and suicidality often remains ignored in clinical assessments."

Robin Gearing and Dana Lizardi
(2009, p. 337)

Religious and spiritual beliefs can affect suicide risk in various ways. For many people, these beliefs are a deterrent to acting on suicidal thoughts, especially when their religious views condemn suicide. Numerous studies have linked greater degrees of religious involvement to lower rates of suicide (Koenig, 2016). One study found that suicide rates among women who attended religious services at least once a week, compared to those who did not, were 84% lower, even when taking into account the social support that religious involvement provides (VanderWeele et al., 2016). At the same time, religion also may *increase* suicide risk in some people (Lawrence et al., 2016). Some suicidal people feel forsaken, or even punished, by God. Other people suffer no estrangement from God and, instead, believe that God will understand or even that God is "calling" them to die.

Beliefs about what happens after death also are important. If a person believes in a heaven where reunions with loved ones occur, then belief in the afterlife can increase a vulnerable person's risk for suicide. Conceptions of an afterlife can buffer suicide risk if a person believes that those who die by suicide suffer divine punishment. In a similar fashion, a person's stance on reincarnation also can enhance or reduce risk. Some people believe that they will be reborn into a better life, while others believe that if they die by suicide, they will be reincarnated into a life of equal, or even harsher, suffering.

To explore how religious and spiritual beliefs affect a person's suicide risk, social workers Robin Gearing and Dana Lizardi (2009) recommend assessing the importance of religion to the person, the ways that religion helps or harms the person, the role of religion and religious coping during times of stress, and the religion's stance toward suicide. Possible questions include:

- *"How religious of a person are you?"*
- *"How do your religious beliefs help you to cope with stress, if at all?"*
- *"Are there ways that your religious beliefs or community add to your stress?"*
- *"What does your religion say about suicide? ... Do you agree?"*

If the person identifies with a religion that condemns suicide, explore the discrepancy between the religion's sanctions and the person's thoughts of suicide. Do not do this as a means to talk the person out of suicide. Instead, seek to understand if this discrepancy causes distress, which could then affect suicidal desire.

Be careful to maintain cultural sensitivity when discussing the person's religious and spiritual beliefs. It is not appropriate to try to talk people out of these beliefs. It is appropriate, though, to tap into any ambivalence about suicide that their beliefs generate, and to observe inconsistencies in how they apply their beliefs. For example, some people apply religious beliefs about grace and forgiveness to others, but not to themselves. Exploring the person's religious and spiritual stance on suicide can amplify your understanding of the person's suicide risk.

"Because Hell is Forever"

Sanjay, 78, spoke softly as he described a stream of tormenting thoughts that he would be better off dead, and that his children and grandchildren would be better off, too, if he were no longer around. His wife of 53 years had died six months earlier. Now, immobilized by grief, Sanjay saw no hope of ever again enjoying being alive.

To get a better picture of Sanjay's risk of acting on his suicidal thoughts, his grief counselor asked him about his religious beliefs. "Some people who think of suicide have religious or spiritual beliefs that affect how much they want to act on their suicidal thoughts," the counselor said. "Is that true for you?"

"That's the thing," Sanjay said. "I'm afraid of going to hell if I kill myself."

"That's a significant fear," she said.

"It certainly is," Sanjay said. "Because hell is forever. No way out. And I'm certain my wife is not in hell. So I would never see her again."

"Do you have a specific religion that you follow?"

"No, I do not," Sanjay said. "Now that I think about it, I simply have absorbed the religious messages about hell."

"Are your fears of hell enough to stop you from acting on your suicidal thoughts, do you think?" the grief counselor asked. "Or are they sort of small fears that you can push aside?"

Sanjay shook his head. "I would say they're rather big fears. To be more precise, the fear of going to hell is the only thing that keeps me here. No matter how bad things get here, hell on earth can't be as bad as hell in the afterlife."

The counselor knew from years of experience that this could change, even if Sanjay thought it couldn't. She would remain on guard for changes both in Sanjay's suicidal thoughts and fears of suicide's aftermath. But, at least for now, Sanjay's fears of hell appeared to be a wall in suicide's path.

Works Cited

Gearing, R. E., & Lizardi, D. (2009). Religion and suicide. *Journal of Religion and Health, 48*(3), 332–341.

Koenig, H. G. (2016). Association of religious involvement and suicide. *JAMA Psychiatry, 73*(8), 775–776.

Lawrence, R. E., Oquendo, M. A., & Stanley, B. (2016). Religion and suicide risk: A systematic review. *Archives of Suicide Research, 20*(1), 1–21.

VanderWeele, T. J., Li, S., Tsai, A. C., & Kawachi, I. (2016). Association between religious service attendance and lower suicide rates among US women. *JAMA Psychiatry, 73*(8), 845–851.

six
Putting It All Together
Estimating Risk

Tip 31: Solicit the Person's Own Assessment of Suicide Risk

"With a lifetime of experience, individuals may be in a better position than are external evaluators to predict their own behavior."
Jillian Peterson and colleagues
(2011, p. 627)

With all the different questions and methods for obtaining a picture of a person's suicide risk, one that is often overlooked is to ask the suicidal person. People's predictions of whether they will attempt suicide are as accurate, and sometimes even more so, than standardized instruments that assess suicide risk (Peterson et al., 2011). As the psychiatrist Robert Hirschfeld (2001) says, "The best way to determine if a patient is at imminent risk of suicide is simply to ask him or her" (p. 192). Possible questions include:

- *"How likely is it that you will kill yourself after you leave this office? ... How about in the next couple of days?"*
- *"How safe do you think you are from acting on your suicidal thoughts today? ... How about tomorrow? ... This week?"*

Whatever the person's response, a helpful follow-up question is, "What is the basis for your answer?" (Peterson et al., 2011, p. 629). Explore, too, what could happen that would make the probability of suicide higher in the future.

Conversely, it is also useful to ask what could lower the chances that the person will act on their suicidal thoughts.

"Not Very High at All"

After it was all said and done, after engaging Daniel, 51, in a narrative interview about how he came to think of suicide, after looking at his history of suicidal behavior, after examining warning signs, risk factors, and protective factors, and after talking with his psychiatrist and his wife, Daniel's level of suicide risk still was unclear. The clinical social worker who interviewed him thought Daniel was at moderate acute risk for suicide. *Maybe.* Despite her years of experience, she wasn't quite sure. Of course, no one can ever be sure. But she wanted to be closer to sure. So she asked him.

"Daniel," the social worker said, "what do you think are the chances that you'll kill yourself within the next few months?"

"Not very high," he said. "Not very high at all."

"So, the weather man will say there's a 20% chance of rain, or 50%, or whatever. What percent would you put a suicide attempt at?"

"Really, I wouldn't say more than 20% or 30%. Maybe not even that high."

"What's the basis for your putting that at 20–30%?" the social worker asked.

"Oh, things would have to get a lot worse before I'd actually do myself in," Daniel said. "I'd have to lose my job, and my wife, and my hope, too, before I would end it all."

"How about in the long term?" she asked. "Thinking ahead, what do you think is the probability that you'll die by suicide eventually?"

"Well, that's different. I'd put that at 70 or 80%," Daniel said. "Maybe even higher. Once I hit old age and can't take care of myself, I don't see much point in being here anymore."

The social worker wouldn't dare rest her assessment solely on Daniel's predictions. Combined with the other details she had collected from Daniel, his psychiatrist, and his wife, Daniel's rating of his suicide risk reinforced her own.

Works Cited

Hirschfeld, R. M. A. (2001). When to hospitalize patients at risk for suicide. *Annals of the New York Academy of Sciences, 932*(1), 188–199.

Peterson, J., Skeem, J., & Manchak, S. (2011). If you want to know, consider asking: How likely is it that patients will hurt themselves in the future? *Psychological Assessment, 23*(3), 626–634.

Tip 32: Estimate Acute Risk for Suicide

"When all the questions have been asked and answered, the final decision regarding degree of suicide risk is a subjective one."

Jerome Motto
(1991, p. 77)

Often, an urgent question tantalizes, even taunts, someone helping a suicidal person: *"How likely is this person to act on suicidal thoughts after they leave this room?"* Unfortunately, there is no formula or algorithm for determining who will or will not attempt suicide. The best we can do is *estimate* the risk for suicide. Given the inability to predict human behavior, estimates of suicide risk are fallible, and some experts question their utility (e.g., Large & Ryan, 2014). Still, some formulation of risk is necessary in order to determine next steps.

Estimates of acute suicide risk tend to fall under the categories of low, medium, high, and imminent (or something similar, like mild, moderate, severe, and extreme) (e.g., Bryan & Rudd, 2006; Berman & Silverman, 2014). What you do next will depend on how high you judge the person's suicide risk to be, especially when deciding whether outpatient care is suitable or hospitalization is necessary (*Tips 35–36*). You should also estimate the person's level of suicide risk in the long term, based on the person's longstanding or recurrent suicidal thoughts, multiple suicide attempts, or other ongoing risk factors for suicide (*Tip 33*).

The material below *generally* describes the various levels of risk in the near term. But first, a warning: There are exceptions to all generalities. Many different variables can affect your estimate of a person's suicide risk. Just a few examples include the strength of the therapeutic alliance, your trust in the person's disclosures, the nature of the person's current crisis, the person's insight into their difficulties, and their willingness and ability to abide by a safety plan. Always individualize your estimate of risk to the person's unique symptoms and situation.

Low (or Mild) Acute Risk

The prototypical person at low risk for suicide, despite having suicidal ideation, has only vague, overly general, and fleeting suicidal thoughts or imagery, no self-reported intent to act on those thoughts, no objective indicators of suicidal intent such as making plans and preparations to attempt suicide, no prior suicide attempt, few or no major warning signs for suicide beyond suicidal ideation, and few or no major psychiatric symptoms. The low-risk person typically has ample hopefulness, resources (e.g., social support), reasons for living, and other protective factors.

Even when a person's risk of suicide appears to be very low, it is not appropriate to say that someone is at *no* risk for suicide. Just as we cannot ever know with certainty who will attempt or die by suicide, we also cannot say with certainty who will not. If you truly believe that a specific person's risk for suicide is very low, say that, and explain why.

Example: Low Acute Risk

At first, Yuan exulted in her new role as an emergency room physician. She was happy to have her long years of training behind her, and she felt increasingly confident in her skills. As the stress of her new job wore on her, she started having trouble sleeping. Then came symptoms of depression, including mere wisps of thoughts of killing herself. When she lay down to sleep at night, the thoughts would come to her: *"I want to die." "It would be easier if I killed myself."* She instantly brushed off the thoughts. They felt so random, so foreign to her, so *alien*. These thoughts were not her. Now, she easily lists off to her primary care physician the reasons she does not want to kill herself: her love for her husband; her pride and satisfaction about her career; her involvement in her Buddhist temple and in charitable groups; her convictions that suffering in life is inevitable, but that life still is to be savored. She has no history of suicidal thoughts or behavior, no prior depression, no family history of mental illness or suicide. She insists she has no intention of acting on these thoughts, which come only a few times a night and last no more than a few seconds each time. She acknowledges that she is developing other symptoms of depression, such as poor appetite and loss of energy, and she agrees to see a psychiatrist for an evaluation for possible medication.

Medium Acute Risk

The moderate risk category captures people whose suicidal thoughts have become more enduring or specific, but who do not have strong subjective or objective indicators of intent to attempt suicide. Typically, a few suicide warning signs are present (*Tip 22*), and psychiatric symptoms are worsening. The person might have thought of ways to die by suicide and even possess some intent to act on the suicidal thoughts, but the suicidal intent is faint and co-exists with an outright desire to live. Another situation where moderate suicide risk can be assumed is when a person has recently attempted suicide (e.g., within days or weeks), reports no longer having strong suicidal desire or intent, and gives the professional reason to believe that their reports are trustworthy. By virtue of the person's recent suicidal behavior, the risk for suicide is elevated.

Example: Moderate Acute Risk

Darnell's mind torments him, transforming ordinary objects into weapons he could use against himself. That tree outside his bedroom window. That bottle of aspirin by his bathroom sink. That knife on the kitchen counter. That balcony outside his office window. He tells the nurse at the community clinic that he constantly has thoughts of killing himself, and he wants help resisting them. Diagnosed currently with a major depressive disorder, he has a history of two suicide attempts 10 years earlier when he was a teenager. "I don't really want to die," he says. "My depression is just telling me I do." Darnell experiences no hallucinations and feels he can control whether he acts on his suicidal thoughts. He readily engages in safety planning and gives permission to the nurse to call his girlfriend and ask her to remove or secure potential weapons from the home, which the girlfriend agrees to do before Darnell returns home. Darnell makes an appointment for one week later, at which point the nurse will assess his suicide risk again.

High (or Severe) Acute Risk

A common high-risk scenario is when a person has intense suicidal thoughts, a plan and the means to carry it out, and intends to attempt suicide, but not any time soon. Another common high-risk scenario is when someone who recently attempted suicide regrets having survived, and wants to attempt suicide again but lacks the ability or intent to do so. Other factors can place someone at high risk for suicide, such as command hallucinations to kill oneself and, in concert with suicidal ideation, substance use and impulsivity. When someone is at acutely high risk for suicide, protective factors can no longer be presumed to diminish the risk (Berman & Silverman, 2014).

Example: High Acute Risk

Iliana, 63, remains hooked up to monitoring devices in the intensive care unit, where she has been a patient for two days as a result of an overdose of medication. Her children and husband are maintaining a bedside vigil, and she appreciates the warmth of their company. But she still wants to die. "I wish I had never woken up," she tells her physician when he checks on her for his daily rounds. With the constant vigilance of her family, she has no plans to try to kill herself again immediately. She knows that, as long as she is in the ICU, she would be thwarted. But her risk for suicide is too high for her to go home after her medical treatment ends, so the physician arranges for her to be transferred to an inpatient psychiatric hospital.

Imminent Risk

A person should be considered at imminent risk for suicide if you reasonably believe that they will attempt suicide within hours or days (generally 48–72 hours) if they are not protected (Berman & Silverman, 2014). Imminent *risk* of suicide is not the same as imminent suicide. To state that someone's suicide is imminent is to predict the unpredictable. Nobody can know with certainty that, barring intervention, someone will die by suicide (Simon, 2006).

Example: Imminent Risk

Carlos, 22, was diagnosed with bipolar disorder as a teenager. He stopped taking his mood-stabilizing medications two months ago, saying, "I don't need them anymore." Now in a depressive episode, he tells his psychologist at his weekly session that he bought a .38 caliber pistol at a pawn shop a couple days ago. Further, he says he is going to shoot himself in the head after he takes his dog to a friend's house later that afternoon. "God has called me home," he says of a voice that he hears incessantly. He has attempted suicide four times in his life, most recently when he stabbed himself nine months ago. He refuses to engage in any problem-solving around his safety. "I'm going to die," he says. "This is the way God wants it."

Your estimation of the person's suicide risk will inform what steps you should take to help keep the person safe, especially in terms of whether you need to move toward hospitalization. *Tips 35–36* address hospitalization, and *Tips 37–43* describe other techniques that can support the person's safety.

Works Cited

Berman, A. L., & Silverman, M. M. (2014). Suicide risk assessment and risk formulation part II: Suicide risk formulation and the determination of levels of risk. *Suicide and Life-Threatening Behavior, 44*(4), 432–443.

Bryan, C. J., & Rudd, M. D. (2006). Advances in the assessment of suicide risk. *Journal of Clinical Psychology, 62*(2), 185–200.

Large, M. M., & Ryan, C. J. (2014). Suicide risk categorisation of psychiatric inpatients: What it might mean and why it is of no use. *Australasian Psychiatry: Bulletin of Royal Australian and New Zealand College of Psychiatrists, 22*(4), 390–392.

Motto, J. A. (1991). An integrated approach to estimating suicide risk. *Suicide and Life-Threatening Behavior, 21*(1), 74–89.

Simon, R. I. (2006). Imminent suicide: The illusion of short-term prediction. *Suicide and Life-Threatening Behavior, 36*(3), 296–301.

Tip 33: Estimate Chronic Risk for Suicide

"All patients have different levels of vulnerability to experience another suicidal crisis in the future."

M. David Rudd
(2008, p. 409)

Paradoxically, a person can be at low risk for suicide in the short term but still have high chronic risk for many years to come, sometimes even a lifetime. The distinction between warning signs and risk factors explains the discrepancy. As *Tip 22* explains, warning signs are thoughts, behaviors, and symptoms that signify potential danger of suicide in the near future. Risk factors, on the other hand, are longstanding, often immutable characteristics about a person's psychosocial history or demographics. Even after warning signs such as suicidal planning, hopelessness, agitation, and insomnia go away, the risk factors remain.

Just as you estimate someone's level of acute risk for suicide, you should also categorize their chronic risk. The psychiatrist Hal Wortzel and colleagues (2014) specify categories of low, intermediate, and high chronic risk.

Low Chronic Risk

Among people with prior suicidal thoughts, those in the low risk category lack chronic suicidal ideation, a history of suicide attempt, persistent and severe mental illness, and severely impulsive behaviors. These individuals have a solid array of protective factors, including good psychosocial functioning and coping skills.

Intermediate Chronic Risk

The intermediate category includes people who have significant mental health problems, such as chronic suicidal ideation, suicide attempt history, mental illness, and substance use disorder. However, their problems are relatively balanced by protective factors, coping skills, and psychosocial stability, all of which buffer the person's risk of attempting suicide in the event of another suicidal crisis. Even so, the person should continue to have a safety plan (*Tip 38*).

High Chronic Risk

In the absence of adequate coping skills and resources, many problems can place someone at high chronic risk for suicide. These include chronic suicidal ideation, a history of suicide attempt, ongoing mental or medical illness, and psychosocial problems such as turbulent relationships, unstable living situations, and financial instability. People at high chronic risk for suicide should keep their safety plan in place (*Tip 38*), maintain a gun-free home (*Tip 40*), and continue to reduce access to other lethal means (*Tip 41*). Typically, high chronic risk in the absence of high acute risk does not require hospitalization. However, be on the lookout for high acute risk – what Craig Bryan and David Rudd (2006) call "acute exacerbation of chronic risk" (p. 193). High acute risk could very well demand hospitalization (*Tip 35*).

A Fragile Peace

Maxwell came into his social worker's office reeking of vodka. As he walked toward the sofa, he wobbled. When he spoke, he slurred his words. "It's all over," he pronounced. "I only came to say goodbye." He intended to shoot himself with his hunting rifle once he got back to his apartment. Sobbing, he thanked Shanti for all her help.

Shanti persuaded Maxwell to wait for an ambulance to take him to the nearby emergency room, from which he was transferred to an alcohol rehabilitation center. One month later, he was back in her office. He felt better, he said. He looked better, too. This time, he hoped to break his record and stay sober longer than seven months.

"How much do you want to kill yourself?" Shanti asked.

"Not one bit," Maxwell said. "I feel great. Blessed. I hit rock bottom, and I've been given another chance."

Whereas one month earlier Maxwell's acute risk for suicide was very high, now it was low, assuming that he stayed on the same course. But there's the rub. How long would he stay in this place of stability and happiness? Now 54, Maxwell had struggled with alcoholism for more than 30 years. He also had bipolar disorder. Although Maxwell took lithium regularly now, he had stopped many times in the past, each time relapsing into psychotic depression or mania. He had attempted suicide three times.

Maxwell is a good example of the need to estimate both acute and chronic suicide risk. Otherwise, based on Maxwell's current desire to live, sobriety, stabilization on medication, and hopefulness, his acute risk would be classified as low. His chronic risk is hardly low. Numerous risk factors raise concern, especially his multiple suicide attempts, recurrent suicidal ideation, alcoholism, and bipolar disorder. Socially isolated and often unemployed, Maxwell is vulnerable to another suicidal crisis if he again starts drinking or stops taking his medication.

Based on Maxwell's high chronic risk for suicide, Shanti knew to remain ever vigilant for signs of relapse, to regularly ask about suicidal thoughts even when Maxwell had gone long periods without them, and to persuade him to get that hunting rifle out of his apartment.

Works Cited

Bryan, C. J., & Rudd, M. D. (2006). Advances in the assessment of suicide risk. *Journal of Clinical Psychology, 62*(2), 185–200.

Rudd, M. D. (2008). The fluid nature of suicide risk: Implications for clinical practice. *Professional Psychology: Research and Practice, 39*(4), 409–410.

Wortzel, H. S., Homaifar, B., Matarazzo, B., & Brenner, L. A. (2014). Therapeutic risk management of the suicidal patient: Stratifying risk in terms of severity and temporality. *Journal of Psychiatric Practice, 20*(1), 63–67.

Tip 34: Document Generously

"In a legal sense, 'if it isn't written down, it didn't happen.'"
Skip Simpson and Michael Stacy
(2004, p. 186)

Solid documentation of suicide risk and interventions is essential. Inherently, documentation helps the suicidal person. The act of writing about your assessment and interventions compels you to analyze your clinical decisions, detect omissions, and identify areas for improvement. The process of documentation also benefits *you*. The potential audience for what you write includes, among others, plaintiff's attorneys, jurors in a malpractice trial, and your state's licensing board, in the event that your client were to die by suicide and someone filed a lawsuit or complaint against you. In such a case, your documentation would serve as testimony to the care you provided. You would want that testimony to help your case, not hurt it.

The adage that something didn't happen if it wasn't written down has big ramifications for documenting suicide risk. If you assess a person's suicide risk and estimate the probability of suicide to be low, and then the worst happens and your client dies by suicide, your justification for judging the person's suicide risk to be low is meaningless if you didn't document the assessment. It would look as though you never assessed suicide risk at all, an act of negligence that makes a clinician vulnerable to a lawsuit following a client's suicide (Ellis & Patel, 2012). The same applies to the safety measures you take and the techniques that you use. Write them down contemporaneously to maintain a living record of your work with the suicidal person.

What to Document

First, remember the basics. Any suicide risk assessment must have at its foundation the fundamental areas of the psychosocial assessment. These basics include the person's presenting problem, recent stressors, mental status, psychiatric diagnoses, substance use, trauma, history of mental health problems and treatment, non-psychiatric medical problems, relevant family history, relationship status and history, strengths, resources, and other aspects of the person's history or situation that are germane to psychological, social, and physical functioning. Also include in the chart any signed forms, such as an intake form and the client's signed form conveying informed consent.

Specific to suicide risk, the documentation should cover all components of the risk assessment process, starting with details about the person's current suicidal ideation and behaviors. Document first whether suicidal ideation is present. If not, write down how you know this, including what the person said (see more on this below). Record any prior suicidal episodes, as well as warning signs, risk factors, protective factors, and cultural factors relevant to the possible occurrence of suicidal thoughts in the future. Be sure to describe the timeline if there is a history of suicidal thoughts or behavior. To write only that the person has attempted suicide three times, for example, is far less meaningful than stating that the person attempted suicide 10 years ago, two months ago, and one month ago.

If the person does report a wish to die, document the frequency, intensity, and duration of the person's thoughts. Record the person's self-reported level of intent to die by suicide, as well as when the person intends to act, if you know. (And if you don't know, then document that, too.) Describe any supporting or contradictory evidence of the person's intent. For example, if the person reports no intent to die by suicide but refuses to discard old, potentially lethal medications, document that fact and consider it in your estimate of risk (*Tip 32*). Take care to note whether thoughts of suicide have extended into considering methods, settling on a method, obtaining the means, making other preparations for suicide (and what those preparations are), and making a specific plan as to when and where the suicide would occur. Also address prior episodes of suicidal ideation, any history of suicide attempts or non-suicidal self-injury, warning signs, risk factors, reasons for living, other protective factors, cultural factors, access to firearms or other lethal means, and collateral information from others, such as family and treating professionals.

If the person lacks an important marker of suicide risk, say so. The psychiatrist Shawn Shea (2011) calls these "pertinent negatives" (p. 266). For example, say you ask the person if they own a firearm or otherwise could get hold of one, and the person says no. If you do not record this information in the chart (e.g., *"Client reports not owning a firearm or having access to one"*), then the documentation gives the appearance that you neglected to ask whether the person had access to a firearm, not that you asked and the answer was no.

Based on the extent of the person's suicidal thoughts and planning, psychiatric symptoms, impulsivity, and other indicators of danger, you should record your estimate of the person's risk for dying by suicide in the near future (that is, acute risk for suicide) (*Tips 32*). Make note of reasons you trust – or do not trust – the person's responses, possibly including the person's mental competence, the quality of the therapeutic alliance, and the degree of honesty that the person has demonstrated in the past. Based on the person's enduring risk factors, also estimate the level of chronic risk for suicide (*Tip 33*).

The chart also should contain copies of any risk assessment questionnaires, the person's safety plan, and the treatment plan. Carefully explicate all measures that you take to help ensure the person's safety, as well as your rationale. These safety measures might include pursuing hospitalization of the person (*Tip 35*), collaboratively creating a safety plan (*Tip 38*), reducing access to lethal means (*Tip 45*), and involving the person's family (*Tip 48*). Also explain measures that you considered and rejected, such as inpatient hospitalization, and your reasoning (more on that below).

Over time, documentation also should tell the story of the person's goals in treatment, the techniques you use to help the person achieve them, and why. At each session, document changes in progress or suicide risk, and note the resolution of specific problems that place the person at acute or chronic risk for suicide. Include, too, notes about any consultation or supervision that you receive from other professionals, including their recommendations and any changes you made as a result.

Use the Suicidal Person's Own Words

When the person says something especially meaningful or illustrative, include their verbatim words. Be sure to mark these words off with quotation marks, to make clear that these words came from the person, not you. These direct quotes can serve as a memory aid for you and help other professionals down the road who review your chart to learn about the client. Direct quotes also are important if a malpractice trial should occur, as though the person is directly talking to jurors (Simpson & Stacy, 2004).

Show, Don't Just Tell

Many mental health professionals take a minimalist approach to documentation of suicide risk. They might write a few words about the person's suicidal thoughts (or lack thereof) and leave it at that. These phrases are commonly used: *"Client denied suicidal ideation"*; *"Client reported fleeting suicidal thoughts"*; *"Client reports suicidal ideation but lacks plan or intent."* By themselves, such phrases are inadequate. It is important to write illustrative notes that show what led you to believe those assertions. Use of the person's own words is especially helpful here.

Examples: Minimalist vs. Illustrative

Minimalist: *Client denied SI.*
Illustrative: *When asked, the client said she has not had any suicidal thoughts or imagery: "I would never, ever think of suicide." She said she "always" has hope that things will get better.*

Minimalist: *Client reported fleeting suicidal thoughts.*
Illustrative: *The client said he thinks about suicide 3–4 times a day, for a few seconds each time. "I push the idea out of my head right away," he said. Asked how he does that, he said he focuses harder on whatever he is doing at the moment.*

Minimalist: *Client reports suicidal ideation but lacks plan or intent.*
Illustrative: *The client acknowledges thinking of suicide for the past two weeks, several times throughout the day for "a couple of minutes" each time. She said she has not given any thought to a method and has no plan or intent to attempt suicide: "I would never actually do anything to kill myself."*

Provide a Rationale for Your Decisions

Many mental health professionals worry that their documentation will come back to haunt them if the suicidal person ends up making a suicide attempt or dying by suicide. For example, say a person reveals intense suicidal thoughts but explicitly states they have no intention of dying by suicide. There is no evidence to contradict the person's report, and there also are no other markers of extreme risk. As a result, you estimate the person's acute risk to be moderate, decide that the person does not require hospitalization, and proceed with helping the person create a safety plan. You write all this down in the person's chart. The next day, the person dies by suicide. The documentation proves you were wrong, right? Not necessarily. It's possible that the person genuinely did not have any suicidal intent and then something unforeseeable happened that dramatically escalated suicide risk. This is why it is crucial to explain your reasoning. You also are not expected to foretell the future. It is impossible to predict suicide (Simon, 2006). You can only estimate the person's risk, using the information available at the time (*Tips 32–33*). Being wrong is not an act of negligence, if you based your estimate on a sound risk assessment (Knoll, 2015).

Where the best course of action is not obvious, the psychiatrist Thomas Gutheil (1980) recommends elaborating on the process of your decision-making, including the risks and benefits of the different options you considered. He adds, "As a general rule, the more uncertainty there is, the more one should think out loud in the record" (Gutheil, 1980, p. 482).

Sample Documentation: Suicide Risk Assessment

The following documentation of a risk assessment interview uses the SOAP format: Subjective (what the client reports), Objective (what the clinician observes), Assessment (what the clinician thinks), and Plan (what the clinician and client will do, or did already) (Cameron & Turtle-Song, 2002).

Subjective: Kenya reported feeling "extremely depressed." She stated she became depressed a month ago, several weeks after abruptly stopping her antidepressant, Wellbutrin XR, 300 mg, because she thought she didn't need it anymore. Six days ago, she started having suicidal ideation, 3–4 times a day, lasting a few minutes each time, with no identified trigger. Yesterday for the first time she thought of overdosing on Tylenol. When asked separately for each method, she denied considering using a firearm, hanging, cutting, or jumping from a tall height to kill herself. She and her wife Sharmaine do not own a firearm (Sharmaine confirmed this by phone near the end of the session), and Kenya said she does not have access to one. Kenya said she has not made any plans or taken any preparations for suicide. On a scale of 0 to 10, Kenya rated her desire to be dead at 8, her desire to kill herself at 5, and her intent to kill herself at 0: "I do believe this will pass." She denied any prior suicide attempt or other self-harm. She said her reasons for living are her wife, her job as a biomedical engineer, and her pets.

Kenya said she has experienced several episodes of major depression with suicidal ideation, beginning at age 15. Her last episode was three years ago. She said she sees her psychiatrist, Dr. Caitlin Rivera, every three months and has not been in therapy previously. Kenya stated she does not use alcohol or other drugs, and her wife confirmed this. Kenya reported a family history of depression (mother, maternal aunt), bipolar disorder (maternal grandfather), and suicide (maternal grandfather).

Objective: Kenya was alert and oriented to person, place, time, and situation. Her affect was congruent with depressed mood (tearful most of session). Thought content was coherent, logical, and goal-oriented. No symptoms of psychosis were evident.

Assessment: Kenya's diagnosis is major depressive disorder, severe, recurrent, without psychosis. Her depression symptoms are depressed mood, suicidal ideation, reduced appetite, insomnia, decreased energy, and feelings of guilt. She has no history of mania, hypomania, or psychosis. Based on the information available to me at this time, I judge Kenya to be at medium risk for suicide in the short term, due to current major depressive episode with daily thoughts of suicide for six days and vague plan of taking an overdose of Tylenol; family history of suicide and depression; and recurrent depression. Protective factors include her stated desire to stay alive, hopefulness about feeling better, previous recoveries from depression, commitment to safety planning, and support from wife. Also, she does not have substance use problems, impulsivity, or psychotic thought processes. These protective factors, combined with Kenya's lack of suicidal planning, preparations, or intent, are why I do not judge her acute risk to be high or imminent. I view Kenya's self-reports to be credible because she was cooperative and engaged during the interview, and readily allowed me to talk with her wife by phone in session. Even after this acute episode resolves, her chronic risk remains moderate due to her recurrent depressive episodes with suicidal ideation and her family history of suicide.

Plan: At this time, outpatient treatment is appropriate because Kenya's suicide risk is not high, and she will benefit from staying connected to her wife, job, and community. Kenya completed a safety plan with me (attached in chart). Sharmaine confirmed by phone that she removed all medications and sharps from their home. Kenya will follow the safety plan and see her psychiatrist in three days re: possibly resuming antidepressant or other medication. I will call psychiatrist today to discuss. Outpatient therapy will target suicidal ideation and depression with cognitive behavior techniques to increase hope, improve mood, and build coping skills. Kenya will call me at 5 p.m. Jan. 29 to check in re: safety, and Kenya's wife agreed to contact me if she observes any deterioration. Next session is in one week at 12 p.m. Feb 3.

Works Cited

Cameron, S., & Turtle-Song, I. (2002). Learning to write case notes using the SOAP format. *Journal of Counseling and Development, 80*(3), 286–292.

Ellis, T. E., & Patel, A. B. (2012). Client suicide: What now? *Cognitive and Behavioral Practice, 19*(2), 277–287.

Gutheil, T. G. (1980). Paranoia and progress notes: A guide to forensically informed psychiatric recordkeeping. *Psychiatric Services, 31*(7), 479–482.

Knoll, J. L., IV. (2015). Lessons from litigation. *Psychiatric Times, 32*(5), 41–51.

Shea, S. C. (2011). *The practical art of suicide assessment: A guide for mental health professionals and substance abuse counselors.* Stoddard, NH: Mental Health Presses.

Simon, R. I. (2006). Imminent suicide: The illusion of short-term prediction. *Suicide and Life-Threatening Behavior, 36*(3), 296–301.

Simpson, S., & Stacy, M. (2004). Avoiding the malpractice snare: Documenting suicide risk assessment. *Journal of Psychiatric Practice, 10*(3), 185–189.

seven
Attending to Immediate Safety

Tip 35: Know When and Why to Pursue Hospitalization

"The clearest indication for hospitalization is the clinician's judgment that the patient is not likely to survive as an outpatient."
Bruce Bongar and Glenn Sullivan
(2013, p. 203)

Criteria for hospitalization can vary by geographical area and hospital but, in general, to warrant hospitalization for suicide risk, the person must be at high or imminent risk of acting on suicidal thoughts in the near future. Common scenarios include:

- A person has a specific plan to die by suicide, the means to do so, and the intent to carry out the plan very soon.
- The person very recently made a suicide attempt, regrets having survived, and intends to make another attempt the next time nobody is around.
- Command hallucinations instruct the person to die by suicide, and the person experiences these hallucinations as actual, meaningful instructions to follow instead of a symptom to observe and treat.

Many other circumstances call for hospitalization, and it is impossible to envision them all. As an example, admissions criteria sometimes are laxer for suicidal children and adolescents, whose behavior is impulsive and unpredictable.

Hospitalization is by no means a cure. On average, individuals stay in a psychiatric hospital no more than 5–7 days (U.S. Department of Health & Human Services, 2016). Except for the occasional long-term hospital or residential treatment facility, the primary goals of inpatient care are safety and crisis stabilization, not treatment or recovery (Glick et al., 2011). There is no evidence that hospitalization actually saves lives (Ward-Ciesielski & Linehan, 2014), but professional, ethical, and in some cases legal obligations to preserve the person's safety compel professionals to take advantage of the higher level of protection that an inpatient stay typically provides.

Ideally, if hospitalization truly is warranted, the suicidal person will agree. Otherwise, you may need to pursue involuntary hospitalization. Avoid involuntary hospitalization whenever possible. Forcing people to receive inpatient care deprives them of civil liberties, disrupts their lives, and is fraught with potential for negative effects (Rüsch et al., 2014). It also can damage the therapeutic alliance beyond repair and close the door to a suicidal person seeking help in the future. Pursue involuntary hospitalization only after careful analysis that the benefits will outweigh the considerable risks. If time permits, consultation is advised (*Tip 43*).

Once you have determined that hospitalization is indicated, be sure to facilitate the process. If possible, do not let the person leave your office alone. Even if family members want to take the person to the hospital, recommend an ambulance. There are too many opportunities for the suicidal person to flee, even to make a suicide attempt, between your office and the hospital. If the person refuses your recommendation and leaves, notify the police and the person's emergency contact. In medical emergencies, you can disclose confidential information without the person's permission, but only what is needed to help keep the person safe. If a child or adolescent is in serious danger of suicide and the parents reject the idea of hospitalization, you might be required to notify child protective services about suspected child neglect, depending on the laws in your jurisdiction.

Before the suicidal person arrives at the hospital, you should call and give a social worker, nurse, or other appropriate staff detailed information about the person's suicide risk. Your report to hospital staff is essential, because the person might not make the same disclosures to hospital staff that they did to you. If the hospital admits the person for inpatient care, you should coordinate with hospital staff to help ensure continuity of care. Staying in touch with the person's family is also recommended, if the person consents.

Once discharge occurs, try to see the person within 24–48 hours. The period immediately following hospitalization is perilous for many suicidal people. One study found that women were 246 times more likely than average – and men were 102 times more likely – to die by suicide in the first week after discharge (Qin & Nordentoft, 2005). According to the study, chances of suicide remain markedly high for at least a month following discharge from a psychiatric hospital, and some degree of increased risk persists for at least a year. To address the heightened risk following psychiatric hospitalization, step up the frequency of sessions, between-session check-ins, or both (*Tip 45*). Consider exploring community support resources, such as intensive outpatient or partial hospitalization programs, as a more gradual "step-down" from being in the hospital as an inpatient. Review with the person any safety plan developed at the hospital. Explore with the person how hospitalization helped, in order to build on gains. Also look at how the hospitalization did not help or even hurt the person (*Tip 36*). Finally, talk with the person about how to deal with possible setbacks in the days, weeks, and months after hospitalization.

These instructions apply when suicidal individuals truly need inpatient care. Often, professionals recommend hospitalization for unnecessary reasons, which the next tip addresses.

"It's All I Can Think About"

In her quarterly appointment with her psychiatrist, Mary Jo, 54, disclosed that she was having obsessive thoughts of suicide. "I would kill myself this instant if I could. It's all I can think about," she said without any emotion, only numbness and the crushing fatigue of months of insomnia. Now, she said, she heard a voice telling her to jump off the balcony of her high-rise apartment when she returned home. Asked how well she could resist this voice, she looked at her psychiatrist blankly. "Why would I resist?" she asked. "This has to end."

The psychiatrist, Dr. Maalouf, was concerned. Although the patient's husband watched out for her, his job as an airline pilot kept him away from home for days at a time. He was leaving town the next day for a flight to Japan. Even if someone else could stay with Mary Jo, she could bolt when the person slept or had to use the bathroom.

Dr. Maalouf told Mary Jo he thought she should be hospitalized. Without any emotion, she said, "Fine." The doctor brought her husband Phillip in from the waiting room and told him the plan. Phillip wanted to take her directly to the hospital, but the psychiatrist cautioned him that it was too dangerous.

Within 15 minutes, an ambulance came and transported Mary Jo to the nearest emergency room; her husband rode with her. The psychiatrist called the hospital and spoke with a social worker who would conduct the psychosocial assessment. Thereafter, he remained in contact with the inpatient unit where Mary Jo was admitted, and he saw her eight days later on the morning following her discharge.

Works Cited

Bongar, B., & Sullivan, G. (2013). *The suicidal patient: Clinical and legal standards of care.* Washington, DC: American Psychological Association.

Glick, I. D., Sharfstein, S. S., & Schwartz, H. I. (2011). Inpatient psychiatric care in the 21st century: The need for reform. *Psychiatric Services, 62*(2), 206–209.

Qin, P., & Nordentoft, M. (2005). Suicide risk in relation to psychiatric hospitalization: Evidence based on longitudinal registers. *Archives of General Psychiatry, 62*(4), 427–432.

Rüsch, N., Müller, M., Lay, B., Corrigan, P. W., Zahn, R., Schönenberger, T., ... & Rössler, W. (2014). Emotional reactions to involuntary psychiatric hospitalization and stigma-related stress among people with mental illness. *European Archives of Psychiatry and Clinical Neuroscience, 264*(1), 35–43.

U.S. Department of Health & Human Services. (2016). National statistics on mental health hospitalizations. Retrieved on December 17, 2016, from http://hcupnet.ahrq.gov.

Ward-Ciesielski, E. F., & Linehan, M. M. (2014). Psychological treatment of suicidal behaviors. In M. K. Nock (Ed.), *The Oxford handbook of suicide and self-injury* (pp. 367–384). Oxford: Oxford University Press.

Tip 36: Know When and Why *Not* to Pursue Hospitalization

"Anxiety about losing a patient to suicide often leads to the decision to send patients to the hospital every time they threaten to end their lives."

Joel Paris
(2007, p. 87)

Even people at high acute risk for suicide can be treated on an outpatient basis (Rudd, 2014). Generally speaking, the main features distinguishing between needing hospitalization and not needing hospitalization are a lack of intent to act on suicidal thoughts in the short term, and the ability to abide by one's safety plan (Wortzel et al., 2014). If these conditions are met, then outpatient treatment typically is appropriate with a collaborative safety plan that the person agrees to follow (*Tip 38*), removal of access to firearms and other means for suicide where possible (*Tips 40–41*), increased frequency of sessions and between-sessions contacts (*Tip 45*), and involvement of significant others (*Tip 47*).

Some mental health professionals pursue hospitalization when the person is not in true immediate danger because they fear the personal, professional, and legal repercussions of losing a client to suicide. This is widely referred to as "defensive practice." Putting it bluntly, the psychiatrist Richard Mullen and colleagues (2008) write, "Defensive practice occurs whenever a practitioner gives a higher priority to self-protection from blame than to the best interests of the patient" (p. 85). The operating belief is: *Better safe than sorry.* The question needs to be asked: *For whom is it better?*

Recommending hospitalization may allay your anxiety, but it may hurt the suicidal person. Hospitalization does offer the potential for increased safety, supervision, and treatment. Yet even when people receive the best of care, hospitalization can have negative effects. The fear, stigma, isolation, disempowerment, and loss of income that often come with hospitalization can intensify feelings of anxiety and hopelessness. Especially for children, adolescents, and parents of young children, the isolation from family can create new wounds. On top of that, measures intended to protect the suicidal person can be experienced as harmful. For example, suicidal people often are not allowed to use the toilet or shower without an attendant looking on at all times. Although patients may perceive this constant observation as evidence of staff's supportive concern for their safety, others consider it degrading and intrusive (Cardell & Pitula, 1999).

Some of the advantages of hospitalization paradoxically can create negative effects, too. For some people, the nurturance from caring staff, the relief from daily stress and responsibilities, and the focused attention on healing foster dependency and even reinforce suicidal behavior (Chiles & Strosahl, 2005). This is especially true among people with borderline personality disorder and others for whom suicidality has become a means to cope or to communicate distress to others (Paris, 2007).

It is important to understand the potential for harm, and to carefully examine both the risks and benefits, when considering hospitalization. Everyone should be treated in the least restrictive environment possible. This might mean that you need to endure considerable anxiety when a person who is at high risk for suicide, but not high enough risk to truly justify hospitalization, walks out of your office. Bearing that anxiety is part of the job.

"There Are No Guarantees..."

Zeke, 44, kept thinking of the rafters. The garage was unfinished, leaving exposed the wood rafters, each strong enough to bear his weight if he hanged himself from one. He emphatically stated this *would* happen. He *would* hang himself. As he spoke, his psychologist ticked off in his head the list of criteria for hospitalization: Ideation? *Yes.* Plan? *Yes.* Means? *Yes.* Intent to die? *Yes.*

But some important elements of risk were missing. Zeke had not made any preparations for suicide or for its aftermath. Another important element was timing. When would Zeke act on his plan? "Not until after our daughter graduates from high school," Zeke said when asked. The psychologist did a quick calculation. It was February. Graduation was in May. Three months. A plan to die by suicide so far off in the future does not constitute imminent risk.

The psychologist probed further. Was there anything that would cause him to act sooner? Zeke was steadfast that he would not "destroy" his daughter's senior year of high school. He said that, at least for the next few months, he would follow his safety plan if his suicidal urges grew stronger. But Zeke offered a slight hedge: "This is the way I feel now. There are no guarantees about how I'll feel later."

No guarantees, indeed. The psychologist knew that suicidal urges can change unpredictably. Zeke's reasons today for not killing himself might become meaningless in the face of overwhelming mental pain, hopelessness, or stress another day.

The psychologist felt frightened. He desperately did not want Zeke to kill himself. With dread, he imagined the grief, self-doubt, and potential legal troubles that would follow if he could not prevent his client's suicide. He was tempted to pursue hospitalization. Not only would Zeke be supervised and safer in a hospital. The psychologist also would pass the liability on to someone else.

But the psychologist also knew that he could not have Zeke locked up simply for his own peace of mind. So, he went over Zeke's safety plan with him, stepped up the frequency of sessions and check-in calls, coordinated care with Zeke's psychiatrist, involved his wife in the treatment (with Zeke's consent), and set about helping Zeke to heal and rediscover hope, even though there were no guarantees.

Works Cited

Cardell, R., & Pitula, C. R. (1999). Suicidal inpatients' perceptions of therapeutic and nontherapeutic aspects of constant observation. *Psychiatric Services, 50*(8), 1066–1070.

Chiles, J. A., & Strosahl, K. D. (2005). *Clinical manual for assessment and treatment of suicidal patients.* Washington, DC: American Psychiatric Publishing.

Mullen, R., Admiraal, A., & Trevena, J. (2008). Defensive practice in mental health. *The New Zealand Medical Journal, 121*(1286), 85–91.

Paris, J. (2007). *Half in love with death: Managing the chronically suicidal patient.* New York, NY: Routledge.

Rudd, M. D. (2014). Core competencies, warning signs, and a framework for suicide risk assessment in clinical practice. In M.K. Nock (Ed.), *The Oxford handbook of suicide and self-injury* (pp. 323–326). Oxford: Oxford University Press.

Wortzel, H. S., Homaifar, B., Matarazzo, B., & Brenner, L. A. (2014). Therapeutic risk management of the suicidal patient: Stratifying risk in terms of severity and temporality. *Journal of Psychiatric Practice, 20*(1), 63–67.

Tip 37: Do Not Use a No-Suicide Contract

"Attempts to pressure a suicidal patient whom one barely knows into making a no-suicide contract could be interpreted by the patient as a clinical retreat into legalisms rather than an expression of genuine concern."

Jerome Kroll

(2000, p. 1685)

After decades of widespread use of no-suicide contracts, most experts now discourage practitioners from using them (e.g., Rudd et al., 2006; McMyler & Pryjmachuk, 2008). With a no-suicide contract (also called a safety contract or no-harm agreement), the client promises, either orally or in writing, not to act on their suicidal thoughts within a specified period of time. This is a simple proposition: A person promises not to attempt suicide, so therefore that means the person is safe and will not attempt suicide. If only it were that simple! Far fewer suicidal people would seek professional help if they could resist their impulses so easily. They would be able to call on their strengths, resources, self-control, and social supports to resist suicidal urges. Yet the role of therapy is to help people build those assets, not to presume that they already exist.

There is little evidence that no-suicide contracts work. Instead, there is evidence that they do *not* work. A survey of psychiatrists found that 40% had a patient die by suicide or make a serious attempt even after committing to a verbal or written no-suicide contract (Kroll, 2000). In another study, 65% of psychiatric inpatients who attempted suicide while hospitalized had agreed to a no-suicide contract (Drew, 2001). The inpatients who "contracted for safety" were 5–7 times *more* likely to attempt suicide than those who did not.

In addition to lacking effectiveness, no-suicide contracts can do harm. Some suicidal individuals report that they felt coerced, pushed aside, and misunderstood when asked to agree to a no-suicide contract (Farrow et al., 2002). The person may feel forced to make a promise in order to receive care. Worst of all, a client who agrees to a no-suicide contract may subsequently hide suicidal acts that constitute a "violation" of the contract, out of fear of angering or disappointing the therapist.

Finally, no-suicide contracts do not protect you from liability in the event that a suicide occurs (Garvey et al., 2009). In fact, the use of such a contract can increase liability if you relied on the person's promise without also regularly assessing suicide risk and using interventions to lessen the risk. A suicidal person's promise to not act on suicidal thoughts can create a false sense of security for you, giving rise to dangerous complacency.

Instead of pushing for a promise about what the person will not do and expecting the person to comply, it is more useful to help them make a plan for how to cope when suicidal thoughts come. This is where safety planning comes in, which is discussed in the next tip.

"You Want Me to Tell You What You Want to Hear"

As a matter of course, Maria Gonzales, a psychologist, asked suicidal clients to sign a written agreement in which they promise not to attempt suicide. She believed that this created a sense of responsibility in the client to not act on their suicidal thoughts, lest they violate their agreement.

So when her new client, Mikhail, voiced suicidal thoughts, Dr. Gonzales broached the question. "Can you make a promise to me that you won't try to kill yourself in the coming week, before we meet again? If you were having urges to make a suicide attempt, I ask that you call me first so that I can try to help you keep that promise."

"I don't know," Mikhail said. "I mean, if it's 3 a.m. and all I can think of is killing myself, I'm not going to call and wake you up."

"I'd like for you to do that," Maria said. "I want to be able to help you stay alive."

"It's not just that. It feels childish," said Mikhail, who, at 48, worked as an anesthesiologist at a nearby hospital. "And it seems like you just want me to tell you what you want to hear, so you don't have to worry about getting sued if I die."

"I can understand how it feels that way," Dr. Gonzales said. "But it's really to help you stay safe."

"What if I say no?" Mikhail asked. "Then what?"

Dr. Gonzales saw that a power struggle was brewing. She could tell him that she would treat him only if he agreed to contract for safety. But she realized that two things could happen. He could make a hollow promise simply for the purpose of telling her, as he'd said, what she wanted to hear. Or he could walk out the door and never come back. Neither option would help him get better. So she resisted the urge to push him further.

"You know, if it doesn't feel right to you to make a promise like that, then I don't want to push it," Dr. Gonzales said. "Let's talk instead about what you can do to stay safe if your suicidal thoughts do become so strong that you are in danger of killing yourself…"

Works Cited

Drew, B. L. (2001). Self-harm behavior and no-suicide contracting in psychiatric inpatient settings. *Archives of Psychiatric Nursing, 15*(3), 99–106.

Farrow, T. L., Simpson, A. I., & Warren, H. B. (2002). The effects of the use of "no-suicide contracts" in community crisis situations: The experience of clinicians and consumers. *Brief Treatment and Crisis Intervention, 2*(3), 241–246.

Garvey, K. A., Penn, J. V., Campbell, A. L., Esposito-Smythers, C., & Spirito, A. (2009). Contracting for safety with patients: Clinical practice and forensic implications. *Journal of the American Academy of Psychiatry and the Law, 37*(3), 363–370.

Kroll, J. (2000). Use of no-suicide contracts by psychiatrists in Minnesota. *American Journal of Psychiatry, 157*(10), 1684–1686.

McMyler, C., & Pryjmachuk, S. (2008). Do "no-suicide" contracts work? *Journal of Psychiatric and Mental Health Nursing, 15*(6), 512–522.

Rudd, M. D., Mandrusiak, M., & Joiner, T. E, Jr. (2006). The case against no-suicide contracts: the commitment to treatment statement as a practice alternative. *Journal of Clinical Psychology, 62*(2), 243–251.

Tip 38: Collaboratively Develop a Safety Plan

"The development of the safety plan is perhaps the single most important activity that occurs in the early sessions of treatment."
Amy Wenzel and Shari Jager-Hyman
(2012, p. 124)

As an alternative to a no-suicide contract, safety planning offers a concrete way to collaborate with the suicidal person about ways to resist acting on suicidal urges. The differences between a safety *contract* and a safety *plan* can seem like hair-splitting semantics, but in reality a safety plan is more practical and empowering: A contract specifies that the suicidal person promises not to act on suicidal thoughts (*Tip 37*); a safety plan spells out *how* to not act on suicidal thoughts. And a safety plan is not a promise, so if the person does act on suicidal thoughts, they can tell you without fear of your disappointment or rebuke for having violated a "contract."

Creating the safety plan also can inform your assessment of the person's suicide risk. If the person is apathetic about their safety, for example, or unable to identify friends or family who can help, then that gives you a clearer picture of the person's suicide risk and lack of social support. The same principle applies when you ask the person what activities they can do for distraction, or what self-talk they can use to cope. If nothing comes to mind for the person, consider that to be important data.

Getting Started with Safety Planning

In the spirit of collaboration, explain the safety planning process and ask the person if you can make a safety plan together. Some people say no. Obviously, if the person declines because they have no interest in staying safe, then that warrants further exploring suicide risk. But people might say no because they have other things they want to discuss instead. In such situations, look for the opportunity to work safety planning into conversation by asking questions such as, *"So, the next time you have suicidal thoughts, what will you do?"* *"What can you do to take care of yourself?"* *"Where can you go?"* and so on. That way you are helping the person to plan for safety without making it explicit. Co-creating a safety plan and writing it down is ideal, but an unwritten, implicit plan is better than none.

Different Types of Safety Plans

A safety plan can take different forms. Informally, it can be as simple as a list of activities to do and people to call (with phone numbers) in case suicidal thoughts flare up. Sometimes, the person writes it down on the back of the therapist's business card:

Example: An Informal Safety Plan

Just in case...

1. Remind myself this will pass
2. Look at pictures on phone of Jake and our dog
3. Call Mom
4. Call (therapist) Nancy, 888-888-8888
5. Call national suicide hotline, 800-273-8255

A structured version of a safety plan also is popular in the suicide prevention field. This version, developed by psychologists Barbara Stanley and Gregory Brown (2012), contains a series of steps, starting with the person identifying warning signs that suicidal thoughts may emerge or worsen. Warning signs include any thoughts, images, emotions, behaviors, or physical sensations that tend to accompany suicidal thoughts in the person. Situations that trigger suicidal thoughts also should be listed here.

Next, the safety plan calls for the person to specify things they can do for distraction. Ideally, the person will not choose alcohol, drugs, or other risky behaviors. Substance use can impair judgment, diminish the effectiveness of psychiatric medications, increase depression, worsen sleep, and have a disinhibiting effect that makes people more prone to acting on suicidal impulses. Alcohol provides a powerful example. On average, in numerous studies of people who died by suicide, roughly 40% had consumed alcohol before the act (Cherpitel et al., 2004). Provide education about the dangers of substance use and other destructive behaviors, and encourage the person to turn to constructive alternatives. If the person is reluctant, elicit the pros and cons of how they are coping, explore ambivalence, and give your professional opinion that their unhealthy behaviors are endangering their life.

After coming up with ways to distract oneself alone, the plan moves on to people and places the person can turn to for distraction, without disclosing their need for help to others. In the next step, the person then decides which friends, family, and other non-professionals they can reach out to for help, since these might be different people they can go to just to get their mind off of things. The person next identifies professionals, agencies, and hotlines they can call or visit for help. By practicing skills in distraction, coping, and socializing before asking others for help, the person can build a sense of self-efficacy about their ability to resist suicidal thoughts (Stanley & Brown, 2012). Skipping ahead to later steps is OK, too. Encourage the person to do so if they urgently need help.

Finally, the safety plan moves on to ways the person can keep the environment safe, usually by removing lethal means for suicide from the person's reach (*Tips 40–41*). Although the person should take action on this immediately, this element comes last in the safety planning process by design. Completing the other steps of the safety plan first can help the person to build motivation and recognize other options besides suicide (Stanley & Brown, 2012).

Sometimes, a client has difficulty coming up with resources and options. For example, the person might get stymied about who to contact in a crisis. Although the safety plan is intended to be completed sequentially, if the person has difficulty finishing one step, move on to the next step. Otherwise, the person might get hung up on that one piece of the safety plan and stop the process entirely. If possible, the person can fill in the missing information later.

A template for this safety plan is available for free at www.suicidesafetyplan.com. An example is provided further below.

Assessing Motivation to Follow the Plan

At each step of the safety planning process, ask the person how likely they are to follow through with that portion of the plan. Equally important, examine what obstacles the person might face when trying to stick to the safety plan, and help the person make changes as necessary:

- *"On a scale of 0 to 10, with 0 being not at all and 10 being completely, how likely is it that you will do this step the next time you have thoughts of suicide?"*
- *"What would make it hard to do this step of your safety plan?"*

Also ask the person to identify where the plan will be kept so that they can access it easily. Some people type it directly into their phone or take a picture of the written plan. It is also common for people to keep a written plan in their wallet, in an easily accessible drawer, or even on their refrigerator door. If the suicidal person is a child or adolescent, the safety plan should be shared with the youth's parent or other caregiver. If the suicidal person is an adult, it can be useful for them to let friends or family in on their plan, especially if they live with someone, but the person might decide to keep it private.

Inoculate the person against self-attack or fear of your disappointment if they do not follow the plan. You can do this by making clear that the safety plan is a work in progress, subject to corrections and changes.

There's an App for That!

Many safety planning applications are available, often for free, for iPhones, Android phones, and other electronic devices. People can use the apps to record different coping strategies. Some offer additional features such as information on crisis and non-crisis support services, linkage to contacts in the device's address book, and music and guided meditations for relaxation and distraction (Larsen et al., 2016).

Example: A Structured Safety Plan

The following is a safety plan for a young woman who has thoughts of overdosing on prescription pain medication that is in her bathroom cabinet.

Step 1: Warning signs:
1. Anxious feeling in my head
2. Sleeping till noon or taking long naps
3. Irritable about little things that usually don't bother me

Step 2: Internal coping strategies: Things I can do to take my mind off my problems without contacting another person:
1. Listen to upbeat music
2. Do sudoku puzzles on my phone
3. Take Juniper for a walk

Step 3: People and social settings that provide distraction:
1. Name: Jake   Phone: 111-111-1111
2. Name: Mom   Phone: 888-888-8888
3. Place: Starbucks
4. Place: Lake Jewel Park

Step 4: People whom I can ask for help:
1. Name: Armando   Phone: 111-111-1111
2. Name: Rory   Phone: 333-333-3333
3. Name: Lolly   Phone: 555-555-5555

Step 5: Professionals or agencies I can contact during a crisis:
1. Clinician Name: Dr. S   Phone: 777-777-7777
   Clinician Pager or Emergency Contact: Same
2. Clinician Name: Dr. M   Phone: 444-444-4444
   Clinician Pager or Emergency Contact: 222-222-2222
3. Suicide Prevention Lifeline: 1-800-273-TALK (8255)
4. Local Emergency Service: Lincoln Hospital ER
   Emergency Services Address: 75 E. Lincoln St.
   Emergency Services Phone: 999-999-9999

Making the environment safe:
1. Give migraine medication to Jake to hold onto for me
2. Throw away the Vicodin

This safety plan uses the template developed by psychologists Barbara Stanley and Gregory Brown (2012). It is reprinted here with their permission. The template is freely available at their website, www.suicidesafetyplan.com.

Works Cited

Cherpitel, C. J., Borges, G. L., & Wilcox, H. C. (2004). Acute alcohol use and suicidal behavior: A review of the literature. *Alcoholism: Clinical and Experimental Research, 28*(5), 18s–28s.

Larsen, M. E., Nicholas, J., & Christensen, H. (2016). A systematic assessment of smartphone tools for suicide prevention. *PLoS One, 11*(4), e0152285.

Stanley, B., & Brown, G. K. (2012). Safety planning intervention: A brief intervention to mitigate suicide risk. *Cognitive and Behavioral Practice, 19*(2), 256–264.

Wenzel, A., & Jager-Hyman, S. (2012). Cognitive therapy for suicidal patients: Current status. *The Behavior Therapist/AABT, 35*(7), 121–130.

Tip 39: Encourage Delay

"In my mind, one of the most powerful clinical interventions one can make when working with a suicidal person is to overtly negotiate with the patient the notion of putting off suicide to a later point in time."

David Jobes
(2016, p. 77)

Even though suicide is always an option (*Tip 18*), you can urge the suicidal person to at least wait. The psychologist David Jobes (2016) notes that delaying suicide "does not eliminate from the already vulnerable patient his or her sense of power and autonomy that the option of suicide psychologically assures" (p. 77). The person can always choose to die by suicide later. Meanwhile, the delay buys time for the person to give treatment a chance. In asking the person to wait, you convey that the work you do together in the meantime can help them to change, to heal, and to want to live again.

The psychologist Donald Meichenbaum offers this example of how to ask the suicidal person to hold off, at least temporarily:

> While suicide is an available option and given your view of your situation that is understandable, it is critical that you allow us some time to work on reducing your emotional pain.... Would you be willing to partner with me and hold off on the suicide option in order to allow yourself the time that is needed to address these issues?
>
> (Meichenbaum, 2005, p. 70)

What if the person rejects your idea to take suicide off the table temporarily? Some professionals refuse to work with a suicidal person without the person's commitment to put suicide off for a certain amount of time. To my mind, that is equivalent to requiring a no-suicide contract or promise, which is actively discouraged for many reasons (*Tip 37*). It is unfair to require someone to abstain from behavior before they have the skills to do so. Instead, I recommend encouraging the person to take suicide off the table temporarily, exploring with curiosity any reluctance or ambivalence the person might have, and continuing to revisit the topic as needed.

"Would You Be Willing to Give This a Chance...?"

Arturo, 46, likened suicide to an escape hatch. "If things get too bad," he said, "I can make my exit any time."

"Arturo, I know you don't want to give up suicide as an option," his social worker said. "And I think that the work we do together in therapy can help you to find reasons to live. There are no guarantees, but there are a lot of ways that the therapy can help. Would you be willing to give this a chance to work before doing anything to end your life?"

"That all sounds good," Arturo said, "but I don't know if I can make that promise."

"I'm not asking for a promise," the social worker said. "I'm really just asking you to consider giving this therapy a chance for 3–4 months. It's your choice whether to die by suicide, but I hope that you will give the therapy time to help you." And then, borrowing a couple lines from David Jobes' writings, she said, "So why not give it a try? You have everything to gain and really nothing to lose" (Jobes, 2016, p. 5).

"I guess you're right," Arturo said. "Even though I've wanted to kill myself a long time, I'm still here. If I can turn things around, I'd like to. I'll give this a fighting chance for the next few months. I can always kill myself later."

"That's true," the social worker said. "And I do believe that you can begin to feel better in the meantime. Let's talk about that…"

Works Cited

Jobes, D. A. (2016). *Managing suicidal risk: A collaborative approach* (2nd ed.). New York, NY: Guilford Press.

Meichenbaum, D. (2005). 35 years of working with suicidal patients: Lessons learned. *Canadian Psychology/Psychologie Canadienne, 46*(2), 64–72.

Tip 40: Problem-Solve Around Access to Firearms

"It is a clinical axiom that there is no safe gun storage at a suicidal patient's home."

Robert Simon
(2011, p. 141)

There are few second chances when somebody uses a firearm to die by suicide. About 85% of people who intentionally shoot themselves die; in comparison, the fatality rate for people who intentionally overdose on medication or poison is 2% (Miller et al., 2012). Among those who survive after shooting themselves, many suffer irreversible injuries such as brain damage, blindness, and paralysis. These stark facts underscore the importance of trying to reduce the suicidal person's access to firearms.

Some state and federal laws in the U.S. limit gun ownership among people with mental illness or risk of violence. Laws change, so if you are in the U.S., check to see the current status in your area; the Law Center to Prevent Gun Violence maintains a database of such laws at http://smartgunlaws.org/search-gun-law-by-state. If no laws in your area allow for authorities to take a person's gun away when suicide risk is present, then it falls on you to explore with the person the dangerous combination of gun ownership and suicidal urges, and to collaboratively problem-solve about what the person can do to reduce that danger.

First, Try to Get Buy-In

Many people resist removing firearms from their home, even temporarily. To help avoid a power struggle, motivational interviewing calls for engaging the person through active listening, collaboratively negotiating a focus on problem-solving about firearms (vs. taking an authoritarian, directive approach), eliciting from the suicidal person the pros and cons of keeping firearms at home, and evoking and reinforcing "change talk" (Britton et al., 2016). After going through this process, key questions are:

- *"In light of the suicidal thoughts you've been having, what are the advantages and disadvantages of having easy access to your firearm?"*
- *"So, with what you've said about the pros and cons of keeping your gun in the house, what do you want to do?"*
- *"What are your next steps?"*

The psychologist Peter Britton and colleagues (2016) note that the goal is not necessarily for the person to decide immediately to get firearms out of the house. They write, "Sometimes the clinician's goal is to encourage the patient to begin thinking about means [safety], allowing them to decide for themselves after the session" (p. 56).

Others take a more directive approach. The psychologist David Jobes (2016) provides dialogue with a hypothetical client, in which he insists that the man get his guns out of his house. Jobes acknowledges the man's pain and desperation and adds,

> Yet something brought you in here in spite of everything! Shouldn't we try to honor the part of you that brought you in and try to do what we can to save your life? You see right now, that handgun in your desk drawer is competing with our potentially life-saving treatment, and we need to remove that temptation if we intend to save your life … I can say without a doubt that this treatment doesn't work if you shoot yourself!
>
> (Jobes, 2016, pp. 97–98)

To help the person maintain a safe distance from firearms, you have several scenarios to pursue:

1. The firearm is removed from the home.
2. The firearm is rendered unusable.
3. The firearm is locked up in the home.
4. The firearm is stored with reminders of reasons for living.

Option #1: The Firearm is Removed from the Home

Without question, the best solution is for the person to have no access to a firearm in the home or elsewhere. A friend or family member could hold on to the person's firearm (or firearms) until the suicidal crisis resolves. The person could give the firearm to the local police, although the police may not be willing to return it. Another option for making the person's home gun-free is for the person to store it unloaded in a storage facility, safe deposit box, or gun range, assuming that it's legal to do so and the facility permits it. A friend or family member could hold on to the key or claim tag.

State laws in the U.S. vary on whether it is legal to give someone else a firearm, and not everybody can legally possess a firearm. If legal, someone else could hold onto the suicidal person's gun. That person should get the firearm out of the house before the suicidal person returns home, because merely handling the firearm places the suicidal person in danger. If your client permits, try to speak directly with the person removing the firearm to confirm that it will not be accessible.

Never hold on to a firearm for a suicidal person in your professional role. The potential for problems is enormous. Taking temporary ownership of a person's gun would expose you to considerable danger, liability, and complications in the therapeutic relationship.

Option #2: The Firearm is Rendered Unusable

A key piece of the gun, such as the slide or firing pin, can be removed and kept by a trusted person. This requires some knowledge of the firearm's mechanics, which can complicate matters if the trusted person does not know much about guns. (Remember, the suicidal person should not have contact with the gun, if possible.) Getting rid of ammunition is a good step if the person declines other options, but it will not render the gun unusable. Ammunition is very easy to buy again. Still, the time it would take to replenish the supply could protect the suicidal person from a purely impulsive decision.

Option #3: The Firearm is Locked in the Home

Another possibility is for the person to lock the firearm (or firearms) and give someone else the key or combination. To do this, a gun lock or gun safe is used. Gun locks include trigger locks, chamber locks, and cable locks. Unfortunately, locks can be defeated, so these options are inferior to getting firearms out of the house and to making the gun unusable by removing a key part.

Option #4: The Gun is Stored with Reminders of Reasons for Living

If all else fails and the person makes clear that the firearm will remain fully assembled and loaded in the home, you might have better luck persuading the person to at least situate the weapon next to reminders of reasons for living. This could include photographs of loved ones or inspirational coping statements (e.g., "This feeling won't last forever"; see *Tip 69*). Individuals can put stickers on their firearm with information that could deter them from pulling the trigger, such as the name of a loved one or the number for a crisis hotline (e.g., in the U.S., 1-800-273-TALK). A group called Cover Me Veterans (www.covermeveterans.org) gives veterans "gun skins" designed to deter people from suicide. The skins, which wrap around the grip, are customized with photos of loved ones or other reasons for living.

Keep in Mind...

On the one hand, refusal to limit access to one's firearm could signal a level of suicidal intent that warrants psychiatric hospitalization. On the other hand, it could simply mean that the person is passionate about gun ownership rights or the ability to protect their home. It is up to you to assess suicide risk and interpret the person's refusal in the context of that assessment. Whatever happens, be sure to document the process.

Children, Adolescents, and Guns: A Special Case

Even when a child is in danger of suicide, many parents resist removing their firearm from their home, as psychiatrist David Brent and colleagues (2000) discovered. Brent's research team studied an intervention for adolescents with major depressive disorder. On intake, parents were asked if there was a gun in the home. For those who said yes, the treating clinician firmly advised the parents to get all firearms out of the house. If the parents resisted, the clinician gave examples of cases where a gun was hidden, locked, or otherwise seemingly out of reach, and still a child got hold of it and died by suicide. Even with this information, and even with an adolescent diagnosed with major depression (many of whom had suicidal thoughts or behavior), only one in four parents with a firearm in the home removed it.

If you are working with a suicidal child or adolescent and the parents or guardians refuse to make a firearm in the home inaccessible, you might be required by law to call your local child protective services agency. Child protective service workers have the authority to require parents and guardians to maintain a safe environment for the children in their care. Leaving a loaded gun in a suicidal child's midst is decidedly unsafe.

Works Cited

Brent, D. A., Baugher, M., Birmaher, B., Kolko, D. J., & Bridge, J. (2000). Compliance with recommendations to remove firearms in families participating in a clinical trial for adolescent depression. *Journal of the American Academy of Child & Adolescent Psychiatry, 39*(10), 1220–1226.

Britton, P. C., Bryan, C. J., & Valenstein, M. (2016). Motivational interviewing for means restriction counseling with patients at risk for suicide. *Cognitive and Behavioral Practice, 23*(1), 51–61.

Jobes, D. A. (2016). *Managing suicidal risk: A collaborative approach* (2nd ed.). New York, NY: Guilford Press.

Miller, M., Azrael, D., & Barber, C. (2012). Suicide mortality in the United States: The importance of attending to method in understanding population-level disparities in the burden of suicide. *Annual Review of Public Health, 33*, 393–408.

Simon, R. I. (2011). *Preventing patient suicide: Clinical assessment and management.* Arlington, VA: American Psychiatric Publishing.

Tip 41: Discuss Access to Other Means for Suicide, Too

"Because of the widespread availability of poisons (e.g., acetami- nophen in large quantities), tall structures (e.g., any building over three stories), strangulation devices (e.g., plastic bags or noose- tying lessons on YouTube), and sharp objects (e.g., kitchen knives, broom handles, broken glass), a suicidal patient's environment can never be considered nonlethal."

Bruce Bongar and Glenn Sullivan
(2013, p. 178)

Once a person develops suicidal intent, countless everyday objects become a poten- tial weapon: a moving car, a bridge, a pair of scissors, a broken shard of glass, a belt. Someone who wants to die by suicide can find countless ways to do so, depending on their creativity. With these limitations in mind, professionals can still give guidance to a suicidal person, and to the person's loved ones, on reducing access to everyday objects that can be transformed into a weapon against oneself.

As *Tip 40* explains, firearms should be removed or made inaccessible when- ever possible. Additionally, depending on the suicidal person's level of risk, other objects that can pose a danger include medications, household chemicals, sharp objects such as knives and razor blades, and ropes, sheets, and other means for hanging or strangulating oneself. Even plastic pencil sharpeners are dangerous, because of the thick blade that can easily be removed from them. Many non- prescription medications are unsafe. In particular, acetaminophen (e.g., Tylenol) and ibuprofen (e.g., Advil) can be lethal in smaller doses than many people realize. For example, a study of adolescents found that almost one in five incor- rectly thought that an overdose of acetaminophen could never be fatal, and an additional 20% overestimated the number of pills that a person could take without suffering harm or dying (Myers et al., 1992).

To secure potentially dangerous items from a suicidal person, loved ones can either remove the objects from the home altogether or lock them up. A small safe can be purchased for $50–100 for the purpose of safely storing medications, knives, and razors. If no safe is available, a loved one can keep the objects at a neighbor's home or in the trunk of their car. Keeping the objects in the home but hidden and unlocked is not the ideal choice, but it is better than leaving them easily accessible.

Unfortunately, objects that can be used as a weapon against the self are ubi- quitous in daily life. Practically speaking, for example, it is very difficult to remove from a home all means for hanging and suffocation, which in addition to ropes and sheets can include belts, plastic bags, extension cords, ripped sheets, and even shoelaces. If a person is at such high risk for suicide that their life is in danger in the presence of a pencil sharpener, belt, or plastic bag, then more intensive care is probably needed.

"I Guess I Need to Thwart the Other Me"

Imani's psychologist had a good memory. So when Imani, 62, developed suicidal thoughts and the two worked on a safety plan together, the psychologist knew something was not quite right. Imani said she had no potentially lethal medications at home. The psychologist remembered that six months earlier, Imani had an infected tooth extracted.

"What about the pain medicine from your dental work last fall? Did you use it all?" the psychologist asked.

"Oh … that. I wasn't really thinking of those pills," Imani said. "I do still have a lot. And I don't quite want to give them up."

"What are the pros and cons of keeping the medication?" he asked.

Imani hesitated. "I might need it again sometimes," she said, "and it's so hard to get. Doctors don't just hand out narcotics."

"That's true," the psychologist said. "What would be the advantages of getting rid of it?"

Imani explored both sides. Ultimately, her decision hinged on her realization that, as she put it, "The 'me' you're talking to doesn't really want to die. It's the other 'me' I become late at night when I'm lonely and depressed that scares me. I guess I need to thwart the other me."

Immediately after the session, Imani went home and flushed the remaining pills down the toilet.

Works Cited

Bongar, B., & Sullivan, G. (2013). *The suicidal patient: Clinical and legal standards of care.* Washington, DC: American Psychological Association.

Myers, W. C., Otto, T. A., Harris, E., Diaco, D., & Moreno, A. (1992). Acetaminophen overdose as a suicidal gesture: a survey of adolescents' knowledge of its potential for toxicity. *Journal of the American Academy of Child & Adolescent Psychiatry, 31*(4), 686–690.

Tip 42: In Case of Terminal Illness, Proceed Differently (Perhaps)

"People who are not terminally ill and commit suicide will shorten a life that could continue on for many years and even decades, whereas people who are terminally ill and commit suicide are likely only hastening a death that is months, or even just weeks or even days, away."

Lisa Campo-Engelstein and colleagues
(2016, p. 172)

The overriding message of suicide prevention is: *"Don't do it!"* People are urged not to kill themselves – not to believe the pessimistic falsehoods of the suicidal mind, not to cut short a life with so much potential left unlived. Quite plainly, suicide prevention calls for preventing suicide. Yet, when a person has a terminal illness, visions of intractable pain and progressive deterioration often are not cognitive distortions. They reflect, in many situations, the reality of what is to come soon. As a result, some people argue that, in the context of terminal illness, the act of intentionally ending one's life is not really suicide. Instead, the person is hastening death, and the normal rules of suicide prevention sometimes are suspended.

Around the world and within the U.S., several jurisdictions permit what is commonly called "physician-assisted suicide," "hastened death," "death with dignity," "physician-assisted death," or "aid in dying."[1] In the U.S., as of June 2017, laws in Oregon, Washington, Vermont, California, Colorado, and Washington, D.C., permit a physician to prescribe a lethal dose of medication to a terminally ill person under the condition that the person is expected to die from the illness within six months and is mentally competent. Although Montana did not enact a law, its state Supreme Court ruled in 2009 that physician-assisted suicide is permissible. Around the world, a handful of countries permit assisted suicide, such as Canada, Switzerland, the Netherlands, Belgium, and Luxembourg.

Even in states where physician-assisted suicide is illegal, individuals who are mentally competent are free to make medical decisions that will result in their death. So, as examples, a person has the right to discontinue dialysis or reject life-saving cancer treatment. People who are mentally competent to make such a decision also have the right to stop eating and drinking as a means to end their life (Pope & Anderson, 2011). These actions – refusing medical treatment, food, and water – are acts of *omission*, unlike the act of taking a fatal overdose of medication.

With both physician-assisted suicide and other types of hastened death, the person must be mentally competent to move forward without professionals' intervening to, at least for now, save their life. Complicating matters, a large proportion of people with terminal illness who want to end their life also have major depression or another mental disorder (Wilson et al., 2016). Mental illness such as depression does not automatically render somebody incompetent to make a rational medical decision (Levene & Parker, 2011), but it does require careful assessment of the person's decision-making capacity. Many people argue that depression should be treated and resolved before the person is permitted to end their life, but others note that depression can be a natural consequence of the physical pain and emotional distress of a terminal illness (Stefan, 2016).

In the absence of factors that do impair rational decision-making, the legalities of assisted suicide call into question the role of suicide prevention in cases of terminal illness. In general, in the U.S. when a person is in extreme danger of dying by suicide very soon, the mental health professional is expected to initiate the process of voluntary or involuntary hospitalization (Bongar & Sullivan, 2013). However, in states where physician-assisted suicide is legal, the terminally ill person has the right to take a legally prescribed fatal dose of medication without interference or intervention if the person is mentally competent. Suicide prevention efforts do not apply in these situations.

Even in states where assisted suicide is not legal, the psychologists James Werth, Jr. and Jessica Richmond (2009) assert that mental health professionals are not obligated to prevent a terminally ill person's suicide as long as the professional has judged the person to be capable of making the decision rationally. Werth and Richmond base their opinion on a review of state laws and professional organizations' codes of ethics, policy statements, and *amicus* briefs in related legal cases, but you should be well-versed in the laws in your area, review your professional code of ethics, and seek legal consultation if this issue arises for you.

"I'm Not Going to Wait for Death to Take Me"

Alvin, 35, started losing sight in one eye four months ago, a symptom that led to his diagnosis of terminal brain cancer. His oncologist told him he has, at most, 3–6 months left to live. "I'm not going to wait for death to take me," Alvin tells the hospice social worker on one of her home visits. "I'm not going to give my wife and kids the lasting nightmare of watching me suffer." Instead, Alvin tells the social worker that at some point in the coming months when his condition worsens, he will end his life peacefully at home using canisters of helium that he will purchase online. Alvin would prefer to use a lethal dose of medication prescribed by his oncologist, but the state where he lives does not permit physicians to assist a person's suicide. Sitting by her husband's side, Alvin's wife tells the social worker that she supports his plan to, as she puts it, "die on his own terms."

The social worker is in a quandary. Her assessment reveals that Alvin's thinking is logical, clear, and focused. She observes no psychosis, depression, or other illnesses that might taint his ability to rationally think through the consequences of his decision. Regardless, a colleague tells the social worker that she has a legal and ethical obligation to prevent Alvin from ending his life. If the social worker does have a duty to protect Alvin, she would need to initiate the process of admission to a psychiatric hospital once Alvin decides to set his plan into motion. The thought sickens the social worker. She does not want to compound tragedy with trauma. Moreover, she supports Alvin's right to end his life on his terms.

If you were Alvin's social worker, what would you do?

Works Cited

Bongar, B., & Sullivan, G. (2013). *The suicidal patient: Clinical and legal standards of care.* Washington, DC: American Psychological Association.

Campo-Engelstein, L., Jankowski, J., & Mullen, M. (2016). Should health care providers uphold the DNR of a terminally ill patient who attempts suicide? *HEC Forum, 28* (2), 169–174.

Levene, I., & Parker, M. (2011). Prevalence of depression in granted and refused requests for euthanasia and assisted suicide: A systematic review. *Journal of Medical Ethics, 37*(4), 205–211.

Pope, T. M., & Anderson, L. E. (2011). Voluntarily stopping eating and drinking: A legal treatment option at the end of life. *Widener Law Review, 17,* 363.

Stefan, S. (2016). *Rational suicide, irrational laws: Examining current approaches to suicide in policy and law.* New York, NY: Oxford University Press.

Werth, J. L., Jr., & Richmond, J. M. (2009). End-of-life decisions and the duty to protect. In J. L. Werth, Jr., E. R. Welfel, & G. A. H. Benjamin (Eds.)., *The duty to protect: Ethical, legal, and professional considerations for mental health professionals* (pp. 195–208). Washington, DC: American Psychological Association.

Wilson, K. G., Dalgleish, T. L., Chochinov, H. M., Chary, S., Gagnon, P. R., Macmillan, K., … & Fainsinger, R. L. (2016). Mental disorders and the desire for death in patients receiving palliative care for cancer. *BMJ Supportive & Palliative Care, 6*(2), 170–177.

Note

1. In this tip, I use the term "assisted suicide" instead of terms like "death with dignity" or "hastened death" to distinguish between acts of omission that hasten death (e.g., refusing medical treatment) but do not fall under the definition of suicide, and actions the person proactively takes (e.g., taking an overdose) to end their life that do fall under the definition of suicide.

Tip 43: Seek Consultation

"There is almost no instance in a therapist's professional life when consultation with a peer is as important as when he is dealing with a highly suicidal patient."

Edwin Shneidman
(1996, p. 424)

Never worry alone. This pithy advice from psychiatrist Thomas Gutheil (2014, p. 380) underscores the importance of seeking the counsel of another professional about a suicidal client. Enlisting the experience and wisdom of others helps ensure that you are providing the best care possible. Also important, failure to avail yourself of consultation could make you vulnerable to a malpractice judgment in the event of a client suicide and subsequent lawsuit. Obtaining consultation demonstrates that you were not complacent or ignorant about addressing a person's suicide risk.

Consultation can take different forms. Formal consultation involves paying a professional for their time and knowledge. With this type of consultation, the professional may have expertise in clinical suicidology, and typically provides a written summary of the consult for your records. Informal consultation – a chat with a colleague, a staffing in a weekly team meeting – also can infuse your conceptualization of the client with a much-needed fresh perspective. So can discussions of a particular client in clinical supervision, peer supervision groups, or case presentations. A drawback of informal consultation is that some professionals will not consent to being named in your documentation as a consultant, lest they incur liability if the treatment goes awry.

When talking with a consultant, do not reveal identifying details about your client. It is also advisable to have a statement in your informed consent form that you might discuss the person's case with a consultant and that you will disguise the person's identifying information. Be sure to document when you receive consultation, as well as the content of your discussions and decisions.

All topics are fair game. The psychologists Bruce Bongar and Glenn Sullivan (2013) suggest that professionals review the following topics with a consultant:

- **Risk assessment and safety planning.** A consultant can provide a second opinion about the client's level of suicidal danger, indications and contraindications for psychiatric hospitalization, and steps to take in safety planning.
- **Treatment planning.** For example, have you overlooked specific interventions or techniques that could help your client?
- **Specific challenges with the client.** An outside view is especially recommended if your client demonstrates chronic suicidality, hostility toward you, an unwillingness to follow the treatment plan, or other complex dynamics.

- **Emotional reactions toward the client.** These might include feelings of fear, helplessness, incompetence, anxiety, burnout, or even anger (*Tip 4*).
- **Risk-management issues.** Issues related to informed consent, confidentiality, and documentation are common fare for consultation. If the client consents, you might ask a consultant to review the file and judge whether your documentation is adequate.

Sometimes consultation with an attorney is needed, especially around issues related to exceptions to confidentiality to ensure safety, and involuntary hospitalization. Many malpractice insurance companies provide a certain number of free consultations with an attorney.

Gutheil (2004) notes that documentation and consultation are "the eternal mainstays of protection for the clinician" (p. 254). It is true that documentation (*Tip 34*) and consultation can help protect the clinician in the event of a malpractice lawsuit or complaint with a licensing board. More importantly, consultation protects the suicidal person by strengthening the care that they receive from you.

"Continuing In This Way Would Be Unethical"

Even after four years of therapy with a clinical psychologist, Sheila continued to deteriorate. She attempted suicide multiple times, required repeated hospitalizations, and had become so disabled by her psychiatric challenges that she could no longer hold a job. Her psychologist, David Jobes, felt he was at his wits' end (Jobes, 2011). He cared about her. He viewed the possibility of her suicide as devastating not only to him personally, but also to his professional worth as a suicidologist. Worse, he felt "blackmailed" by Sheila's constant suicidal expressions and behaviors. Dr. Jobes sought advice from colleagues, and one consultant in particular had valuable advice for him: "To knowingly continue as you are would be unprofessional – without some sort of major therapeutic change, continuing in this way would be *unethical*," the consultant told him. This advice inspired Dr. Jobes to overcome his terror of Sheila's suicide and to take risks in the service of helping her heal. "Armed with his support and insightful feedback, I began a new process ... with new clinical resolve and determination," Dr. Jobes writes. He set new limits and changed Sheila's treatment plan, focusing on concrete behavioral goals rather than exploration of her traumatic past. Within a year, Sheila had improved. And in the ensuing years, she returned to work, developed a loving relationship, married, and also flourished professionally. "Finally, and most critically from my view of these things," Dr. Jobes writes of her status 12 years later, long after the therapy ended, "she feels extremely grateful to be *alive*." The consultation that Dr. Jobes received helped numerous people: him, his client, and countless clients to come.

Works Cited

Bongar, B., & Sullivan, G. (2013). *The suicidal patient: Clinical and legal standards of care.* Washington, DC: American Psychological Association.

Gutheil, T. G. (2004). Suicide, suicide litigation, and borderline personality disorder. *Journal of Personality Disorders, 18*(3), 248–256.

Gutheil, T. G. (2014). Boundary issues. In J. M. Oldham, A. E. Skodol, & D. S. Bender (Eds.), *The American Psychiatric Publishing textbook of personality disorders* (pp. 369–381). Arlington, VA: American Psychiatric Publishing.

Jobes, D. A. (2011). Suicidal blackmail: Ethical and risk management issues in contemporary clinical care. In W. B. Johnson, & G. P. Koocher (Eds.), *Ethical conundrums, quandaries, and predicaments in mental health practice: A casebook from the files of experts* (pp. 33–40). New York, NY: Oxford University Press.

Shneidman, E. S. (1996). Psychotherapy with suicidal patients. In J. T. Maltsberger & M. J. Goldblatt (Eds.), *Essential papers on suicide* (pp. 417–426). New York, NY: New York University Press.

eight
Planning for Treatment

Tip 44: Make Suicidality the Focus

"Suicidal behavior should be targeted directly in the treatment plan. Simply treating an underlying condition, such as depression, on the assumption that suicidal risk will abate as the condition improves is insufficient."

Mark Oordt and colleagues
(2005, p. 215)

For decades, the prevailing approach to treating suicidality has been to not actually treat suicidality. Instead, the advice was – and still is, in many quarters – to treat psychiatric disorders that give rise to suicidal thoughts, such as major depression. Once the disorder resolves, the thinking goes, so will the suicidal thoughts (e.g., Wasserman et al., 2012). In contrast, increasing amounts of research and theory reflect a growing awareness that suicidality itself must be the primary focus of treatment.

A team of researchers looked at studies of psychotherapies that directly targeted suicidal thoughts and behaviors and compared them to interventions that indirectly addressed suicidality by focusing instead on correlates of suicide risk such as mental illness symptoms and skills deficits (Meerwijk et al., 2016). The results showed that individuals' suicidal behaviors dropped more swiftly in treatments that directly targeted suicidality. Other researchers looked at interventions designed to treat depression. Although suicidal individuals' hopelessness decreased with treatment, reductions in suicidal ideation were small and not statistically significant (Cuijpers et al., 2013).

Making suicidality the focus of treatment means proactively engaging the person in ongoing discussions of suicidal thoughts, reasons for living and dying, safety planning, and suicide risk. It also means addressing specifically what's causing the person to want to die, working toward resolving those problems, and helping the person to tap into goals, hopes, and plans that give life meaning. Other conditions linked to suicidal thoughts, such as depression and substance use, certainly ought to be addressed, too. But it should not be assumed that treating these conditions will resolve the person's wish to die.

Suicide "Drivers"

The Collaborative Assessment and Management of Suicidality (CAMS) offers a useful framework for keeping the focus on suicidality (Jobes, 2016). CAMS calls for assessing the person's suicidality every session, using the Suicide Status Form, (*Tip 21*). In addition, the treatment calls for targeting direct and indirect "drivers" of suicide. Direct drivers are "suicide-specific thoughts, feelings, and behaviors" (Jobes et al., 2011, p. 389). Indirect drivers are the psychosocial stressors (such as substance use or trauma) that make a person vulnerable to developing suicidal thoughts, feelings, and behaviors.

To ascertain the person's direct drivers, CAMS therapists ask the person to identify the two problems that most account for the person's desire to die (Jobes, 2016). CAMS does not prescribe a specific set of techniques for ameliorating the person's direct and indirect drivers of suicidality, making the approach what its developer, psychologist David Jobes, calls "nondenominational."

Jobes and colleagues (2011) note that some professionals "feel uncomfortable with the persistent emphasis on suicide" (p. 387). Jobes' team has a compelling rejoinder: "We remind them that a patient's other issues are better addressed if they are alive."

Works Cited

Cuijpers, P., de Beurs, D. P., van Spijker, B. A., Berking, M., Andersson, G., & Kerkhof, A. J. (2013). The effects of psychotherapy for adult depression on suicidality and hopelessness: A systematic review and meta-analysis. *Journal of Affective Disorders, 144*(3), 183–190.

Jobes, D. A. (2016). *Managing suicidal risk: A collaborative approach* (2nd ed.). New York, NY: Guilford Press.

Jobes, D. A., Comtois, K. A., Brenner, L. A., & Gutierrez, P. M. (2011). Clinical trial feasibility studies of the Collaborative Assessment and Management of Suicidality. In R. C. O'Connor, S. Platt, & J. Gordon (Eds.) *International handbook of suicide prevention: Research, policy and practice* (pp. 383–400). Hoboken, NJ: John Wiley.

Meerwijk, E. L., Parekh, A., Oquendo, M. A., Allen, I. E., Franck, L. S., & Lee, K. A. (2016). Direct versus indirect psychosocial and behavioural interventions to prevent suicide and suicide attempts: A systematic review and meta-analysis. *The Lancet Psychiatry, 3*(6), 544–554.

Oordt, M. S., Jobes, D. A., Rudd, M. D., Fonseca, V. P., Runyan, C. N., Stea, J. B., ... & Talcott, G. W. (2005). Development of a clinical guide to enhance care for suicidal patients. *Professional Psychology: Research and Practice, 36*(2), 208–218.

Wasserman, D., Rihmer, Z., Rujescu, D., Sarchiapone, M., Sokolowski, M., Titelman, D., ... & Carli, V. (2012). The European Psychiatric Association (EPA) guidance on suicide treatment and prevention. *European Psychiatry, 27*(2), 129–141.

Tip 45: As Needed, Increase Frequency of Contact

"If therapists feel that being available for telephone contact is an imposition, then they're in the wrong field or they're treating the wrong patient. They should treat only well people."

Bruce Danto
(quoted in Colt, 1991, p. 320)

A weekly psychotherapy session provides support only 50–60 minutes out of 168 hours. In the midst of a suicidal crisis, clients often need more than that. While being mindful of boundaries (*Tip 5*), professionals should make themselves available for brief between-sessions check-ins by phone, text, or email; skills coaching calls; crisis calls; and more frequent sessions. These increases in contact can help the person stay safe on an outpatient basis.

In dialectical behavior therapy (DBT), therapists regularly are available by phone between sessions for telephone coaching or other support (Linehan, 1993). DBT uses the "24-hour rule." Clients are told at the start of therapy that if they have already harmed themselves, they are not to call their therapist for at least 24 hours unless the injuries are life-threatening. This serves two functions. First, it encourages people to reach out for help before acting on urges to harm themselves. Second, it avoids sending the message that the therapist will care and spend ample time with the person only if self-harm occurs, which could reinforce such behaviors.

Many professionals worry that between-sessions contact can trigger excessive phone calls, dependency, and intrusions on their time. Research indicates, however, that therapists who make themselves available to clients between sessions experience *fewer* calls than those who direct clients not to contact them (Reitzel et al., 2004). It may be that simply knowing that they can call their therapist if needed helps soothe individuals, enabling them to cope on their own.

For guidance on how to structure between-sessions contact with a suicidal person, consider these recommendations, which draw from the writings of psychologist Thomas Joiner and colleagues (2009) and psychologist Marsha Linehan (1993):

- Increase the frequency of sessions as needed, especially if suicide risk is elevated so much that the person is on the border of needing hospitalization.
- Schedule between-sessions phone check-ins at specific times if the client is at moderate or high risk of suicide. The calls should be goal-oriented and brief (generally 5–10 minutes, and no longer than 15–20 minutes). A common structure would be to assess the person's current and recent suicidal ideation, planning, intent, and behaviors; express empathy and concern; and go over what the person will do next to cope.

- Invite the person to call you if needed between sessions for unscheduled calls, while also being careful not to portray yourself as unconditionally available. Although it might seem like stating the obvious, let the person know that you may be in session or otherwise unavailable to talk, and that you will return the call as soon as you can.

- Depending on your stance toward electronic communications, encourage the person to send a text or email to reach you during a crisis or to check in.

- In case the person is in dire need of help and you are unavailable, instruct them to call a crisis hotline or emergency services, or to go to the nearest emergency room. In the U.S., the National Suicide Prevention Lifeline number is 1-800-273-TALK (8255), and dialing 911 connects the person to emergency services.

Between-sessions contact can shore up the person's safety, and it also can be therapeutic. Phone calls and other contacts help the person to feel a sense of belonging, an important salve for the "thwarted belongingness" that suicidal individuals commonly experience (Joiner et al., 2009). Between-sessions contact also can be an opportunity to support the person's autonomy, provide skills coaching, and express empathy and support.

Extra contact with clients can have negative effects if it erodes boundaries and feeds a desire in you to rescue the suicidal person (*Tip 5*). Also be mindful that some people with chronic suicidality may become more helpless and dependent with too much extra contact (*Tip 46*). To help protect your boundaries and foster the suicidal person's resilience, focus on skills the person can practice to cope better (vs. what you can do to help the person feel better), and raise the issue in sessions if the person is relying too much on you rather than building their own skills, support network, and resources.

"Just Knowing You Were There Helped A Lot"

Kayla, 19, adamantly stated she did not want to kill herself, but thoughts of stabbing herself with a knife or hanging herself came every day without invitation. The thoughts frightened her. Although she did not meet criteria for hospitalization, she needed more than once-a-week therapy. Collaboratively, she and the counselor made a plan for Kayla to check in with him by phone in two days, and then to return for another therapy session two days after that. Kayla signed a consent form permitting the counselor to call her emergency contact (Kayla's mother) if Kayla did not call at 2 p.m. If Kayla had not consented to his contacting her mother or someone else she knew personally, then the plan would have been for the counselor to call the police and request a welfare check. During the check-in call, the counselor asked Kayla how she was doing and feeling, conducted a rapid suicide risk assessment, and reviewed how Kayla had used her safety plan. At the next session a couple days later, he evaluated whether Kayla's danger had increased to the point of her needing a more intensive level of care. She remained at a moderate level of risk, still having intrusive thoughts of suicide, still following her safety plan, and still feeling afraid, so they repeated the previous week's plan. At various times over the next few months, Kayla came more frequently for sessions, scheduled between-sessions phone calls, and texted her counselor. She reached out sparingly, never more than once or twice a week, and she did not resist when the counselor moved to end the calls. Finally, as Kayla worked through personal issues and her new skills took hold, the suicidal thoughts subsided. Kayla told her counselor, "Just knowing you were there helped a lot."

Works Cited

Colt, G. H. (1991). *The enigma of suicide.* New York, NY: Touchstone/Simon & Schuster.

Joiner, T. E. Jr., Van Orden, K. A., Witte, T. K., & Rudd, M. D. (2009). *The interpersonal theory of suicide: Guidance for working with suicidal clients.* Washington, DC: American Psychological Association.

Linehan, M. M. (1993). *Cognitive-behavioral treatment of borderline personality disorder.* New York, NY: Guilford Press.

Reitzel, L. R., Burns, A. B., Repper, K. K., Wingate, L. R., & Joiner, T. E., Jr. (2004). The effect of therapist availability on the frequency of patient-initiated between-session contact. *Professional Psychology: Research and Practice, 35*(3), 291–206.

Tip 46: Treat Chronic Suicidality Differently

"Methods generally recommended for the management of suicidality are ineffective and counterproductive in chronically suicidal patients."

Joel Paris

(2007, p. xiv)

For some people, suicidal thoughts are not an emergency but, instead, a "way of life" (Schwartz et al., 1974). People with chronic suicidality have thought of suicide for many years. They might have already made multiple attempts, perhaps even more than they can remember. This longstanding suicidality differs from acute suicidality in important ways. When a person has an acute suicidal crisis, the goal is for the person to return safely to their baseline or better. When a person has chronic suicidal thoughts, suicidality *is* the baseline.

Persistent suicidal thoughts and behaviors are especially common in people with borderline personality disorder. The diagnosis is the only one for which recurrent suicidality is a symptom (American Psychiatric Association, 2013). Chronic suicidal ideation can also occur in concert with major depression, bipolar disorder, post-traumatic stress disorder, and other psychiatric problems.

Some clinicians dismiss chronic suicidality as more "attention seeking" and "manipulative" than actually dangerous, especially when the person attempts suicide multiple times. These pejorative labels can mask genuine danger. Rather than being a benign gesture, multiple suicide attempts increase the risk that the person will eventually die by suicide (Zahl & Hawton, 2004). Among people treated for borderline personality disorder, roughly 8–10% die by suicide, one of the highest suicide rates among any diagnostic group (Paris & Zweig-Frank, 2001; Pompili et al., 2005). In comparison, 2% of people with major depression die by suicide (Bostwick & Pankratz, 2000).

Acute and chronic suicidality diverge not only in their form, but also in their treatment. With a person in acute suicidal crisis, clinicians often are called upon to take control in order to protect the person and save a life (e.g., Shneidman, 1996). For people with chronic suicidal episodes, the therapist often needs to give up control and take more risks in order to prevent regression, dependency, and reinforcement of suicidal behaviors (Paris, 2007). Measures typically recommended for an acutely suicidal person can reinforce the use of suicidal ideation and communications as a means to cope. For example, *Tip 45* addresses increasing the frequency of sessions and between-session contact when a person's suicide risk is elevated. The psychiatrist Joel Paris (2007) notes that such an approach could have the reverse effect for someone with chronic thoughts of suicide: "The more frequently a patient is seen, the more suicidal behaviors are elicited, because they have become a ticket to obtaining care and connection" (p. 153).

The psychiatrist Thomas Gutheil (in Koekkoek et al., 2008) contrasts acute and chronic suicidality as a crisis of despair vs. responsibility. Acute suicidality is a time-limited crisis, like pneumonia. Chronic suicidality endures, like diabetes. As a result, chronically suicidal individuals need to take responsibility for managing their challenges. Gutheil elaborates:

> The patient must take ultimate responsibility over a lifetime for managing the illness. Like irresponsible management of one's diabetes, the irresponsible management of chronic suicidality may have a fatal result; however, neither "taking over" the patient's life nor attempts at "rescue" are likely to succeed.
>
> (Gutheil, in Koekkoek et al., 2008, p. 203)

Dialectical behavior therapy offers important strategies for helping chronically suicidal people learn how to manage their emotions, find purpose in living, and reduce self-harming behaviors (*Tip 73*). An empirically supported treatment, DBT was developed specifically for individuals with borderline personality disorder and chronic suicidality, though research supports its use with a broader range of problems (Linehan, 1993). It is wise to include DBT in your work with anyone who has chronic suicidality, whether you practice DBT exclusively, integrate its techniques selectively, or refer your client for adjunctive DBT skills training.

"Staying Alive" vs. "Having a Life"

At 29, Justin has attempted suicide many times in the last five years. Each time, he was hospitalized in a psychiatric inpatient unit, where the focus was on keeping him alive. The nurturance of staff and the escape from daily burdens gave Justin a much-needed sense of relief. But he didn't get better. To the contrary, although he seemed to improve while in the hospital, he deteriorated almost immediately upon returning home. His therapist, a clinical social worker, noted a cycle of dependency and helplessness. She decided to counter this by exploring the problem-solving nature of Justin's suicidal behaviors (*Tip 60*), building skills in problem-solving (*Tips 61–62*) and distress tolerance (*Tip 73*), focusing on goals and plans to make life more meaningful (*Tip 63*), and recommending hospitalization only in the case of extreme risk (*Tip 35*). This approach meant taking less responsibility for Justin's life, so that he could take more. His therapist was sure to document her rationale, noting that Justin's risk for suicide seemed only to grow when his chronic suicidality was consistently treated as an acute emergency. Over time, as Justin gained practical coping skills and overcame his dependency on hospitalizations, he continued to have suicidal thoughts occasionally but no longer felt compelled to act on them. "Before I was just barely staying alive," he said. "Now I have a life."

Works Cited

American Psychiatric Association. (2013). *Diagnostic and statistical manual of mental disorders (DSM-5).* Washington, DC: American Psychiatric Publishing.

Bostwick, J. M., & Pankratz, V. S. (2000). Affective disorders and suicide risk: A reexamination. *American Journal of Psychiatry, 157*(12), 1925–1932.

Koekkoek, B., Gunderson, J. G., Kaasenbrood, A., & Gutheil, T. G. (2008). Chronic suicidality in a physician: An alliance yet to become therapeutic. *Harvard Review of Psychiatry, 16*(3), 195–204.

Linehan, M. M. (1993). *Cognitive-behavioral treatment of borderline personality disorder.* New York, NY: Guilford Press.

Paris, J. (2007). *Half in love with death: Managing the chronically suicidal patient.* New York, NY: Routledge.

Paris, J., & Zweig-Frank, H. (2001). A 27-year follow-up of patients with borderline personality disorder. *Comprehensive Psychiatry, 42*(6), 482–487.

Pompili, M., Girardi, P., Ruberto, A., & Tatarelli, R. (2005). Suicide in borderline personality disorder: A meta-analysis. *Nordic Journal of Psychiatry, 59*(5), 319–324.

Schwartz, D. A., Flinn, D. E., & Slawson, P. F. (1974). Treatment of the suicidal character. *American Journal of Psychotherapy, 28*(2), 194–207.

Shneidman, E. S. (1996). Psychotherapy with suicidal patients. In J. T. Maltsberger & M. J. Goldblatt (Eds.), *Essential papers on suicide* (pp. 417–426). New York, NY: New York University Press.

Zahl, D. L., & Hawton, K. (2004). Repetition of deliberate self-harm and subsequent suicide risk: Long-term follow-up study of 11,583 patients. *The British Journal of Psychiatry, 185*(1), 70–75.

Tip 47: Involve Loved Ones

"Take advantage of the opportunity to rally and organize the patient's social support system by routinely integrating family members into the treatment process during periods of heightened risk."

M. David Rudd and colleagues
(2001, p. 105)

Family and significant others can help inform your assessment of the suicidal person's risk (*Tip 26*). If possible, their involvement should not end there. Throughout the person's treatment, family and other loved ones can provide valuable information about the person's suicidal statements and actions over time, alert you to changes in the person's mood and functioning, help the person follow the safety plan, and in general help the person use other skills and tactics to solve problems without resorting to self-harm. This has the added advantage of widening the suicidal person's circle of care and, as a result, potentially increasing their sense of connection and belonging. Involving the person's support system can range from occasional phone conversations about the person's progress and problems, to actually including significant others in sessions with the suicidal person.

Confidentiality laws apply, and you need the person's permission to involve others in their treatment (*Tip 26*). Some clients may choose to preserve their privacy. In other cases, including family or other loved ones in the person's treatment can do harm. Most notably this is true if the person's relationships with loved ones are abusive or otherwise toxic. Tragically, some family members encourage the person to act on suicidal thoughts, shame the person for receiving care, or otherwise are emotionally or physically abusive. In extreme cases, some family members have provided a suicidal person with a firearm or other means for suicide. Before involving family, assess whether they are a "hinderer or helper in the treatment process" (Shneidman, 1993, p. 146).

Even when family or others are involved, do not rely on them too much. Loved ones should never be expected to keep a dangerously suicidal person from acting on suicidal thoughts. It is simply not possible for friends or family to monitor a suicidal person 24 hours a day without interruption. If a suicidal person is in so much danger that family are expected to never leave the person alone, then hospitalization is usually necessary (*Tip 35*).

"I Don't Want to Burden Him"

Lydia's husband had no idea. He did not even know that Lydia, 48, was depressed, let alone thinking of suicide. Lydia was, as she told her therapist, a "master at hiding." She smiled. She laughed. She joked. And when she cried, she did it only where nobody could see.

Lydia's psychiatrist asked what stopped her from telling her husband, Demetrius. "I don't want to burden him," Lydia said. "He has enough to worry about." Asked how it might help her to let Demetrius in on her depression and suicidal thoughts, Lydia could not think of one reason.

Her psychiatrist did not push it. It was only their first session together. "I hope you'll think about it," he told her. "You don't have to bear this alone."

A few weeks later, Lydia came into the session feeling worse than ever. Her suicidal thinking had deteriorated. Now she had a method in mind, and the means. She insisted she did not intend to act on her suicidal thoughts, but her psychiatrist felt uneasy.

"I really think it could help you if we brought Demetrius into the loop," he said.

This time, Lydia did not protest. She called Demetrius, put the call on speaker, and tearfully shared the reason for the call. Demetrius expressed sadness to Lydia that she was hurting so badly and that he hadn't known. The psychiatrist asked Demetrius to let him know if he observed anything of concern in Lydia. Lydia and Demetrius decided it would be good for Demetrius to join the next session.

After the call ended, Lydia told her psychiatrist, "I guess it's good he knows. It takes a lot of energy to hide all the time."

Works Cited

Rudd, M. D., Joiner, T., & Rajab, M. H. (2001). *Treating suicidal behavior: An effective, time-limited approach.* New York, NY: Guilford Press.

Shneidman, E. S. (1993). *Suicide as psychache: A clinical approach to self-destructive behavior.* Lanham, MD: Rowman & Littlefield Publishers.

Tip 48: Suggest a Physical Exam

*"Physical illness may first manifest itself as a disturbance in mood,
thought processes, or behavior."*

Stephen Krummel and Roger Kathol
(1987, p. 275)

The mind–body connection is so well established that to even distinguish between physical and mental health is an artificial division. Mental health, the provenance of the brain, *is* an aspect of physical health. With that said, several aspects of physical health besides mental illness can cause, contribute to, or exacerbate suicidal thoughts. This calls for advising the suicidal person to get a physical exam, if they haven't already done so.

Several physical conditions create psychiatric symptoms that can lead to suicidal ideation and behavior or related conditions. For example, depression and attendant suicidal thoughts can arise from hypothyroidism, hyperthyroidism, Cushing's disease, and other endocrine disorders (Lauriat & Samson, 2017). Vitamin D deficiency appears to be associated with increased suicide risk (Umhau et al., 2013). Increasingly, research is linking inflammatory processes to suicidality (Brundin et al., 2017). Other physical conditions, such as migraines, fibromyalgia, and arthritis, can create chronic pain that feeds suicidal thoughts (Ratcliffe et al., 2008). Better management of these conditions has the potential to lessen suicide risk.

Medications can affect suicidal thoughts, too. It is fairly well known that antidepressants trigger suicidal thoughts and behaviors in a very small proportion of the people who take them (Pompili et al., 2016). What is less well known is that some medications for physical conditions besides mental illness also have been incriminated. Although research studies are inconclusive, increases in suicidal thoughts and behaviors have been linked to medications for asthma, epilepsy, and acne (Gorton et al., 2016). Encourage suicidal individuals to talk with their prescribing physician about whether any of their medications could be responsible for psychological side effects, including suicidal thoughts.

A Blood Test, and a Revelation

Jing, 33, sat fully clothed on the toilet in the stall, crying, hoping that no one else would come into the women's restroom. For several weeks, crying spells punctuated her mornings. She felt morose and empty, and she could not tie her sad mood to any change in her life. Now, she found herself wishing she was dead and even thinking of ways to make it happen. This alarmed her, so she sought help from a clinical social worker at her company's employee assistance program. Based on symptoms that Jing reported, such as depressed mood, suicidal ideation, poor concentration, lethargy, and hypersomnia, the social worker diagnosed depression. He judged Jing to be safe for outpatient treatment, prescribed a course of cognitive behavior therapy, and recommended that Jing see her physician to make sure that no physical condition accounted for her depression. The physician sent her for blood tests, and the results revealed that Jing had hypothyroidism. For treatment, Jing began taking the medication levothyroxine (e.g., Levothroid or Synthroid), a synthetic form of thyroid hormone. Within weeks, she no longer found herself rushing to the bathroom in tears or, worse, thinking of killing herself. As her thyroid levels improved, so did her mood.

Works Cited

Brundin, L., Bryleva, E. Y., & Rajamani, K. T. (2017). Role of inflammation in suicide: From mechanisms to treatment. *Neuropsychopharmacology, 42*(1), 271–283.

Gorton, H. C., Webb, R. T., Kapur, N., & Ashcroft, D. M. (2016). Non-psychotropic medication and risk of suicide or attempted suicide: A systematic review. *BMJ Open, 6*(1), e009074.

Krummel, S., & Kathol, R. G. (1987). What you should know about physical evaluations in psychiatric patients: Results of a survey. *General Hospital Psychiatry, 9*(4), 275–279.

Lauriat, T. L., & Samson, J. A. (2017). Endocrine disorders associated with psychological/behavioral problems. In P. M. Kleespies (Ed.), *The Oxford handbook of behavioral emergencies and crises* (pp. 426–448). New York, NY: Oxford University Press.

Pompili, M., Giordano, G., & Lamis, D. A. (2016). Antidepressants and suicide risk: A challenge. In P. Courtet (Ed.), *Understanding suicide: From diagnosis to personalized treatment* (pp. 291–302). Cham: Springer.

Ratcliffe, G. E., Enns, M. W., Belik, S. L., & Sareen, J. (2008). Chronic pain conditions and suicidal ideation and suicide attempts: An epidemiologic perspective. *Clinical Journal of Pain, 24*(3), 204–210.

Umhau, J. C., George, D. T., Heaney, R. P., Lewis, M. D., Ursano, R. J., Heilig, M., ... & Schwandt, M. L. (2013). Low vitamin D status and suicide: A case-control study of active duty military service members. *PLoS One, 8*(1), e51543.

Tip 49: Recommend an Evaluation for Medication

"Medications to treat symptoms such as psychic pain, anxiety and turmoil, panic attacks, agitation, impulsiveness, aggression, and feelings of hopelessness can be extremely helpful in managing the patient with suicidal tendencies."

H. Florence Kim and colleagues
(2012, p. 212)

Dozens of medications are designed to improve mental health conditions associated with suicidal thoughts. The potential risks and benefits are complex. At least one medication, lithium, appears to directly decrease suicidal thoughts, even without improving related conditions such as a mood disorder (Bauer & Gitlin, 2016). Complicating matters, research suggests that some psychiatric drugs such as antidepressants reduce suicidal thoughts in some people *and* trigger new suicidal thoughts in a very small proportion of others (Pompili et al., 2016). A further complication is that some psychotropic drugs, such as lithium and tricyclic antidepressants, can be taken in excess to die by suicide. Despite these risks, and despite controversy around the use of psychiatric medications, the use of medication is commonly recommended for suicidal individuals (Kim et al., 2012).

Just as you would do the suicidal person a disservice if you did not recommend an exam to rule out physical causes of their psychiatric symptoms and suicidal thoughts (*Tip 48*), you also have a responsibility to inform them of all treatment options, including medications. Even if you do not have prescribing privileges, you can still discuss the potential benefits of an evaluation for medication by a psychiatrist, primary care physician, or other prescriber.

"I Don't Want to Just Take a Pill"

Tirique, 44, had classic symptoms of depression. He was eating less, sleeping more, moving and thinking more slowly, and getting very little pleasure out of things that he once enjoyed. And then there were the feelings of emptiness and guilt, not to mention the suicidal thoughts. His therapist, a licensed professional counselor, shared with him her diagnosis of major depression and explored his reaction. He agreed.

"You know, Tirique, often when people have serious depression, they benefit from an antidepressant," the counselor said. "There can be negative side effects, but the general consensus is that antidepressants help more than they hurt."

"I don't want to just take a pill," Tirique said. "That's the reason I came to see you instead of a psychiatrist."

"It sounds like you've already given this some thought," she said. "And it's certainly your choice. It's just, I would be remiss if I didn't bring up medication as an option. The thing about medication is, there's research that shows that antidepressants alone and psychotherapy alone can both reduce depression. But the research shows that each reduces depression more when used together."

"Well, I'd like to give therapy a try first," Tirique said. "Then maybe we can see later if it seems like I need to take a pill, too."

"That sounds like a good plan," she said. "I understand that it's important to you to try to get better without medication. Let's talk about the different things we can do to help make that happen ..."

Works Cited

Bauer, M., & Gitlin, M. (2016). Suicide prevention with lithium. In *The essential guide to lithium treatment* (pp. 81–89). Cham: Springer.

Kim, H. F., Chen, F., & Yudofsky, S. C. (2012). Psychopharmacotherapy and electroconvulsive therapy. In R. I. Simon & R. E. Hales (Eds.), *The American Psychiatric Publishing textbook of suicide assessment and management* (2nd ed., pp. 211–232). Arlington, VA: American Psychiatric Publishing.

Pompili, M., Giordano, G., & Lamis, D. A. (2016). Antidepressants and suicide risk: A challenge. In P. Courtet (Ed.), *Understanding suicide: From diagnosis to personalized treatment* (pp. 291–302). Cham: Springer.

Tip 50: Continue to Monitor Suicidal Ideation

"Because risk of self-harm can ebb and flow over time, clinicians must assess risk repeatedly over time."

Jillian Peterson and colleagues
(2011, p. 627)

Suicidal thoughts come and go. They are fluid, dynamic, and unpredictable. These vicissitudes require constant vigilance throughout treatment. Mini-assessments, standardized questionnaires, and diary cards present different methods for monitoring suicide risk on an ongoing basis.

Mini-Assessments

It's necessary to assess suicidal thoughts and behaviors every session, at least until well after the suicidal crisis resolves. The assessment need not be a formal or lengthy process. Possible questions include:

- *"Tell me what your suicidal thoughts have been like this week."*
- *"How much have you thought about suicide since our last meeting?"*
- *"On a scale of 1 to 10, how intense have your suicidal thoughts been?"*
- *"What methods for suicide do you have in mind?"*
- *"What, if anything, have you done to act on your suicidal thoughts or prepare for suicide?"*
- *"How much do you intend to act on your suicidal thoughts? ... When?"*
- *"What has stopped you from trying to die by suicide?"*

When suicidal thinking persists, also be sure to determine whether the person's choice of methods and access to means have changed.

Suicide-Related Questionnaires

Tip 21 described several questionnaires used to assess suicidal thoughts: the Suicide Status Form, the Columbia Suicide Severity Rating Scale, and the Beck Scale for Suicidal Ideation. The Beck Scale can be administered repeatedly. The Columbia Scale and the Suicide Status Form come in shortened versions specifically designed to track suicidality across sessions.

Diary Cards

Widely used in dialectical behavior therapy, diary cards provide a quick and easy way for the suicidal person to record regularly the extent of suicidal thinking and related problems, such as hopelessness. Every day, the person checks off whether they had suicidal thoughts or provides a numeric rating. The diary card gives a picture of the intensity of the person's suicidal thoughts and related emotions during the time between sessions. From there, it is important to explore with the person the specific nature and content of the suicidal thoughts. The diary card provides an easy starting point for doing so.

Example: Diary Card

Rate on a scale of 0 to 10 how much each of the following applied to you, with 0 = "not at all" and 10 = "completely." Please fill this out every night while your memory of the day is fresh.

	M	T	W	Th	F	Sat	Sun
Wanted to kill myself	6	5	3	3	1	1	6
Felt ... depressed	10	9	7	6	4	3	10
anxious	5	4	3	4	3	2	9
hopeful	0	1	1	3	4	4	0
happy	0	0	1	2	4	4	0

Now, please check off any of the following actions that you took that day:

	M	T	W	Th	F	Sat	Sun
Thought about how to kill myself	x	x	x				x
Made preparations to kill myself	x						x
Tried to kill myself							
Hurt myself (not a suicide attempt)							x

The diary card example focuses solely on suicidal thoughts and relevant emotions. A far more comprehensive diary card is available in the *DBT Skills Training Manual* (Linehan, 2015). Additionally, there are many hundreds of diary card formats available online for free, from the very complex to the very simple; simply do a Google search with "diary card" as the keyword. Some have emoticons or graphics for children. Diary card apps also are available for cell phones, tablets, and computers.

Asking about Suicidal Thoughts: How Much is Too Much?

Some clinicians fear that repeatedly assessing suicide risk can exacerbate a person's suicidal thoughts. A study investigated that very possibility (Law et al., 2015). Using a handheld, computerized device similar to a smart phone, almost 130 adults answered questions *five times a day* – every three hours from 10 a.m. to 10 p.m. – about whether they had considered suicide or actually made an attempt in the previous hour. Along with another group of comparable adults, they also answered questions about their positive and negative psychological experiences (e.g., shame, irritability, happiness, impulsive behaviors). At the end of a two-week period and in monthly follow-up interviews for six months, researchers compared the "intensive suicide assessment" group with the group that had answered no suicide questions. The rates of suicidal ideation and suicide attempts in both groups were the same, meaning that intensively asking individuals about suicidal thoughts and behavior did not lead to more suicidal thoughts or behavior.

The circumstances in this study were fairly extreme; outside of inpatient settings, few if any clinicians need to ask clients about suicidal thoughts and behaviors five times a day. Still, it is reassuring that assessing suicidality an abundance of times does not appear to intensify the person's wish to die.

Works Cited

Law, M. K., Furr, R. M., Arnold, E. M., Mneimne, M., Jaquett, C., & Fleeson, W. (2015). Does assessing suicidality frequently and repeatedly cause harm? A randomized control study. *Psychological Assessment, 27*(4), 1171–1181.

Linehan, M. M. (2015). *DBT skills training manual* (2nd ed.). New York, NY: Guilford Press.

Peterson, J., Skeem, J., & Manchak, S. (2011). If you want to know, consider asking: How likely is it that patients will hurt themselves in the future? *Psychological Assessment, 23*(3), 626–634.

nine
Alleviating Psychological Pain

Tip 51: After Safety, Address Suffering

"Reduce the level of suffering and the individual will choose to live."

Maurizio Pompili

(2015, p. 227)

Anguish, misery, desperation, psychic trauma, mental torture – these are a few of the ways people describe the psychological pain that incubates the suicidal wish. The pain is intolerable to the suicidal person, and the person urgently seeks an escape (Hendin et al., 2004). The psychologist Edwin Shneidman (1993) argued that this psychological pain takes precedence over any other risk factor for suicide. It might seem like common sense to attend fully to the suicidal person's mental pain. Instead, professionals often shy away from exploring the person's pain, prematurely resorting instead to reassurance, advice, problem-solving, and intellectualization (Neimeyer & Pfeiffer, 1994).

Many people innately fear emotional contagion. In reality, it does hurt to vicariously experience the suffering and hopelessness that engulf the suicidal person. It is the professional's job to manage those experiences of vicarious pain, not to avoid them. This requires inviting the person to express their pain and responding with validation and empathy. Helpful questions include:

- *"How badly are you hurting emotionally?"*
- *"How would you describe your mental pain?"*

- *"What hurts the most?"*
- *"What does it feel like?"*

Examine what underlies the person's psychological pain. In a study looking at people who died by suicide, the most prominent affective states were feelings of self-hatred, hopelessness, rage, loneliness, guilt, and humiliation (Hendin et al., 2004). The potential role of trauma and its attendant feelings of panic and anguish also cannot be ignored (Maltsberger et al., 2011). Whatever form a person's mental pain takes, it often comes with a sense of entrapment, abandonment, emotional flooding, loss of control, and belief that the pain is irreversible (Orbach, 2001).

In time, after you have facilitated and understood the person's expression of pain, you will need to move from exploring pain to making efforts to alleviate it. The psychologist Israel Orbach advocates for helping the client to work through "pain to its fullest intensity" (Orbach, 2011, p. 125). For people who have experienced trauma, this can involve a formal trauma intervention such as prolonged exposure (Foa et al., 2007) or cognitive processing therapy (Resick et al., 2016). More generally, you can help the person work through pain by helping them to discern, accept, put into words, and fully experience their various emotions (Greenberg, 2015).

Other means for diminishing the person's pain are covered in numerous tips in this book. These tips address helping the person to increase a sense of social connection and worth (*Tip 53*), learn grounding techniques (*Tip 54*), solve problems that create pain (*Tips 60–62*), rediscover hope (*Tips 63–65*), challenge or disarm destructive thought processes (*Tips 66–72*), improve coping skills (*Tip 73*), develop a habit of mindfulness (*Tip 74*), stimulate positive emotions (*Tip 75*), and reconnect with meaningful activities (*Tip 76*). Another approach is to identify and help remedy the person's unmet needs, which is the topic of the next tip.

A Conversation with Ernest Hemingway

In the days before the novelist Ernest Hemingway fatally shot himself, he and the writer A. E. Hotchner had what would be their final conversation. Hotchner visited his friend while Hemingway, 62, was hospitalized for depression. During that time, Hemingway let Hotchner in on his mental pain (Hotchner, 2005, pp. 297–300). It was hard for Hotchner to hear. So, when Hemingway despaired that he could no longer write, Hotchner offered reassurance. He emphatically told Hemingway that he was a good writer. When Hemingway stated that "existence is impossible" if he could not live on his own terms (and he firmly believed that he couldn't), Hotchner offered advice: Put writing aside for now, take time off and travel, or even retire altogether. He went on to tell Hemingway, "And you should work hard to think about the things you care about and like to do, and not about all those negative things."

On examining this conversation, the psychiatrist Douglas Jacobs concludes, "Hotchner desperately wanted to be helpful but had difficulty hearing Hemingway" (Jacobs, 1989, p. 332). Jacobs goes on to note that Hotchner's responses sent this message to Hemingway: "I don't hear you, I don't want to listen, I can't accept that you, a great man are so miserable" (p. 333).

Hemingway's friend was not a mental health professional. He could not be expected to use the foundational counseling skills of accurate empathy, reflective listening, and validation (e.g., Corey, 2015). But many trained professionals, too, have difficulty bearing witness to a person's intense emotional pain. With good intentions, they offer reassurance, advice, and encouragement, without first trying to understand and empathize. "I hear how much you are hurting," a therapist might have said to Hemingway. "You feel totally hopeless, don't you?"

Difficulty hearing a person's pain, without immediately trying to weaken the pain, is common. It reflects a compassionate desire to pull the person out of the dark abyss, and a self-protective maneuver to not fall into the abyss, too. This resistance can create a painful sense of loneliness, estrangement, and hopelessness in the suffering person. As mental health professionals, it is our job to do the difficult – to join with the person in that darkness before, side by side, helping the person climb out.

Works Cited

Corey, G. (2015). *Theory and practice of counseling and psychotherapy* (10th ed.). Boston, MA: Cengage Learning.

Foa, E. B., Hembree, E. A., & Rothbaum, B. O. (2007). *Prolonged exposure therapy for adolescents with PTSD: Emotional processing of traumatic experiences – therapist guide.* New York, NY: Oxford University Press.

Greenberg, L. S. (2015). *Emotion-focused therapy: Coaching clients to work through their feelings.* Washington, DC: American Psychological Association.

Hendin, H., Maltsberger, J. T., Haas, A. P., Szanto, K., & Rabinowicz, H. (2004). Desperation and other affective states in suicidal patients. *Suicide and Life-Threatening Behavior, 34*(4), 386–394.

Hotchner, A. E. (2005). *Papa Hemingway: A personal memoir.* Boston, MA: De Capo Press.

Jacobs, D. (1989). Psychotherapy with suicidal patients: The empathic method. In D. Jacobs & H. N. Brown (Eds.), *Suicide: Understanding and responding* (pp. 329–342). Madison, CT: International Universities Press.

Maltsberger, J. T., Goldblatt, M. J., Ronningstam, E., Weinberg, I., & Schechter, M. (2011). Traumatic subjective experiences invite suicide. *The Journal of the American Academy of Psychoanalysis and Dynamic Psychiatry, 39*(4), 671–693.

Neimeyer, R. A., & Pfeiffer, A. M. (1994). The ten most common errors of suicide interventionists. In A. A. Leenaars, J. T. Maltsberg, & R. A. Neimeyer (Eds.), *Treatment of suicidal people* (pp. 207–224). New York, NY: Routledge.

Orbach, I. (2001). Therapeutic empathy with the suicidal wish: Principles of therapy with suicidal individuals. *American Journal of Psychotherapy, 55*(2), 166–184.

Orbach, I. (2011). Taking an inside view: Stories of pain. In K. Michel & D. A. Jobes (Eds.), *Building a therapeutic alliance with the suicidal patient* (pp. 111–128). Washington, DC: American Psychological Association.

Pompili, M. (2015). Our empathic brain and suicidal individuals. *Crisis, 36*(4), 227–230.

Resick, P. A., Monson, C. M., & Chard, K. M. (2016). *Cognitive processing therapy for PTSD: A comprehensive manual.* New York, NY: Guilford Press.

Shneidman, E. S. (1993). *Suicide as psychache: A clinical approach to self-destructive behavior.* Lanham, MD: Jason Aronson.

Tip 52: Look for Unmet Needs

"In doing psychotherapy with a suicidal person a therapist would do well to have a tailormade template of that patient's frustrated needs in mind and to focus the therapy toward mollifying those painful frustrations."

Edwin Shneidman
(1998, p. 249)

All you need is love, the saying goes, and it is true that the absence of love in a person's life can cause untold pain. But people need far more than love, from basic necessities such as food, shelter, and health, to more complex needs such as perceived competence and autonomy. Based on the psychologist Edwin Shneidman's assertion that the mental pain fueling suicidal desire arises from unmet psychological needs, it is crucial to assess what ingredients are painfully missing from the person's life, and to help the person move toward getting those needs met.

A key question for uncovering unmet needs is simple: *"What is missing from your life that, if you could have it tomorrow, would make you want to live?"* Along the same lines, the Suicide Status Form (Jobes, 2016) calls for the suicidal person to complete this sentence: *"The one thing that would help me no longer feel suicidal would be..."* Most often, the person's response to that prompt reveals needs in the areas of intimate relationships, other social relationships, and economic, professional, or academic stability (Kulish et al., 2012, cited in Jobes, 2012).

Research and theory illuminate other important psychological needs. Shneidman based his conceptualization of unmet needs on the work of Henry Murray (1938), a psychologist who specified 20 psychological needs. These include the needs to love and be loved, to accomplish, to play, to be autonomous, to avoid harm and shame, and to be able to make sense of what happens. More recently, self-determination theory has identified three principal psychological needs: autonomy, competence, and relatedness (Deci & Ryan, 2000). Additional research has pointed to people's need to have positive self-esteem and a sense of security in their lives (Sheldon et al., 2001).

Also look at needs that you can meet through the vehicle of the therapeutic relationship. This can help lessen the person's sense of isolation. Helpful questions include:

- *"How can I help you to get some of your needs met?"*
- *"What do you need from me as your therapist?"*
- *"What can we do together to help you fill up some of the holes in your life?"*

Never underestimate the potential of the therapeutic relationship to heal. The psychologists Bruce Bongar and Glenn Sullivan (2013) note, "A sensitive and deeply caring therapeutic relationship … is still the best form of suicide prevention" (p. 199).

In addition to psychological needs, survival needs are also important. These can include physical and mental health care, food, shelter, employment, education, transportation, child care, and elder care. A good psychosocial assessment will have already uncovered gaps in these areas. Probe further about how these deficits specifically relate to the person's wish to die, and provide information about any available community resources that can help the person secure basic necessities.

Learning about the person's unmet needs enables you to collaboratively establish treatment goals with the suicidal person, engage in problem-solving, and help the person generate ways to get what they need. The more the person's needs are met, the less likely suicide is to beckon.

"Everything's So Out of Control"

On a sunny, fall day, Yuliya, 54, went for a hike in the woods near her New Jersey house. Unbeknownst to her, a tiny deer tick attached itself to her thigh, stealing small amounts of blood and giving her *Borrelia burgdorferi* bacteria in return. Infected with Lyme disease, Yuliya now suffers from debilitating arthritis.

"Before I got Lyme," she told her psychologist, "I would get depressed but never, ever wanted to die. Now it's all I think about."

"What do you need in your life to make you want to live again?" the psychologist asked her.

"My health," Yuliya said, without a moment's hesitation. "If I were not hurting and sick all the time, I'd be happy to be alive."

This was a tough one. It was beyond the psychologist's and Yuliya's control to undo her Lyme disease. He delved a little more.

"So, health is incredibly important, especially when you're in pain. What do you need that could make your health problems more manageable?"

"I don't feel like there's anything," Yuliya said. "Everything's so out of control."

"Everyone needs some sense of control – of mastery – over at least some aspects of their life," the psychologist said. "Of course, nobody can control everything, but to be able to control something, even just a little something here and there, about our situation helps. Let's talk about ways that you could get more of that in your life."

Yuliya and her psychologist talked at length about areas where she could be pro-active with her health. In the coming weeks, she joined a water exercise class for people with arthritis. This built up her strength. She felt more empowered after joining a support group for people with Lyme disease. The group gave her valuable tips for ways to cope with the disease. She talked with her rheumatologist about her severe pain. The doctor started her on a different medication as a result and also referred her to a pain-management clinic.

Yuliya couldn't take control over her disease, but she could play an active part in her recovery. This increased her sense of mastery, which, in combination with other aspects of her psychotherapy, led her to discard suicide as an option.

Works Cited

Bongar, B., & Sullivan, G. (2013). *The suicidal patient: Clinical and legal standards of care.* Washington, DC: American Psychological Association.

Deci, E. L., & Ryan, R. M. (2000). The "what" and "why" of goal pursuits: Human needs and the self-determination of behavior. *Psychological Inquiry, 11*(4), 227–268.

Jobes, D. A. (2012). The Collaborative Assessment and Management of Suicidality (CAMS): An evolving evidence-based clinical approach to suicidal risk. *Suicide and Life-Threatening Behavior, 42*(6), 640–653.

Jobes, D. A. (2016). *Managing suicidal risk: A collaborative approach* (2nd ed.). New York, NY: Guilford Press.

Kulish, A., Jobes, D. A., & Lineberry, T. (2012, April). Development of a reliable coding system for the SSF "one thing" response. Poster presented at the annual conference of the American Association of Suicidology, Baltimore, MD.

Murray, H. A. (1938). *Explorations in personality.* New York, NY: Oxford University Press.

Sheldon, K. M., Elliot, A. J., Kim, Y., & Kasser, T. (2001). What is satisfying about satisfying events? Testing 10 candidate psychological needs. *Journal of Personality and Social Psychology, 80*(2), 325.

Shneidman, E. S. (1998). Further reflections on suicide and psychache. *Suicide and Life-Threatening Behavior, 28*(3), 245–250.

Tip 53: Target Social Isolation

"Indeed, a persuasive case can be made that, of all the risk factors for suicidal behavior, ranging from the molecular to the cultural levels, the strongest and most uniform support has emerged for indices related to social isolation."

Thomas Joiner and Kimberly Van Orden
(2008, p. 85)

According to the interpersonal theory of suicide, three conditions must be present for suicide to occur: The person feels disconnected from others ("thwarted belongingness"); the person believes they contribute nothing to the lives of others or even make life worse for loved ones ("perceived burdensomeness"); and the person has become so used to pain and risky behaviors that suicide is no longer frightening ("acquired capacity for suicide") (Joiner, 2005). It is difficult to directly change a person's capacity for suicide, but the interpersonal aspects are very malleable. Change one of those – increase the person's sense of belongingness or help the person to recognize their value to others – and the interpersonal theory asserts that suicide will not occur.

It is unknown whether these three conditions truly are required ingredients for suicide, but abundant research connects feelings of perceived burdensomeness and thwarted belongingness to suicidal ideation and behavior (Ma et al., 2016). And we know that various causes of social disconnection, such as a relationship breakup, death of a loved one, public humiliation, and loneliness, increase the risk for suicide (Trout, 1980; King & Merchant, 2008). For these reasons, you should endeavor to increase a suicidal person's sense of belonging and value to others.

Increasing Belongingness

There are many ways to help increase the person's sense of connection to others. For starters, try to involve significant others in the treatment, if the person consents and their loved ones would be constructive to the healing process (*Tip 47*). Explore the person's past and present social support network, including old friends with whom the person can reconnect and ways to meet new friends. Provide coaching in interpersonal skills, if necessary. Assign what psychologists Thomas Joiner and Kimberly Van Orden (2008) call "belongingness-related homework" (p. 87). This homework includes any activities that increase the person's engagements with others. As an added bonus, some activities (such as helping friends or family or volunteering in the community) can increase the person's sense of value to others, reducing feelings of burdensomeness.

Sometimes, the person's sense of isolation is the product of cognitive distortions (*Tips 66–67*). In these cases, the suicidal person discounts, minimizes, or is simply unable in the moment to experience the love and support that they receive from friends and family. Distorted perceptions of social isolation can be as painful as actual isolation (Hawthorne, 2008). Techniques from cognitive behavior therapy (*Tips 68–70*) can help you guide the person to explore their sense that nobody cares, examine the evidence to determine whether their thoughts are both true and constructive, correct cognitive distortions such as all-or-nothing thinking and catastrophizing, and challenge inaccurate thoughts. Where thoughts are accurate, engage the person in problem-solving to meet new people and revive neglected relationships.

You have another valuable resource at your disposal for decreasing a suicidal person's sense of isolation: yourself. The therapeutic relationship can be a tool for healing, especially when you help engender a sense of belongingness, care, and support. To take full advantage of the therapeutic relationship's power to heal, Joiner and Van Orden (2008) offer several suggestions: Take a collaborative approach (*Tip 14*). Emphasize your connection with the person by often using the terms "we" and "us" (e.g., "we're in this together" and "we'll figure this out"). Frame your relationship with the client as a source of care, help, and support. Try to avoid empathic failures and other injuries to the therapeutic relationship, and make efforts to repair them when they do occur.

Reducing Perceived Burdensomeness

Cognitive-behavioral techniques also are useful in helping a person challenge the sense that they are a burden to others. First, nonjudgmentally and compassionately unearth the person's beliefs about what they contribute to people's lives. Refrain from immediately trying to dissuade the person from their conviction that others would be better off if they were dead. It would be invalidating to not empathize with the torment of feeling worthless. After you have conveyed empathy and explored the person's feelings of being a burden, use CBT techniques to help the person examine the evidence that the belief is true or untrue, recognize where cognitive distortions are occurring, and develop adaptive, realistic beliefs (*Tips 67–70*).

Beyond thoughts, also address actions the person can take. Come up together with activities that can help the person increase their sense of value, even if only in small ways. This will vary from person to person, but some realistic and achievable possibilities include asking the person to give a compliment to three different people every day or to do a good deed for at least one person every day. If the person has wronged or let down another person, they can try to make amends. For contributing on a larger scale, people can do such things as volunteer work for a cause they believe in, get involved at some level in grassroots activities or politics, or even try to find employment for a cause greater than themselves (Joiner & Van Orden, 2008).

"The African Violet Queen"

An elderly woman lived alone in a dilapidated house. In poor health and socially isolated, she lost interest in living. One day, a relative who lived out of town called the psychiatrist Milton Erickson. The relative was concerned about her. Could Dr. Erickson please help?

Dr. Erickson made a house call. He could see from the plants in the woman's house that she liked African violets. Indeed, she grew them as a hobby. When she rejected his offer to help, he made a proposal: He would not bother her again if she would agree to take some African violets to people in her community who had experienced a major life event, such as the birth of a child, a wedding, or a death in the family.

She took him up on the offer, and it changed her life. It got her out of the house. She forged connections with others. And she felt of value to the people who delighted in receiving her African violets. Years later, the story goes, a newspaper article appeared with this headline: "African Violet Queen Dies, Thousands Mourn."

This story, told and retold in various forms by numerous psychotherapists (Fiske, 2008), makes the important point that giving to others is a gift to oneself, as well. Growing the African violets was a passion for this once-isolated woman. In sharing these beautiful flowers with others, her sense of connection and value to others bloomed.

Works Cited

Fiske, H. (2008). *Hope in action: Solution-focused conversations about suicide*. New York, NY: Routledge.

Hawthorne, G. (2008). Perceived social isolation in a community sample: Its prevalence and correlates with aspects of peoples' lives. *Social Psychiatry and Psychiatric Epidemiology, 43*(2), 140–150.

Joiner, T. (2005). *Why people die by suicide*. Cambridge, MA: Harvard University Press.

Joiner, T. E., Jr., & Van Orden, K. A. (2008). The interpersonal–psychological theory of suicidal behavior indicates specific and crucial psychotherapeutic targets. *International Journal of Cognitive Therapy, 1*(1), 80–89.

King, C. A., & Merchant, C. R. (2008). Social and interpersonal factors relating to adolescent suicidality: A review of the literature. *Archives of Suicide Research, 12,* 181–196.

Ma, J., Batterham, P. J., Calear, A. L., & Han, J. (2016). A systematic review of the predictions of the interpersonal–psychological theory of suicidal behavior. *Clinical Psychology Review, 46,* 34–45.

Trout, D. L. (1980). The role of social isolation in suicide. *Suicide and Life-Threatening Behavior, 10,* 10–23.

Tip 54: Use Grounding Exercises

"Our true home is in the present moment."

Thich Nhat Hanh
(2016, p. 131)

Painful emotions often overwhelm the suicidal person. In these times, the person's thoughts and fears can run into the future. *"This feeling won't go away." "I can't bear it any longer." "The only way to escape this pain is to die."* Alternatively, the person may retreat to the past, getting stuck in previous hurts, traumatic memories, and perceived failures. The person becomes unmoored, disconnected from the world around them. In such instances, grounding techniques can anchor the person physically to the safety of the present moment (Lowen, 1972).

There are two categories of grounding techniques to consider: Those you can use with the suicidal person, and those you can teach the suicidal person to use on their own. Grounding techniques are especially important if the person is destabilized and the end of your session or meeting together is approaching. Relatively quick and simple ways to orient the person to the safety of the present moment involve stating the person's name repeatedly while talking with them, asking the person to look into your eyes if it is culturally appropriate to make such a request, and asking the person questions about what is happening in the external environment. You can invite the person to look around your office and describe what they see – objects, colors, shapes, and patterns. Encourage the person to be a witness to their body, paying moment-by-moment attention to how it feels, including specific body parts. As an example, ask the person to place their feet on the ground and sit up straight. Then orient the person to their physical feelings with a series of questions:

- *How do the soles of your feet feel in relation to the ground?*
- *How does your butt feel on the chair? Your thighs? Your back?*
- *What are your hands touching? What does that feel like?*
- *What other physical sensations are you experiencing?*

Outside of sessions, the person can draw from a broader repertoire of techniques. Dialectical behavior therapy calls for teaching people to use the five senses of the body to connect to the here and now (Linehan, 2015):

Touch. The person can hold an ice cube, noting the physical sensations this produces. (Advise the person not to hold it too long in one place, to avoid frostbite!) Another option is for the person to run their fingers over a soft fabric like fleece or velvet, or an abrasive material like a rock or sandpaper, or the soft fur of a cat or dog. All the while, the person turns their mind to the feel of the texture on their skin.

Sight. Looking at a specific object in the room, the person reflects on the object or describes it in detail. The person also can focus on an object's physical movement: the flow of water as it leaves the faucet, hits the surface of the sink, creates tiny bubbles, and circles down the drain; the dancing flame of a candle; leaves quaking on the branches of a tree. Whatever moves, the person can become absorbed in tracking all the facets of its motions.

Smell. The person smells items with distinctive odors, such as specific foods, spices, soaps, perfumes, flowers, and essential oils. Selecting objects with contrasting odors can especially stimulate awareness of the physical sensations.

Taste. The person eats foods that are exceptionally salty, sweet, or pungent, making note of the food's taste at different locations along the lips and tongue.

Hearing. The person homes in on various sounds in the environment, noting the tone, type, and origin of each. Another option is for the person to select songs to listen to, perhaps even songs that the person detests, and become absorbed in the sounds, rhythm, and lyrics of the music.

Fundamentally, grounding techniques are an exercise in mindfulness. But grounding and mindfulness exercises differ in function. Grounding techniques reconnect the person to the safety of their physical environment, specifically as a means to stabilize the person. Mindfulness techniques sustain awareness not only of physical experiences and observations in the here and now, but also of thoughts, emotions, and urges, whether or not those are stabilizing. *Tip 74* addresses mindfulness in more depth.

"I Want to Die Because I Can't Stop Hurting"

When the panic envelops her, Josie wants nothing more than to die. During those times, she sees herself in the small, pale blue dorm room where she lived three years ago – no, she actually *is* in that room again, being raped again. That's how it feels. And in those times, she sees no escape from this pain besides death. The most recent time she fell into this dark place, two days ago, she overdosed on medication in an attempt to die.

"If in those moments you could get some relief from your pain," the social worker asks her in the hospital, "would you still want to die?"

"No offense, but that's kind of a stupid question," Josie, 24, answers. "If I felt better, why would I want to die? I want to die because I can't stop hurting."

"OK, it's clear how important it is to stop reliving that terrible night," the social worker says. "Let's talk about ways you can escape from the horror of that night, to the safety of the here and now."

The social worker discusses various grounding techniques with Josie and asks her for her own ideas, too. Josie settles on several options to try. She can keep her eyes open and note everything she sees and hears in the room. She can watch TV and count the number of times she hears the word "the." She can rub ice on the inside of her hands. And she can caress her dog's wiry fur. These grounding exercises alone will not cure her post-traumatic stress or despair. But the exercises can help bring her focus back to the present moment, a moment free of violence, and a moment far from the past.

Works Cited

Hanh, T. N. (2016). *At home in the world: Stories and essential teachings from a monk's life.* Berkeley, CA: Parallax Press.

Linehan, M. M. (2015). *DBT skills training handouts and worksheets* (2nd ed.). New York, NY: Guilford Press.

Lowen, A. (1972). *Depression and the body: The biological basis of faith and reality.* New York, NY: Coward, McCann & Geoghegan, Inc.

ten
Exploring Motivations and Misgivings

Tip 55: Assume Nothing: Does the Person Want to Give Up Suicide?

"Suicidal thoughts were my drug of choice, and I didn't want to let them go."

Susan Rose Blauner
(2002, p. 69)

Most mental health professionals view suicidal thoughts as a problem to be eliminated or disarmed. Yet many suicidal individuals do not perceive their suicidal thoughts as a problem. Some gain feelings of comfort, peace, or satisfaction from thinking about suicide (e.g., Crane et al., 2014). Especially people with long-standing suicidal ideation may grow attached to their suicidal thoughts as a means to soothe themselves and fend off feelings of entrapment – what the psychiatrist John Maltsberger and colleagues (2010) call "suicide fantasy as a life-sustaining recourse" (p. 611).

To understand the person's attachment to suicidal thinking, helpful questions include:

- *"How much do you want to stop thinking of suicide, if at all?"*
- *"What are the pros and cons of keeping suicide open as an option?"*

Another way to get at the person's desire to change comes from motivational interviewing. With the "readiness ruler," the person rates on a scale from 0 *(not)* to 10 *(very)* the importance of changing their suicidal thinking (Moyers et al., 2009). The person uses the same scale to then rate their confidence that they can change. The scaled responses open the door to further exploring the person's motivations. For example, you can ask the person why their rating was so high, or what would bring it up a number or two higher.

It's also possible that the person does not want to change their suicidal thinking. Don't force the issue, because ultimately suicide is an option whether you like it or not (*Tip 18*). The objective here is to understand the person's motivations, so that you can work to find some common ground. If you and the suicidal person are unwittingly walking alone on separate, diverging paths, it is difficult to join together.

"I Didn't Really Come Here to Stop Thinking of Suicide"

Nikos, 27, first thought of suicide in high school. Nothing in particular happened at the time, no breakup with a romantic partner, no college rejection, no arrest for committing a crime. He simply found himself wondering if life was worth living. Since then, he has thought of suicide often. Although he has never acted on those thoughts, it comforts him to know that he can.

"You've been thinking of suicide for a long time, it sounds like. Do you want to stop?" his therapist, a licensed professional counselor, asked.

"I know this sounds weird, but I didn't really come here to stop thinking of suicide," Nikos said. "I came here so that I could maybe stop feeling like crap."

"I want that, too," the counselor said. "I want you to stop feeling like crap. Of course, speaking as a mental health professional, I hope you'll get to a place where both happen – you feel better *and* you no longer look to suicide."

"It's not like I'm going to do anything," Nikos said. "It's just something I think about."

"So then, on a scale of 0 to 10, how important to you is it to stop thinking of suicide?" the counselor asked.

"Really, it's a 0," Nikos said. "I don't see it as a problem."

"That's good for me to know," the counselor said. "I'm certainly not going to fight you to take suicide off the table. Instead, let's work on putting other options on that table, too."

Works Cited

Blauner, S. R. (2002). *How I stayed alive when my brain was trying to kill me.* New York, NY: Harper Collins.

Crane, C., Barnhofer, T., Duggan, D. S., Eames, C., Hepburn, S., Shah, D., & Williams, J. M. G. (2014). Comfort from suicidal cognition in recurrently depressed patients. *Journal of Affective Disorders, 155,* 241–246.

Maltsberger, J. T., Ronningstam, E., Weinberg, I., Schechter, M., & Goldblatt, M. J. (2010). Suicide fantasy as a life-sustaining recourse. *Psychodynamic Psychiatry, 38*(4), 611.

Moyers, T. B., Martin, J. K., Houck, J. M., Christopher, P. J., & Tonigan, J. S. (2009). From in-session behaviors to drinking outcomes: A causal chain for motivational interviewing. *Journal of Consulting and Clinical Psychology, 77*(6), 1113–1124.

Tip 56: Tap into Ambivalence

"Make the following assumption: 'This person is talking to me because of ambivalence about suicide. If there is an unequivocal desire to commit suicide, this person would probably already be dead.'"

John Chiles and Kirk Strosahl
(2005, pp. 28–29)

Many suicidal people face extremely painful circumstances that fuel their desire to die. They may experience tragedies of unfathomable proportions, unrelenting mental illness, heartrending emotional pain, chronic physical pain without promise of a cure – and more. Even amid this pain and hopelessness, the person is still here, alive. This survival itself is evidence of reason for hope. And it begs the question: *"With all the reasons you have for dying, what has kept you from killing yourself?"* Or, more simply: *"What stops you?"*

Some helpers fear asking these questions, as if they are tantamount to daring the person to act on their suicidal thoughts. To the contrary, asking someone what has stood in the way of suicide can help the person get in touch with what keeps them alive. It shifts the focus, at least momentarily. Tunnel vision is common to suicidal thinking (*Tip 66*). The person's focus narrows to their experience of despair, depression, or other painful states. And this narrowed perspective can blind the person to their own inherent wish to live. Asking what has stopped them from acting on suicidal thoughts casts a light on this ambivalence, enabling the suicidal person to recognize and explore it.

So don't be afraid to ask the person why they have not acted on their suicidal thoughts. The answer may be what keeps them alive.

"I'm Still Here"

Felicia's baby girl was only three months old when Felicia found her lifeless body in her crib. Days later, her husband confessed to police that he had struck their baby against the kitchen counter in anger when she would not stop crying. It has been four months since her daughter's death and husband's arrest, and Felicia's emotional pain is so excruciating that she longs to die.

"I honestly have no reason to live anymore," Felicia, 32, told her grief counselor. "None. Everything I lived for, everything that mattered to me, has been destroyed."

"You've been through so much," the grief counselor said. "It's understandable that you would want to die as a way to end your pain. With all this in mind, what has kept you going?"

Felicia wept. "I honestly don't know," she told him.

"Well, let's try to figure that out together, OK?" he said. "You're still here, sitting in front of me. There must be a reason, or even many reasons. What do you think has stopped you from killing yourself?

"Fear," Felicia said. "I'm scared. I'm a coward."

"OK, one thing that stops you is you're afraid. What is it that scares you about killing yourself?

"I'm afraid that I'll screw up," Felicia said. "That I'll somehow make things even worse for myself. You know, like if I try to kill myself and instead have some kind of awful permanent injuries."

"I understand how that is a horrifying thought," the counselor said. "A lot could go wrong, couldn't it?"

Felicia nodded. "Yes. And I'm scared of something else, too. I'm scared I'll die and then be shown a movie of my life the way it would have been if I had stayed alive. I mean, what if I kill myself and then in the afterlife I learn that I could've gotten through this? But instead I'm being punished because I killed myself. And I see all that I missed out on, and then hate myself for it. Maybe that's what hell is, hating yourself for eternity."

"It's painful to consider, isn't it?" the grief counselor said. "Yet at the same time your fear seems a little like hope. I mean, one reason you're afraid is because you recognize that maybe someday you can feel better, right?"

"Yes. I think so," Felicia said. "It hurts so much that I hadn't really thought of it that way. But it's true. I'm still here."

Work Cited

Chiles, J. A., & Strosahl, K. D. (2005). *Clinical manual for assessment and treatment of suicidal patients*. Washington, DC: American Psychiatric Publishing.

Tip 57: Compare Reasons for Living and Dying

"Perhaps examining both reasons for living and reasons for dying may enable us to better understand the significance of both sides of the suicidal equation – the internal suicidal debate, a gestalt of the suicidal mind."

David Jobes and Rachel Mann
(1999, p. 98)

A common-sense yet powerful approach to uncovering ambivalence about suicide is to ask the person to examine reasons for dying and reasons for living. This simple act can help broaden a suicidal person's perspective, so that the person is not looking at only one side of the equation. Even better, the reasons against suicide – and, as such, reasons for hope – come from the suicidal person, not from you or someone else imposing an anti-suicide agenda on the person.

People who share suicidal thoughts with others often encounter shock, sadness, and efforts at persuasion. This can lead to one person arguing on the side of life, and the suicidal person defending the choice of suicide. By offering an invitation to look at both the good and bad aspects of suicide, you enable the suicidal person to get in touch with both sides of the argument.

One way to guide the exploration of reasons for living and dying is to ask the person to list each. This exercise is a piece of the Collaborative Assessment and Management of Suicidality (CAMS). Using the Suicide Status Form (*Tip 21*), the CAMS clinician asks clients to list five reasons each for living and dying. Then the person is asked to rank each reason in order of importance.

Some writers recommend counting the person's reasons for living and dying and calculating the numeric difference between each in order to gauge the person's ambivalence (e.g., Palmer, 2014). Such a comparison can be deceptive. It fails to take into account that just one reason for living (e.g., the person's children) could overpower in significance all of the person's reasons for dying, and vice versa. For example, in one study, reasons for living ranged from "eating Chinese food" to "my family" (Jobes & Mann, 1999). Rather than relying on a simple count of reasons, it is more meaningful to explore the meaning and value that the person attaches to them.

Another method is to frame the discussion around the pros and cons for suicide *and* for staying alive. It might seem like the pros and cons of suicide and of staying alive would be mirror images of each other. In reality, reasons against dying by suicide often are fear-based (e.g., "I'm afraid I'll permanently screw up my body if I try suicide and survive"), whereas reasons for living tend to be life-affirming (e.g., "I still have things I want to do"). Looking at the advantages and disadvantages of both living and dying encourages a more holistic view, providing space for life-affirming and suicide-rejecting reasons to emerge.

It is important not to challenge the person's views of the advantages of suicide and their reasons for dying during a discussion of pros and cons. For now, the objective is to foster an open conversation, one that lets the person connect with their ambivalence.

"Playing Tug of War"

Juan, 28, went back and forth as he debated whether he really should kill himself. His counselor told him, "It can help to look at the good and bad things about suicide, and also the good and bad things about staying alive. We can learn a lot by having all your arguments in one place." She drew a large square, sectioned off columns for advantages and disadvantages of suicide and staying alive, and gave it to Juan to jot down his thoughts as he spoke. This is what flowed from their discussion:

	Disadvantages	Advantages
Suicide	It would devastate my mother.	No more pain. No more worries.
	My little brother looks up to me and will think suicide is OK.	People will be better off without me.
	I might go to hell.	Relief.
	I could be permanently disabled if I attempt suicide and don't die.	
Staying alive	I am in a hole that I can't get out of financially.	Things might change for the better.
	I can't fix my problems.	There's a lot more that I'd like to see and do.
	More and more pain.	I can show my little brother that life goes on, even when we screw up.

The exercise provided Juan with a clearer picture of his reasons for living and dying and, even more importantly, of his ambivalence. "I thought it was clear that dying is better than living, but it's like these two parts of my mind are playing tug of war," Juan said. "I guess that's a good thing, right?"

Works Cited

Jobes, D. A., & Mann, R. E. (1999). Reasons for living versus reasons for dying: Examining the internal debate of suicide. *Suicide and Life-Threatening Behavior, 29*(2), 97–104.

Palmer, S. (2014). *Suicide: Strategies and interventions for reduction and prevention.* New York, NY: Routledge.

Tip 58: Invite the Person to Look for the "Catch"

"Even though we have tried, we have not yet been able to come up with a single advantage to suicide that did not have at least one major catch."

Thomas Ellis and Cory Newman
(1996, p. 47)

A comparison of reasons for living vs. dying (*Tip 57*) can underscore points of ambivalence. A simple exercise can deepen the person's awareness of this ambivalence even further: The person looks for the disadvantages of the advantages of suicide. In other words, for whatever suicide promises, what is the catch?

The psychologists Thomas Ellis and Cory Newman (1996) look at common reasons that people give in support of suicide, along with a catch for each. For example, one common reason is, "I'll no longer be a burden to others." The catch? "How do I know that my death won't make their burden even greater?" As another example, for someone who thinks, "When I'm dead, they'll be sorry for how they treated me," the catch would be, "I won't be around to enjoy my revenge" (Ellis & Newman, 1996, p. 48).

Rely on the suicidal person to come up with the catch; this will be more powerful than your providing it. If the person has difficulty, then tentatively ask Socratic questions to help. Perhaps the most succinct question is, simply, *"What's the catch?"* Other possibilities include:

- *"When you say suicide would help because _____, what could be the downside to that?"*
- *"Is it possible that you're wrong about what will happen if you kill yourself?"*
- *"Is there anything you might be leaving out?"*

Remember that the goal here is not to persuade the person that suicide is a bad option but, instead, to help the person become more aware of their own misgivings about suicide. This greater awareness may, as a result, motivate the person not to act on suicidal thoughts.

"I Don't Want to Hurt Even More..."

Joel, 54, could see no way out of his pain except for suicide. "If I kill myself," he said, "it's all over. I won't hurt anymore."

His psychologist resisted the urge to say, *"Exactly, it's all over. The good, too. Think of all the good things you'll miss."* Instead, to help Joel arrive at his own answers, she asked, "Is it possible that there's a downside to that?"

"I can't really think of one," Joel said. "I simply can't bear this anymore. It's torture. If you knew you were going to be tortured every day, wouldn't you want to die to avoid going through it again and again?"

"It makes sense that you don't want to be tortured anymore," the psychologist said. "I'm also wondering whether there's anything you lose if you kill yourself to avoid the torture."

"What do you mean?" Joel asked.

"I suppose I mean, what's the catch? Suicide's making this seductive promise to you: *Come with me, and you won't ever suffer again.* Is there a downside to making sure you don't suffer again?"

"I think you might want me to say that if I can't feel pain again, then I can't feel good again, either," Joel said. "So I'd miss out on a lot of good things. But the thing is, I don't think I'm ever going to feel good again, anyway. So it's not much of a catch."

The psychologist was tempted to challenge Joel about whether he really couldn't feel good again. Instead, she simply reflected his hopelessness back to him. "So it sounds like there really isn't a catch for you, then. You're thinking if you kill yourself, your pain will end, and there's no downside."

"Well, maybe there is a downside," Joel said, "I admit, I am afraid of what comes next. What if we're put on this earth to learn from our pain? I'll fail at my lesson if I kill myself. Then what if I'm sent back to live a life of even greater pain? I don't want to hurt even more in the next life."

"So the catch isn't that you could miss out on pleasure down the road in this life, but that you could have to suffer even more in the next life. Is that right?"

"Yes," he said. "And I have to admit, that's quite a catch."

Work Cited

Ellis, T. E., & Newman, C. F. (1996). *Choosing to live: How to defeat suicide through cognitive therapy.* Oakland, CA: New Harbinger Publications, Inc.

Tip 59: Search for Exceptions

"A suicidal person is not constantly suicidal: there will be times when they are less so, or not at all."

John Henden
(2008, p. 84)

Suicidal people typically have moments of respite when their suicidal ideation is less severe, even if only by degrees. Be on the lookout for those exceptions. The times when people's suicidal thoughts weaken or retreat contain clues to what they can do differently to feel differently.

Ask the person when their suicidal thoughts are strongest, and when their suicidal thoughts are weakest. What is different in those moments? What are they doing, thinking, and feeling? The idea is that even a small change can produce big results. The psychotherapist John Henden puts it this way to clients:

> You mentioned earlier there was one occasion only over this past week, that you have felt slightly less suicidal. What I would like you to do between now and when we next meet is to be on the lookout for just a brief time – it may be a fleeting moment only – when you feel just very slightly less suicidal. I want you to notice this time and notice what is different about it compared to the rest of the week. Can you do this for me?
>
> (Henden, 2008, p. 149)

Searching for these kinds of exceptions to problems is a central piece of solution-focused psychotherapy. Solution-focused therapy rests on the premise that dwelling on problems does not lead to solutions. Solution-focused aphorisms include *"If it works, do more of it"*; *"If it's not working, do something different"*; and *"No problem happens all the time"* (De Shazer & Dolan, 2012, pp. 2–3). Although no rigorous studies have examined the effectiveness of solution-focused brief therapy (SFBT) with suicidal individuals, there is some evidence that SFBT reduces conditions that can fuel suicidal thoughts, such as depression (Gingerich & Peterson, 2013).

The purpose of seeking out exceptions is not to convey to the person that things are not as bad or hopeless as the person says. Instead, the purpose is to help the person look for ways to do more of what works. This is the essence of hope.

"In Some Sweet Moments"

Alister, 71, felt desperate. Nothing he did seemed to help. Not the pills. Not the daily exercise. Not the prayer and Bible study. This darkness seemed to be the home in which he would reside forever, he told his psychiatrist, Dr. Youngdeer.

"You've described really painful emotions, so painful that you want to kill yourself," Dr. Youngdeer said. "When you're feeling your worst, on a scale of 0 to 10, with 10 being you absolutely want to live and 0 being you don't want to live at all, where would you put yourself on that scale?"

Without hesitation, Alister said, "A 1. Definitely 1."

"And how high have you gone on that scale?" she asked.

"Sometimes I'd say I'm at a 3 or 4. Maybe even a 5 in some sweet moments."

"What do you attribute that to, those times you are at a 5 on the scale?"

"I think it has to do with being around my daughters or my buddies. Not feeling so alone. My friends and family, they distract me," Alister said.

"Well that's a very important clue, then," Dr. Youngdeer said. "Sounds like if you're around people you love more often, you'll feel suicidal less often."

"Yes, that's true. But it always comes back to wanting to die, it seems," Alister said. "And when it's 3 in the morning and I'm thinking of getting out the hunting rifle, it's not like I can just show up at my daughters' doorstep, or my buddies'."

"Would it help you to remind yourself of your friends and family in those times?" Dr. Youngdeer asked. "Maybe put photos out or look at photos in your phone so you can remind yourself that in the morning, you can connect with someone again?"

"That might help," Alister said. "Maybe just a little, but a little's better than nothing. See, when I'm in that state of mind, it's like I'm the only person in the world. I forget everything and everyone else."

"So those photos could be your memory for you," Dr. Youngdeer said. "Now, let's talk about other times when you're higher on that scale than a 1 ...." And the process repeated.

Works Cited

De Shazer, S., & Dolan, Y. (2012). *More than miracles: The state of the art of solution-focused brief therapy.* New York, NY: Routledge.

Gingerich, W. J., & Peterson, L. T. (2013). Effectiveness of solution-focused brief therapy: A systematic qualitative review of controlled outcome studies. *Research on Social Work Practice, 23*(3), 266–283.

Henden, J. (2008). *Preventing suicide: The solution focused approach.* Chichester: John Wiley & Sons.

eleven
Inspiring Hope

Tip 60: Frame Suicide as a Problem-Solving Behavior

"Suicidal behavior can be thought of as a problem-solving attempt aimed at escape from seemingly intolerable emotional pain."
Jason Luoma and Jennifer Villatte
(2012, p. 267)

A popular saying goes, *"Suicide is a permanent solution to a temporary problem."* Many people in the suicide prevention field detest this saying. They believe it wrongfully advertises suicide, a devastating social problem, as a solution. The reality is, however tragic and destructive, suicide *is* a solution, and problems are not always temporary. An individual turns to suicide when they view their problems as "inescapable, interminable, and intolerable" (Chiles & Strosahl, 2005, p. 96). Suicide promises an escape, an end, and, so far as anyone knows, a cessation of pain. Instead of explicitly embracing an anti-suicide agenda, it is better to recognize the problem-solving nature of suicide and to look for other, more constructive solutions.

To better understand what suicide would "fix" for the person, try asking these questions, based on the suggestions of psychiatrist John Chiles and psychologist Kirk Strosahl:

- *"What problems would suicide solve for you?"*
- *"If those problems could be solved in some other way, would you still want to die?"*

Very often, the answer is no, the person would not want to die if their problems and pain could somehow subside another way. Here, you can convey hope that there are other solutions waiting to be discovered. Chiles and Strosahl word it this way:

> Before you get to that point [of killing yourself], would it make sense for us to work together to explore what you've actually done to try to solve the problem ... and to see if we can come up with something that might work better and doesn't involve you having to be dead?
>
> (Chiles & Strosahl, 2005, p. 80)

Do not jump too soon into problem-solving. First you must demonstrate empathy and understanding of the person's reasons for suicide (*Tip 15*). Thereafter, framing suicide as a problem-solving behavior can foster hope. It expands thinking; the person can consider possibilities, solutions, and even, one hopes, survival. The problem-solving approach forges an alliance where you and the suicidal person work together to uncover solutions that do not require dying.

"I Wouldn't Feel Like Crap Anymore"

Jamal longed to kill himself. He did not know how. He did not know when. For now, he simply prayed every night, as he lay in bed trying to fall asleep, for God to take him. The peer specialist at the community health center asked him, "What problems would dying solve for you?"

"I wouldn't feel like crap anymore," Jamal, 27, told her. "It'd all go away."

"Tell me more," she said.

Jamal described long bouts of feeling hopeless and worthless, estranged from his family and friends, and convinced that, as he put it, "I am not made for this world."

"So if there were another way you could feel better, would you still want to kill yourself?" the peer specialist asked.

"I guess not," he said. "I guess I really want to stop feeling like crap."

"It's good you realize that," the peer specialist said. "Together, we can look at your problems and ways to feel better. Before you do anything to kill yourself, would you like to try some other things first?"

"Yeah," Jamal said. "I guess it's worth a try."

Works Cited

Chiles, J. A., & Strosahl, K. D. (2005). *Clinical manual for assessment and treatment of suicidal patients.* Washington, DC: American Psychiatric Publishing.

Luoma, J. B., & Villatte, J. L. (2012). Mindfulness in the treatment of suicidal individuals. *Cognitive and Behavioral Practice, 19*(2), 265–276.

Tip 61: Help Brainstorm an "Options List"

"The suicidal person's thinking pattern has constricted; often it is dichotomous with only two possibilities: yes or no, life as I want it or death…"

Edwin Shneidman
(1996, p. 61)

People with suicidal thoughts are notorious for viewing things in an all-or-nothing fashion: Stay alive and suffer inexorably, or die by suicide. The person may see very few options, if any, in between those two extremes. One way to help a suicidal person overcome this dichotomous thinking is to help construct an "options list" (Shneidman, 1981).

The idea is this: You work with the person to brainstorm every possible option they have, even options that seem onerous or unacceptable. Then the person orders the possibilities, from best to worst. Keep in mind two important guidelines for brainstorming (Nezu et al., 2012, p. 195):

1. *"Quantity leads to quality."* The more ideas, the better!
2. *"Defer judgment."* The idea is not to generate good ideas but to generate *any* ideas, good or bad.

The quality of ideas is unimportant in this exercise. The objective mainly is to widen the person's perspective. Expansive thinking by definition dissolves cognitive constriction, at least temporarily. And in the midst of the inferior or unrealistic ideas, a good, realistic, and previously unrecognized option might emerge. This sort of brainstorming is a key component of the problem-solving method (*Tip 62*).

Do not object if the person keeps suicide on the list as an option. Realistically speaking, suicide is always an option (*Tip 18*). The options list reveals that in between the extremes of abject misery and suicide, many other options remain to be considered.

"I'd Rather Be Dead than Live on the Streets"

Just as Cindy, 37, was getting her life back together, a sheriff's deputy came to her house and posted a bright orange eviction notice on the door. Cindy had stopped using heroin only three months ago, after many years of addiction. She still lacked a job and had no way to afford other housing. She told her addictions counselor, "I'd rather kill myself than be homeless."

The counselor worked with Cindy to prepare an options list. He wrote down two options:

Be homeless.
Kill myself.

He handed her the yellow notepad and asked her to write other options. Cindy said with sincerity, "I honestly can't think of any other option."

"Well," the addictions counselor said, "if you stay alive, what would be the worst-case scenario?"

"I would have to live on the streets and become a prostitute to stay alive."

"OK, write that down," he said.

"But that's not really an option!" Cindy protested. "I wouldn't really do that. I'd rather be dead."

"That's OK. Let's just brainstorm about every possible option there is. With brainstorming, there are no good or bad ideas."

Eventually, Cindy came up with the following list of possibilities:

- Live on the streets and become a sex worker
- Live in a shelter
- Live in a motel
- Couch surf at friends' houses (not a good option, because they still use drugs)
- Kill myself

The addictions counselor guided Cindy to also think of ways she could make money, besides being a prostitute. When she got stuck, he threw in a few suggestions for her to accept or reject. Eventually she came up with this list:

- Solicit money on street corners
- Work as a day laborer
- Sell drugs
- Steal
- Get any job possible, like at a fast-food restaurant, retail store, or office
- Apply for government assistance
- Do nothing and hope for the best

In a matter of minutes, Cindy's two options – be homeless or suicide – grew to a dozen. Cindy ended up choosing to stay in a shelter, with the understanding that it would be temporary. She would look for a job either at a drug rehab center or at a fast-food restaurant. Living in the shelter seemed awful, but not as awful as living on the streets. And living in the shelter seemed better than dying. She could always kill herself later. First, she wanted to see if her life could get better because she realized, with new-found clarity, that she had other options besides misery and death.

Works Cited

Nezu, A. M., Nezu, C. M., & D'Zurilla, T. (2012). *Problem-solving therapy: A treatment manual.* New York, NY: Springer.

Shneidman, E. S. (1981). Psychotherapy with suicidal patients. *Suicide and Life-Threatening Behavior, 11*(4), 341–348.

Shneidman, E. S. (1996). *The suicidal mind.* New York, NY: Oxford University Press.

Tip 62: Teach the Problem-Solving Method

"As problem-solving skills increase, the risk of suicide declines."
Mark Reinecke
(2006, p. 238)

Suicidal individuals often lack basic skills in problem-solving. The psychologist Mark Reinecke notes that suicide itself results from "a breakdown in adaptive, rational problem solving" (p. 240). In the face of problems that seem insoluble, the person feels hopeless. The hopelessness makes it even harder to come up with possible solutions besides suicide. Providing concrete skills in problem-solving can help break this cycle and create hope.

The problem-solving method provides a structured way for the person to break down a seemingly overwhelming process into manageable steps, as described by the psychologist Arthur Nezu and colleagues (2015):

1. Identify the specific problem to be solved.
2. Brainstorm possible solutions (i.e., create an options list; see *Tip 61*).
3. Evaluate advantages and disadvantages of possible solutions.
4. Select the seemingly best option.
5. Try out the option.
6. Evaluate results and, if the results are not positive, try the next best option on the list.

Explore with the person all the different ways they have tried to solve their problem so far. When, in Step 5 of the process, the person tries to solve the problem, frame this new effort as an experiment where there is no success or failure, only data to help determine what works and what does not work. That way, if the option that the person selected fails to solve the problem, the groundwork is laid to try another.

The problem-solving method might seem elementary. Its value lies with those for whom problem-solving skills do not come naturally. The approach is a core part of problem-solving therapy, an evidence-based treatment for depression (Nezu et al., 2015). In some studies, people who received problem-solving therapy experienced a reduction in suicidal ideation or behavior (Brown & Jager-Hyman, 2014). For more information, see *Problem-Solving Therapy: A Treatment Manual* (Nezu et al., 2013).

The Lonely Widow

Some days, Gisela, 79, hardly wants to get out of bed, let alone her apartment. Her pain seems immutable and inescapable to her, and she considers her suicide inevitable. She lives alone in an assisted-living apartment building.

Her husband died seven months ago, after 56 years of marriage. Gisela's two sons live in California, terribly far from her Florida apartment, and her one remaining sibling, a sister, lives in Germany. Gisela's days lack structure or interactions with others.

Using the problem-solving method with her grief counselor, Gisela identifies her key challenges (*Step 1*). This process helps her realize that grief is not her only problem. Social isolation is another. Gisela and the counselor brainstorm possible ways for her to cope better (*Step 2*). As for her bereavement, options include joining a support group for widows and widowers at the senior center, continuing with the grief counseling, participating in online chat groups for grieving people, and completing a self-help book or workbook on the grief process. As for her isolation, she can phone her sons more often, eat meals in the dining room, participate in the bridge group on her floor, and volunteer as a science tutor for high school students through a program in her building. Gisela examines the pros and cons of each option with the grief counselor (*Step 3*), then selects what seem to be the best choices for now (*Step 4*): joining the weekly grief group, remaining in individual counseling, and eating in the dining room once every other day. She will try these out over the coming weeks (*Step 5*) and then evaluate (*Step 6*) whether these were good solutions, or whether she ought to try some of the other possibilities.

Works Cited

Brown, G. K., & Jager-Hyman, S. (2014). Evidence-based psychotherapies for suicide prevention: Future directions. *American Journal of Preventive Medicine, 47*(3), S186–S194.

Nezu, A. M., Nezu, C. M., & D'Zurilla, T. (2013). *Problem-solving therapy: A treatment manual.* New York, NY: Springer.

Nezu, A. M., Greenfield, A. P., & Nezu, C. M. (2015). Contemporary problem-solving therapy: A transdiagnostic intervention. In C. M. Nezu & A. M. Nezu (Eds.), *The Oxford handbook of cognitive and behavioral therapies* (pp. 160–171). New York, NY: Oxford University Press.

Reinecke, M. A. (2006). Problem-solving: A conceptual approach to suicidality and psychotherapy. In T. E. Ellis (Ed.), *Cognition and suicide: Theory, research, and therapy* (pp. 237–259). Washington, DC: American Psychological Association.

Tip 63: Nourish Future Plans and Goals

"Without goals there is no hope."

David Kondrat and Barbra Teater
(2012, p. 7)

Whatever the pain, loss, or despair that feed a person's wish to die, suicide is essentially a crisis of hope. If only the suicidal person could believe that life can get better, then suicide would lose its allure. Hope is not only the antidote to suicidality, but also its antithesis. A strategy for building hope is to help the person focus on – or develop – meaningful plans and goals for the future (Jobes, 2016).

Research has demonstrated that hope emanates from three pragmatic components: goals, pathways to achieving those goals, and a sense of agency and competence to succeed (Snyder, 2000). Hope generates action, and action goes on to generate yet more hope. Areas to explore with the suicidal person, then, are what plans, goals, and dreams the person holds but has not yet realized. The psychologists Thomas Ellis and Cory Newman (1996) call this the "unfinished business list" (p. 64). They advise suicidal individuals to "keep focusing on the idea that having unfinished business in life is good, because it gives you purpose and goals to pursue" (p. 65). In that vein, ask the person to identify what they have wanted, now or in the past, for important areas of their life: professional, family, romance, friendship, leisure (e.g., travel), health and fitness, and personal growth (McDermott & Snyder, 1999). Then ask the person to prioritize the goals by order of importance.

Goals are not enough. As noted above, for a person to become infused with hope, they must also see a path for achieving their goals. Help the person come up with actions they need to take to meet each goal. Even very small steps can create a sense of agency and competence, the third ingredient necessary for hope to flourish, according to hope theory (Snyder, 2000). Guide the person to identify potential obstacles and what they will do to overcome them. Help the person to craft realistic coping statements (*Tip 69*) about their ability to meet their goals. You can elicit these coping statements using questions from cognitive behavior therapy (*Tip 68*), such as, *"What would you say to a friend who had the same goals as you and was having trouble meeting them?"*

Setting a goal, any goal, no matter how small, can build hope. Achieving the goal can build even more. The suicidal person desperately needs this hope. Accordingly, the psychiatrist John Chiles and psychologist Kirk Strosahl (2005) suggest asking the suicidal person the following question: *"If we could select a small task, that, if you accomplished it, would tell you that things were just a little better, what would that be?"* (p. 106).

"I Know This Sounds Corny, But..."

Mack, 53, leaned back in his chair, held out his hands in front of him, and shook his head. "I got nothing," he said, in response to the simple question, "What are your hopes and goals?"

"Well, let me ask you something," Latoya, the nurse practitioner, said. "What did you hope for before you got to feeling so bad that you made a plan to kill yourself?"

"I can answer that one," Mack said. "I wanted to have a tattoo parlor. I'm tired of tatting someone up and having the boss get almost all the money. And I hoped for a good woman. I know this sounds corny, but ... love. I hoped for that, too."

"Those are all pretty important hopes," Latoya said. "What happened?"

"They just became impossible," Mack said. "It hurts to hope."

"I can understand that. Sort of like a starving man having food waved in front of his face that he can't have?"

"Yeah, just like that. Like, if I can't have it, I don't want to want it," Mack said. "And I know I can't have it – love, money, my own shop. My life is shit."

"You feel so strongly that it won't happen that it feels true, doesn't it?" Latoya asked. "If you weren't so convinced it was impossible, would you still want to have your own tattoo parlor?"

"If I thought it was possible, yeah. I'd want that," he said.

"And what kinds of things would you be doing if you weren't so convinced that there's no hope?" she asked.

This led Mack and his nurse practitioner down a pathway of possibilities, in which Mack set forth the different things he would need to do to work toward this goal – the motorcycles to sell, the debts to pay off, the extra work on the side. And, with her prompting, he described the relationship he hoped for, what qualities the woman would have, and how he could try to meet someone.

"So, these are all important big-picture goals," Latoya said. "It's good to have big things to hope for, to work toward. I'm also curious about what some smaller-picture goals are for you."

Whereas before Mack said, "I got nothing," now he was able to come up with smaller goals. Get back in touch with one of his Army friends. Take his dog Bucky for a walk every day. Go to NA meetings.

In big ways and small, Mack was building goals and making plans. These acts gave him hope.

Works Cited

Chiles, J. A., & Strosahl, K. D. (2005). *Clinical manual for assessment and treatment of suicidal patients.* Washington, DC: American Psychiatric Publishing.

Ellis, T. E., & Newman, C. F. (1996). *Choosing to live: How to defeat suicide through cognitive therapy.* Oakland, CA: New Harbinger Publications, Inc.

Jobes, D. A. (2016). *Managing suicidal risk: A collaborative approach* (2nd ed.). New York, NY: Guilford Press.

Kondrat, D. C., & Teater, B. (2012). Solution-focused therapy in an emergency room setting: Increasing hope in persons presenting with suicidal ideation. *Journal of Social Work, 12*(1), 3–15.

McDermott, D., & Snyder, C. R. (1999). *Making hope happen: A workbook for turning possibilities into reality.* Oakland, CA: New Harbinger Publications, Inc.

Snyder, C. R. (2000). Hypothesis: There is hope. In *Handbook of hope: Theory, measures, and applications* (pp. 3–21). San Diego, CA: Academic Press.

Tip 64: Incorporate a Hope Kit

*"Simply put, treating the person who is suicidal is all about facilit-
ating hope."*

Thomas Joiner and colleagues
(2009, pp. 192–193)

A hope kit is a box or other container that the suicidal person fills with reminders of why life is worth living. A core piece of cognitive therapy for suicide prevention (Wenzel et al., 2009), the hope kit serves two purposes: It stimulates
thinking about the people, places, pets, goals, and other aspects of living that are
important to the person. And, during times of crisis, it can help the person
remember what there is to hope for beyond this very painful moment.

Items that commonly go into hope kits run the gamut. They can include
meaningful poems, song lyrics, inspirational quotes, photos, cards, and letters.
Just about anything goes, as long as the object does not trigger painful emotions
or bad memories. To help the person summon ideas for what to put in the hope
kit, ask questions that get at reasons for living now and in the future:

- *"What hopes sustain you? … What things do you hope to do? … What
  places do you hope to go?"*
- *"What photos, writings, souvenirs, and other objects could remind you of
  what has kept you alive to this point?"*
- *"What objects could serve as symbols for what you hope for in the future?"*

For whatever reason, some people might not want to make a hope kit. In such
cases, the psychologist Amy Wenzel and colleagues (2009) recommend suggesting a substitute, such as a scrapbook, painting, or web page. In one case, an adolescent created "hope shoes"; she decorated a pair of high-top sneakers with
reminders of what gave her life meaning (Wenzel et al., 2009). The actual type of
hope kit is not important. Instead, the value of this technique lies in inspiring
people both to look for reasons for hope and to keep reminders of these hopes
that they can look back on. And if the person declines to put together a hope kit
in any fashion, it can still be meaningful to ask what physical reminders of hope
could go into a hope kit if ever they chose to make one.

There's an App for That!

There are hope kit apps for cell phones, tablets, and computers. One is Virtual
Hope Box (Bush et al., 2015). The app enables people to store favorite photos,
videos, songs, supportive messages, and inspirational quotes all in one place. It
also contains different activities to provide distraction, inspiration, relaxation,
and coping tools.

What If the Person Comes Up with Nothing?

Hopelessness can present itself as a fact, not a feeling. The suicidal person unquestioningly believes – no, the person *knows* – that there is nothing to hope for. At least, that is their inner experience. If the person can't come up with anything to hope for, empathize and explore their feelings of hopelessness. Let the person know that, although they feel hopeless, you feel hopeful that in time they will reclaim dreams, goals, and hopes. And if you don't feel any such hope for the person, challenge your own hopelessness (*Tip 6*), whether alone or with the help of a therapist or consultant (*Tip 43*).

Something to Do, Something to Hope For

Often, when Granger, 47, sank into the dark quicksand of despair, he longed for something concrete he could do to help him climb out of it. He hated the feeling of waiting for the despair to decide it was done with him, as if he was at its mercy. When his counselor talked to him about making a hope kit, the idea alone gave him a smidgen of hope. It would give him something constructive to do, both in making the kit and in reviewing his creation during bouts of hopelessness.

On the way home from his session, he stopped at a hardware store and bought a large, red plastic tool box. Once home, he got to work. He scoured his drawers and closets for mementos, went through his vast collection of emails, printed out photos that meant a lot to him, and considered other questions that his counselor had posed: *"What do you want to be reminded of during the times you feel suicidal? What inspiration would help offer you a lifeline?"*

After spending considerable time on this project, these were some of the things that Granger put in his hope kit:

- Two photos of his younger sister and her children.
- His dog Chewy's first collar and tag.
- Several wise quotations he had saved from Chinese fortune cookies: *"Envision your future self, and make it good." "Without dreams, your dreams cannot come true." "Begin again. And again."*
- His season's pass for Park City ski resort, from the prior winter.
- Lyrics to the song "Don't Try Suicide," by Queen.
- A photo of giant sequoias in the Mariposa Grove at Yosemite Park, which he hoped to visit someday.

Two nights after putting his hope kit together, Granger fell into a dark spiral. Suicidal thoughts tempted him. He decided to try out looking at his new hope kit instead. In the soft light of his bedroom, he found that going through his box gave him something constructive to do … and to hope for.

Works Cited

Bush, N. E., Dobscha, S. K., Crumpton, R., Denneson, L. M., Hoffman, J. E., Crain, A., …
& Kinn, J. T. (2015). A virtual hope box smartphone app as an accessory to therapy:
Proof-of-concept in a clinical sample of veterans. *Suicide and Life-Threatening Behavior*, 45(1), 1–9.

Joiner, T. E., Jr., Van Orden, K. A., Witte, T. K., & Rudd, M. D. (2009). *The interpersonal theory of suicide: Guidance for working with suicidal clients.* Washington, DC: American Psychological Association.

Wenzel, A., Brown, G. K., & Beck, A. T. (2009). *Cognitive therapy for suicidal patients: Scientific and clinical applications.* Washington, DC: American Psychological Association.

Tip 65: Highlight Strengths

"Utilizing a positive framework that promotes the understanding of strengths and virtues rather than investigating weaknesses and vulnerabilities … has great potential for suicide intervention therapies."

Paul Surgenor
(2015, p. 12)

Often, the suicidal person experiences a progressive narrowing of both options and memory (*Tip 66*). The person is unable to see the full picture, not only in terms of options besides suicide but also in terms of all aspects of oneself. Memories of successes, happiness, and positive attributes can become overly general or depart altogether. Part of your task is to help widen the person's perspective.

If the person professes to have no strengths, then it is important to empathize with how painful it must be to feel that way. But also remain skeptical. Everybody alive has strengths in some form or another or else they would not still be alive. Your well-placed prompts and insightful questions can lead the suicidal person to see personal qualities that they have overlooked.

Solution-focused questions home in on the person's abilities to cope and survive (De Shazer & Dolan, 2007):

- *"How have you coped with everything that you are going through?"*
- *"What have you done that has prevented your situation from getting even worse?"*
- *"How have you managed to stay alive amid your suicidal thoughts?"*
- *"Thinking back to other times that you have had suicidal thoughts, what helped you to get through them?"*

Another avenue for exploring strengths is to have the person complete a formal inventory. One resource for this is the Values in Action Survey, available at no cost at www.viacharacter.org. It contains 120 questions that capture 24 character strengths, such as creativity, love of learning, perseverance, kindness, fairness, humility, humor, and gratitude. It takes about 15 minutes to complete, making it an ideal homework assignment, to be reviewed together the next time you meet.

"There's Nothing, Not One Good Thing About Me"

Regrets and criticisms raced through Dalip's mind. *"I shouldn't have lost my temper with my wife."* *"I hurt my son's feelings when I criticized his art work."* *"I'm not a good son."* Even minor details did not escape his criticism:

criticism: *"I forgot to take out the recycling. I'm such a loser."* When the psychiatric nurse in the hospital asked him to name some good things about himself, he replied, "There's nothing, not one good thing about me. It'd make things easier for everybody if I were gone from their lives."

"How very painful," the nurse said. "Your mind is not being kind to you, and we'll talk more about ways to deal with that. But for now I want to understand some of the good things about you."

"I really can't think of anything," Dalip, 47, said.

"Well, one thing I see is that you are a caring person. Your criticisms of yourself mostly revolve around letting other people down."

"I do try really hard," Dalip said. "I do try to be a good person. But I fail so much."

"And I want to hear about those experiences, too, but for now I want to hear about when, in your mind, you succeed at being a good person," the nurse said. "What does that look like?"

"I'm very kind to my friends. Always willing to help them out. I help our next door neighbor, an elderly woman whose husband died last year. And..." Dalip paused.

"Keep going..." the nurse said warmly.

And he did.

Works Cited

De Shazer, S., & Dolan, Y. (2007). *More than miracles: The state of the art of solution-focused brief therapy.* New York, NY: Haworth.

Surgenor, P. W. (2015). Promoting recovery from suicidal ideation through the development of protective factors. *Counselling and Psychotherapy Research, 15*(3), 207–216.

twelve
Drawing from Cognitive Behavior Strategies

Tip 66: Connect Suicidal Thoughts to Other Thinking

"Suicidal people are cognitively different, compared with people who may share the same diagnosis and symptom severity but are not suicidal."

Thomas Ellis
(2006, p. 370)

Whatever painful emotions accompany suicidal ideation, the wish to die is essentially a cognitive phenomenon (Rudd, 2000). The person thinks, at least to some degree, that things will never get better. In this context of hopelessness, the suicidal person often believes that they are unlovable, helpless, a burden to others, and incapable of bearing emotional pain much longer (Rudd, 2004). Other patterns of thought also characterize suicidal individuals, including cognitive constriction, cognitive distortions, overgeneral autobiographical memory, perfectionism, and poor problem-solving (Ellis, 2006).

According to cognitive behavior theory, these ways of thinking strongly influence people's emotions and behaviors (Beck, 2011). This creates a dynamic in which thoughts influence and are influenced by mood and behaviors. The remaining tips in this section describe ways to help the suicidal person challenge, change, or respond differently to the types of thoughts that contribute to suicidality. First, it is important to recognize and understand these patterns, so each is briefly described here.

Cognitive Constriction

Especially common in suicidal individuals, cognitive constriction is akin to blinders on a horse: the person's field of vision is reduced (Shneidman, 1996). The person cannot see the full range of possibilities for viewing their situation, solving problems, and lessening their suffering. *Tip 61* addresses how to help people widen their perspective.

Cognitive Distortions

Cognitive distortions are half-truths or errors of omission that occur in a person's thinking. They include exaggeration, denial, overgeneralization, and all-or-nothing thinking (Burns, 1999). Especially in times of stress, these distortions often breed anxiety, hopelessness, and other painful emotions. *Tip 67* describes cognitive distortions further, and *Tip 68* describes possible remedies.

Overgeneral Autobiographical Memory

Memory is fallible. People may forget the times they endured suffering and prevailed, as well as the times they solved problems successfully – really, the times that could now give them hope. These problems are especially pronounced in suicidal individuals (Richard-Devantoy et al., 2015). Even when suicidal individuals do remember past events that might counteract their hopelessness, those memories tend to be vague or overly general (Williams et al., 2006). *Tip 65* provides questions that can help the person to call on past experiences to solve problems and feel hopeful about the future.

Perfectionism

"Nobody's perfect," the saying goes, but some people expect themselves to be perfect, regardless. They hold themselves to rigid, high standards and berate themselves whenever they fall short of their expectations, or they feel compelled to meet others' impossibly high standards for them (Flett et al., 2014). Perfectionism often provokes feelings of worthlessness, shame, and estrangement from others, and it increases suicide risk (Flett et al., 2014). Techniques to challenge destructive thought processes can help people to think more realistically and compassionately (*Tips 68–70*).

Poor Problem-Solving

Many people with suicidal thoughts have a deficit in problem-solving skills (Pollock & Williams, 2004). They fail to see, let alone try out, diverse ways to remedy their situation. When they do try to resolve problems, suicidal individuals are more inclined than non-suicidal people to resort to escapism, denial, and drastic solutions (Orbach et al., 1990). Without the ability to think flexibly about possible solutions, the person might truly see few if any options besides suicide. Helping the person to explore the problem-solving nature of suicide (*Tip 60*), brainstorm options (*Tip 61*), and follow the problem-solving method (*Tip 62*) can build the person's problem-solving skills.

An Elaboration: Cognitive Behavior Therapy

Cognitive behavior therapy rests on several premises (Beck, 2011): Thoughts strongly influence our actions and reactions. Thoughts often are not accurate or helpful. Changing one's thoughts can change emotions, behaviors, and associated thoughts, such as suicidal ideation.

This might all sound pretty obvious. But people tend to assume that the events and circumstances in their lives – not their *thoughts* about these events and circumstances – directly account for how they feel and act. Also, it's not especially easy for people to change their thoughts when those cognitions are longstanding and address the essence of how they view themselves, the world, and the future (Beck et al., 1979).

To date, hundreds of studies have demonstrated the effectiveness of CBT across a wide range of emotional problems such as depression, anxiety, general stress, and bulimia (Hofmann et al., 2012). In studies that looked at CBT specifically with adults who thought about or attempted suicide, suicide attempt rates over a period of 18–24 months were 50–60% lower in the people who received CBT, compared to those in the control condition (Brown et al., 2005; Rudd et al., 2015).

CBT offers much promise in transforming the lives of suicidal individuals. Many of this book's tips draw from CBT: identifying cognitive distortions (*Tip 67*), challenging destructive thoughts (*Tip 68*), creating coping statements (*Tip 69*), revising suicidal imagery (*Tip 70*), creating a hope box (*Tip 64*), addressing cognitive constriction (*Tip 61*), teaching problem-solving skills (*Tip 62*), using behavioral activation (*Tip 76*), conducting a behavior chain analysis (*Tip 79*), and completing a relapse prevention protocol (*Tip 87*).

The assortment of CBT-related tips in this book does not constitute an empirically tested protocol. One such protocol is described in the book *Cognitive Therapy for Suicidal Patients* (Wenzel et al., 2009).

Works Cited

Beck, A. T., Rush, A. J., Shaw, B. F., & Emery, G. (1979). *Cognitive therapy of depression.* New York, NY: Guilford Press.

Beck, J. S. (2011). *Cognitive behavior therapy: Basics and beyond* (2nd ed.). New York, NY: Guilford Press.

Brown, G. K., Ten Have, T., Henriques, G. R., Xie, S. X., Hollander, J. E., & Beck, A. T. (2005). Cognitive therapy for the prevention of suicide attempts: A randomized controlled trial. *JAMA, 294*(5), 563–570.

Burns, D. D. (1999). *The feeling good handbook* (revised ed.). New York, NY: Plume.

Ellis, T. E. (2006). Epilogue: What have we learned about suicide and cognition and what more do we need to know? In T. E. Ellis (Ed.), *Cognition and suicide: Theory, research, and therapy* (pp. 369–380). Washington, DC: American Psychological Association.

Flett, G. L., Hewitt, P. L., & Heisel, M. J. (2014). The destructiveness of perfectionism revisited: Implications for the assessment of suicide risk and the prevention of suicide. *Review of General Psychology, 18*(3), 156–172.

Hofmann, S. G., Asnaani, A., Vonk, I. J., Sawyer, A. T., & Fang, A. (2012). The efficacy of cognitive behavioral therapy: A review of meta-analyses. *Cognitive Therapy and Research, 36*(5), 427–440.

Orbach, I., Bar-Joseph, H., & Dror, N. (1990). Styles of problem solving in suicidal individuals. *Suicide and Life-Threatening Behavior, 20*(1), 56–64.

Pollock, L. R., & Williams, J. M. G. (2004). Problem-solving in suicide attempters. *Psychological Medicine, 34*(1), 163–167.

Richard-Devantoy, S., Berlim, M. T., & Jollant, F. (2015). Suicidal behaviour and memory: A systematic review and meta-analysis. *The World Journal of Biological Psychiatry, 16*(8), 544–566.

Rudd, M. D. (2000). The suicidal mode: A cognitive-behavioral model of suicidality. *Suicide and Life-Threatening Behavior, 30*(1), 18–33.

Rudd, M. D. (2004). Cognitive therapy for suicidality: An integrative, comprehensive, and practical approach to conceptualization. *Journal of Contemporary Psychotherapy, 34*(1), 59–72.

Rudd, M. D., Bryan, C. J., Wertenberger, E. G., Peterson, A. L., Young-McCaughan, S., Mintz, J., … & Wilkinson, E. (2015). Brief cognitive-behavioral therapy effects on post-treatment suicide attempts in a military sample: Results of a randomized clinical trial with 2-year follow-up. *American Journal of Psychiatry, 172*(5), 441–449.

Shneidman, E. S. (1996). *The suicidal mind.* New York, NY: Oxford University Press.

Wenzel, A., Brown, G. K., & Beck, A. T. (2009). *Cognitive therapy for suicidal patients: Scientific and clinical applications.* Washington, DC: American Psychological Association.

Williams, J. M. G., Barnhofer, T., Crane, C., & Duggan, D. S. (2006). The role of overgeneral memory in suicidality. In T. E. Ellis (Ed.), *Cognition and suicide: Theory, research, and therapy* (pp. 173–192). Washington, DC: American Psychological Association.

Tip 67: Educate about Cognitive Distortions

"Thoughts and facts are not the same. Just because you think something is true does not necessarily mean that it is true."

Robert Leahy
(2003, p. 13)

A basic task in cognitive behavior therapies is to help people recognize the different ways that their mind can mislead them. Everyone's thoughts reflect distortions of reality to some degree, and this happens more often than usual in suicidal individuals (Jager-Hyman et al., 2014). When suicidal individuals can identify the ways that their mind distorts things, they are better equipped to respond differently to thoughts that drive the suicidal wish (*Tips 68–72*). Based on the work of psychologist David Burns (1999) and Judith Beck (2011), common cognitive distortions are described below.

All-or-Nothing Thinking

The person makes judgments on the basis of only two extreme possibilities – good or awful, perfection or failure, always or never – without considering the many different gradations between the polar opposites. Examples: *"If I don't succeed, then I'm worthless"*; *"The only options are to live a miserable life, or to die."*

Overgeneralization

Overgeneralization involves taking one piece of evidence and treating it as an inevitable pattern. Example: *"I tried an antidepressant and it didn't help, so no medication can help me feel better."*

Emotional Reasoning

The person wholeheartedly believes what *feels* true without questioning whether it actually *is* true. Example: *"I feel like I don't deserve to live, so it's true, I don't deserve to live."*

Fortune-Telling

The person presumes to know that they will never feel good again, will always be alone, or some other negative prediction. Nobody knows the future. Negative predictions, with rare exceptions, are beliefs, not facts. Examples: *"Life will not get better"*; *"This pain will never end."*

Catastrophizing

A combination of all-or-nothing thinking and fortune-telling, catastrophizing involves predicting a terrible outcome, without considering the less dire possibilities. Example: *"Because I have bipolar disorder, I will end up alone and miserable, living on the streets."*

Disqualifying the Positive

The person sees only the bad when evaluating their experiences, actions, memories, and personal qualities. Examples: *"I have never been happy. Even when I thought I was, I was deluded"*; *"I'm a failure. The times I succeeded were just flukes."*

Labeling

The person applies a global label to oneself or others rather than allowing for the complex, multidimensional aspects of being human. The label neglects important aspects of their qualities and experiences. Example: *"I'm a loser."*

Magnification/Minimization

Typically, this cognitive distortion involves magnifying negative qualities and minimizing the positive. It can also apply to someone who minimizes the effects of their actions. Example: *"It's not a big deal that I'm going to kill myself. My parents will move on."*

"Should" or "Must" Statements

The charismatic founder of rational emotive therapy, psychologist Albert Ellis, would tell people, "Stop 'shoulding' on yourself" (e.g., Ellis & Velten, 1992). When people would impose unrealistic or harsh expectations on themselves, Ellis called it "musterbation." His provocative statements capture the exacting, painful nature of rigid expectations that many people have for themselves or others. Examples: *"I shouldn't need help"*; *"I must never cry."*

Personalization

Many people think that others are constantly evaluating and responding to them, even when there is no evidence of that. Or they hold themselves responsible for bad things that happened when their role was negligible. Examples: *"My psychiatrist was in a bad mood because of me"*; *"It's my fault when bad things happen."*

Words of Caution

Negative, distressing thoughts are not always cognitive distortions. As an example, consider a woman who tearfully says she did something awful, and then tells you she beat up her partner the night before. She actually did do something awful, and it would benefit her to learn how to prevent the violence from recurring and to make amends, where possible. That does not mean *she* is awful, unlovable, or destined to always be violent, all of which would be cognitive distortions if she told herself those things. When thoughts accurately reflect reality, be careful not to minimize or invalidate the person's legitimate concerns. The same goes for grief and other painful emotions that arise from a difficult truth. A man who receives a diagnosis of terminal cancer, for example, is not demonstrating distorted thinking if he says he is going to die soon. To attempt to cheer the person up would be invalidating. Instead, listen, empathize, explore, and help the person identify what they can do to cope, whether that means finding meaning in their experience, engaging in rituals, reaching out to others, or something else constructive.

"If the Shoe Fits..."

When Matthew's top-choice colleges rejected his applications, he was devastated. "I'm a failure," the 17-year-old said. "I'm never going to amount to anything."

After responding to his painful situation with reflective listening and empathy, his school social worker gave him a handout describing thinking errors, and they went over the list together. She was sure to tell him that these thinking errors are very common, so that he wouldn't fault himself for failing to "think better."

"Let's go back to something you said earlier," she said. "You said you're a failure and will never amount to anything. I know that feels very true to you. Do you see any thinking errors in there?"

Matthew looked down at the list. "Well, I guess I'm labeling myself by calling myself a failure. But if the shoe fits ..."

"I understand," the social worker said. "It seems to you that the label fits. Is it possible that putting the 'failure' label on yourself ignores the ways you are not a failure?"

"I guess so," Matthew said. "So then how would you put it?"

"Well, does it feel different to say that you failed at getting into the colleges that you wanted, instead of saying simply that you are a failure?"

"I guess so. It sucks but it's not as depressing. Like, if I failed at one thing, it doesn't mean I'll fail at everything."

"Exactly," she said. "So, with that in mind, is there a thinking error in telling yourself that you'll never amount to anything?"

"I guess that's fortune-telling. I can't really know what's going to happen, can I?" Matthew asked, and he knew the answer without waiting for a response.

Works Cited

Beck, J. S. (2011). *Cognitive behavior therapy: Basics and beyond* (2nd ed.). New York, NY: Guilford.

Burns, D. D. (1999). *The feeling good handbook* (revised ed.). New York, NY: Plume.

Ellis, A., & Velten, E. (1992). *Rational steps to quitting alcohol.* Fort Lee, NJ: Barricade Books.

Jager-Hyman, S., Cunningham, A., Wenzel, A., Mattei, S., Brown, G. K., & Beck, A. T. (2014). Cognitive distortions and suicide attempts. *Cognitive Therapy and Research, 38*(4), 369–374.

Leahy, R. L. (2003). *Cognitive therapy techniques: A practitioner's guide.* New York, NY: Guilford Press.

Tip 68: Help Challenge Negative Thoughts

"The therapist's major task is to help the patient think of reasonable responses to his negative cognitions."

Aaron Beck and colleagues
(1979, p. 164)

Self-denigrating, hopeless, and other destructive thoughts often fuel or exacerbate a suicidal state of mind. According to CBT, changing one's thinking can set off a chain reaction, transforming what the person feels and does, too. As people change deep-seated, negative ways of thinking, they can feel better about themselves, more hopeful about the future, and less pulled toward suicide (Beck et al., 1979).

Generally speaking, there are two approaches to take to destructive thoughts linked to suicidal ideation. In traditional cognitive behavior therapy, the approach is to help the person change the thoughts, replacing them with healthier and more realistic self-talk. In acceptance-based cognitive behavior therapies, considered the new wave of CBT, the approach is to help people mindfully observe their pessimistic, hopeless, and otherwise destructive thoughts, without believing them or giving them undue weight. The current tip incorporates the traditional CBT approach.

The first step is to guide the person to identify distressing thoughts that affect their mood and behaviors. Next, the person assesses whether the thoughts are both true and constructive. And if not, then the person works on changing the thoughts. This process is captured in the "3 Cs": catch the thought, check it, and change it (Granholm et al., 2004).

Catching Negative Thoughts

Often, people have difficulty identifying thoughts that lead to emotions, behaviors, and further thoughts, such as suicidal ideation. To help the person "catch" these thoughts, consistently ask questions that link moods and behaviors to the thoughts that precede or accompany them. A few helpful questions include:

- *"What were you telling yourself just before you felt that way?"*
- *"What else were you thinking or imagining when you felt so hopeless?"*
- *"What thoughts caused you to do that or to feel that way?"*

In time, the person will come to ask the same questions, and connecting thoughts with emotions and actions will become more natural.

Checking the Validity and Utility of Thoughts

Guide the person to check whether negative thoughts and beliefs are accurate. The simple act of questioning the truth of one's thoughts can be therapeutic. It teaches people to observe their thoughts as fallible ideas, not incontrovertible facts. Questions that get at whether a thought is true include (Beck, 2011):

- *"Is that thought a fact or a belief?"*
- *"What is the evidence that what you are telling yourself is true?"*
- *"What is the evidence that what you're telling yourself is not true, or only partly true?"*

The distressing things people tell themselves may be realistic, but unhelpful. Anxious thoughts are a good example. Some people dwell on a litany of horrible things that could befall them, in a misguided effort to help themselves. The person may view preparing for the worst as a way to buffer themselves from pain if the worst actually happens. Several questions get at whether a person's ways of thinking are useful:

- *"How does it help you to tell yourself that?"*
- *"How does it hurt you?"*
- *"Overall, is telling yourself_____ working well for you?"*
- *"What would be different for you if you stopped telling yourself this so much?"*

Remember, distressing thoughts can be a healthy and constructive response to a realistic problem. *Tip 67* gave the example of a woman who thought she had done something awful by beating up her partner. After exploring and empathizing with the woman's feelings of guilt and regret, an appropriate question for her would be, *"What now? That is, what can you do to address this problem?"* Possibilities include problem-solving, changing one's behavior, making amends, and forgiving oneself. When trauma and loss trigger painful but realistic thoughts, the situation often calls for the person to work through grief, improve coping skills, and practice acceptance of their emotions.

Changing the Thoughts

Assuming that a person's negative thoughts are untrue or unhelpful, the next step in the 3 Cs is to change them. Ask questions designed to generate alternative thoughts and beliefs (Ellis & Newman, 1996; Beck, 2011):

- *"What is another way to look at this?"*

- *"What would you tell someone you love or care about if they were having the same problem?"*
- *"What could you tell yourself about this that does not use one of the cognitive distortions?"*

Helping the person correct cognitive distortions can also give rise to more realistic and flexible ways of thinking. *Tip 67* provided an example of challenging a teen who labeled himself a failure: *"Is it possible that putting the 'failure' label on yourself ignores the ways you are not a failure?"* You can challenge other cognitive distortions with questions that get at what the person overemphasizes, minimizes, or leaves out altogether. For example, for people who engage in all-or-nothing thinking about their future (i.e., catastrophizing), the psychologist Judith Beck (2011) asks questions designed to rein in overwhelming fears:

- *"What's the worst that could happen?"*
- *"What's the best that could happen?"*
- *"On a scale of 0 to 100%, how likely is it that the worst will happen?"*
- *"What will probably happen?"*
- *"If the worst happened, what could you do to cope?"*

When helping people change their thoughts, emphasize self-compassion. Harsh and punitive self-talk often characterizes people who experience suicidal thoughts and behaviors (MacBeth & Gumley, 2012). These questions can help awaken a compassionate response:

- *"What would you say to a person you care about who was in the same situation as you and wanted to die by suicide?"*
- *"What is it that you wish someone would say to you that would be soothing, reassuring, or hopeful? ... Can you tell that to yourself?"*

Words of Caution

CBT is not about thinking positively. It is about thinking *realistically.* This stance departs from that of many motivational speakers in popular culture, who preach that positive affirmations come true if repeated often enough. Telling oneself something untrue, even though positive, can give negative thoughts more force. For example, say a woman who feels intensely flawed adopts a practice of telling herself that she is perfect. The gap between her ideal and her reality can evoke a protest from within: *"Don't be absurd. You're not perfect, and here are all the reasons why..."* A realistic adaptation would be for her to learn to tell herself, *"I'm human, and there are a lot of good things about me. But nobody's perfect."*

Another caution is that logic alone does not bring about emotional healing. An exclusively rational or intellectual approach to a person's psychological torment can be invalidating, as if you are trying to talk the person out of their emotions. Always overlay CBT techniques on top of fundamental counseling skills such as empathy, reflection, and validation of emotions (Corey, 2015).

Keep in mind, too, that people's indictments against themselves *feel* true to them. Telling people that they are wrong seldom produces change. It means more for people to recognize for themselves where their thinking is untrue, unrealistic or unhelpful. To help people come to their own truths, craft incisive questions that guide them to a more realistic way of thinking, rather than telling them the "right" way to think.

Finally, forewarn the person that changing thoughts is not a quick and easy process. Consider a 60-year-old man who tells himself, "I'm weak" whenever he feels sad. He has probably told himself that message many *thousands* of times over the years. Even after he settles on an alternative message (e.g., "Sadness is a normal human emotion"), telling himself this new message once or twice or even 100 times is not going to produce lasting change. Like learning a new language or musical instrument, adopting a new way of thinking takes practice and repetition.

"I'd Tell Them You Are Not Your Addiction"

At 44, Tovah has struggled with alcoholism for years. She has been to rehab several times. She has worked the steps in AA. She has ridden on the roller coaster of sobriety and relapse more times than she can count. Her newest relapse came after 22 months of sobriety. Now she judges herself relentlessly: *"I'll never be sober." "I can't kick it." "I don't deserve to live."*

"I'm curious about your use of the word 'never,'" Estefan, her addictions counselor at the rehab facility, said to her. "It makes me wonder, how can you know for certain that you will never be sober again?"

"I guess I can't know for sure," Tovah said. "But it's how I feel."

"You feel terribly discouraged," Estefan said. "Given all that alcoholism has put you through, I can understand that. I wonder though, how does telling yourself you can't kick drinking help you to kick drinking?"

Tovah chuckled a little. "It doesn't. Ironically, I think it's why I drink. To shut myself up."

In the coming days while Tovah was in rehab, she scrutinized with Estefan her indictments against herself, how those indictments made her feel, and how her life might be different if she did not believe them so strongly. She identified several cognitive distortions in her thinking: labeling, fortune-telling, all-or-nothing thinking, and emotional reasoning. These exercises helped her to distance herself from her thoughts a bit.

"It helps to recognize that I'm unfair to myself," she said. "And I know at one level that the hateful things I tell myself aren't always true. But like I said, it still *feels* true."

"It's so painful," Estefan said. "It's like you have a prosecutor living inside your head, isn't it? Someone who's telling you all the things you've done wrong, and none of the good."

"It really is," Tovah said. "This asshole is always attacking me, and I'm always feeling guilty."

"Do you have a defense attorney?" Estefan asked.

This question resonated with Tovah. "No," she said. "I sure don't. And I really need one."

For homework after one session, she wrote down everything someone might say in her defense: the ways she's been a good mother, the times she's tried hard to stay sober, and the many pieces of herself that addiction cannot touch. Even better, she started saying these things to herself whenever she found herself in the midst of self-attack.

Over time and with much practice, Tovah was able to look at herself more holistically. Asked what she would say to someone she cared about who had the same struggles, she said, "I'd tell them you are not your addiction. You're a person with an addiction. And whatever you do, don't lose sight of that person."

Works Cited

Beck, A. T., Rush, A. J., Shaw, B. F., & Emery, G. (1979). *Cognitive therapy of depression*. New York, NY: Guilford Press.

Beck, J. S. (2011). *Cognitive behavior therapy: Basics and beyond* (2nd ed.). New York, NY: Guilford Press.

Corey, G. (2015). *Theory and practice of counseling and psychotherapy* (10th ed.). Boston, MA: Cengage Learning.

Ellis, T. E., & Newman, C. F. (1996). *Choosing to live: How to defeat suicide through cognitive therapy*. Oakland, CA: New Harbinger Publications, Inc.

Granholm, E., McQuaid, J. R., Auslander, L. A., & McClure, F. S. (2004). Group cognitive-behavioral social skills training for older outpatients with chronic schizophrenia. *Journal of Cognitive Psychotherapy, 18*(3), 265–279.

MacBeth, A., & Gumley, A. (2012). Exploring compassion: A meta-analysis of the association between self-compassion and psychopathology. *Clinical Psychology Review, 32*(6), 545–552.

Tip 69: Elicit Coping Statements

"Assist clients in substituting functional self-statements for self-defeating cognitions."

Dean Hepworth and colleagues
(2010, p. 400)

Condemning, punitive, and pessimistic thoughts often run through suicidal individuals' minds: *"You don't deserve to live." "You'll never feel better." "Everyone would be better off without you."* Coping statements are the opposite. They are soothing yet realistic phrases that people can tell themselves to maintain hope, resist suicidal urges, and feel better.

To avoid the appearance of giving trite advice, elicit coping statements from the person or help the person to come up with phrases that have special meaning. Key questions can help draw coping statements out of the suicidal person (*Tip 68*):

- *"Think of someone you love or care about a lot. If they said they wanted to die by suicide, what would you say to them?"*
- *"What do you most wish someone would say to you right now that would help you get through another day?"*
- *"When you tell yourself _____, what's another way to look at it? What might someone who cares about you say?"*

Coping statements should reflect reality (*Tip 68*). They are not the same as affirmations, which tend to reflect the way people want to be rather than the way they actually are. Coping statements that employ wishful thinking (e.g., "I'm happy and hopeful" in a person who is depressed and suicidal) can worsen a person's sense of despair. The gap between the wish and the reality hurts (Wood et al., 2009). Encourage people to pick coping statements that fundamentally are true.

A Sampling of Coping Statements

Although you should not prescribe coping statements, some people are helped by hearing examples, as long as it is clear that the sayings are simply possibilities to consider and, if wanted, to reject. Here are several:

- *This will pass.*
- *One day at a time.*
- *I won't feel this way forever.*
- *I deserve to live.*
- *Life can get better.*

- *Suicidal thoughts are a symptom, not a solution.*
- *Just because I think it, doesn't mean it's true.*
- *I am a work in progress.*
- *I don't really want to die. I want the pain to end.*
- *I'm working on other ways to end my pain.*
- *Don't believe everything you think.*

Works Cited

Hepworth, D. H., Rooney, R. H., Rooney, G. D., Strom-Gottfried, K., & Larsen, J. A. (2010). *Direct social work practice: Theory and skills* (8th ed.). Belmont, CA: Brooks/ Cole.

Wood, J. V., Perunovic, W. Q. E., & Lee, J. W. (2009). Positive self-statements: Power for some, peril for others. *Psychological Science, 20*(7), 860–866.

Tip 70: Rescript Suicidal Imagery

"The suicidal state is a tense drama in the mind. It is a drama that often can benefit from the talents of a 'rewrite specialist,' a psychotherapist or a consultant who can help recast the faulty final scene into something other than a tragic last act."

Edwin Shneidman
(1998, p. 249)

Cognitive behavior therapy interventions usually focus on what people tell themselves and, in turn, how their self-talk influences behaviors, feelings, and further thoughts. Yet what people *say* to themselves might not be as important as what people *show* to themselves (*Tip 11*). Imagery stimulates stronger emotions than verbal material does (Holmes & Matthews, 2005). You can harness the potency of mental pictures to aid in survival and healing, using a technique called imagery rescripting.

The psychologist Emily Holmes and colleagues (2007) describe two primary ways to rescript images. The first is to mentally transform the imagery into something benign or positive. The second is to change one's relationship to the imagery, meeting it with curiosity and acceptance rather than treating it literally. Imagery rescripting is more commonly used for memories of traumatic events, but images of future events also can be rewritten.

Rescripting the image calls on the person to assert control as the creator of their mind's visual stories. The psychologist Judith Beck invokes the analogy of being a movie director: *"You don't have to be at the mercy of this image. You can change it, if you want. It's as if you're a movie director: You can decide how you want it to be instead"* (Beck, 2011, p. 285).

One way for a person to change their imagery is to imagine doing something differently at a crucial moment. Help guide the suicidal person to build into their current daydreams or mental imagery scenes in which they cope effectively with their suicidal urges, rather than act on them. Once the person has changed the image in a way that resonates with them, ask them to play it in their head several times a day. This helps the person to train the mind, creating a habit for good rather than harm.

For some people, imagining or seeing one's suicide or its aftermath can be a way to cope. They find comfort in the images of escape or in other positive feelings that the suicidal images generate (Crane et al., 2014). Help the person create some kind of substitute image that can fulfill the same needs (Wesslau et al., 2014). For example, a person who finds solace in the idea of escaping their problems through suicide could create a different escapist fantasy.

Another option besides changing imagery is for a suicidal person to look at their imagery differently. They can nonjudgmentally observe and remain curious about what they see in their mind's eye. This stance is consistent with acceptance of suicidal thoughts (*Tip 72*). You can also encourage the person to use coping statements (*Tip 69*) while experiencing images of suicide, as a means of self-soothing. The person can note that the mental pictures are neither real nor a harbinger of things to come (e.g., *"Don't take these images literally"* and *"These images do not dictate my future."*)

Transforming images or one's relationship with them need not occur only in the context of suicidal imagery. These techniques are useful for all kinds of distressing imagery, especially those related to trauma, anxiety, and grief. To learn more, a useful book is the *Oxford Guide to Imagery in Cognitive Therapy* (Hackmann et al., 2011).

"I See Myself Getting a Rope…"

The image came a few times the past week, a scene that haunted Harrison but also enticed him. "I see myself getting a rope from the closet in my basement, tying it in a noose, and hanging it over the steel beam that runs across the basement." Harrison went on to describe to his psychologist the act of hanging himself, and the image of his body dangling from the beam. In his picture, he was at peace.

"What's it like for you to keep having that image?" his psychologist asked.

"It's OK," Harrison, 64, told her. "I know it should probably bother me, but it kind of makes me feel good to go through the motions. You know, like to know that I could do it if I need to."

"The problem is, the more you think of it, the more inviting it might become," she said. "Is it an image you'd like to change?"

"True. It's probably not the healthiest thing for me to be thinking on, you know?" Harrison laughed lightly.

"Can we go through that image again, but this time with you imagining that you do something that helps you rather than kills you?" she asked.

"Well, I suppose I could imagine myself going to the basement to get the rope and not actually taking it out of the closet," he said.

"What happens next?" she asked.

"OK…" Harrison took a moment to think. "I decide I really ought to look at that safety plan in my kitchen drawer. I figure I should take a look at that before doing something so drastic as killing myself."

"That seems like a realistic image. So, walk me through what happens after you have the thought that you ought to get your safety plan."

"I go to the kitchen and get it out of the junk drawer," he said. "Sorry, I don't mean that the plan is junk, it's just where I keep a lot of things. So I look at the safety plan and see that I really ought to call my best friend."

"And if she's not home?" the psychologist asked.

"Well, then I call you. Now that I think of it, I call you even if she is home. I call you after and I say, 'I need to see you as soon as I can, because I almost got out the rope.'"

"During this next week," she said, "when you see yourself going down to the basement to get that rope, can you try changing the story the way you just did with me?"

"I can try," Harrison said. "I reckon it might do me some good."

Works Cited

Beck, J. S. (2011). *Cognitive behavior therapy: Basics and beyond* (2nd ed.). New York, NY: Guilford Press.

Crane, C., Barnhofer, T., Duggan, D. S., Eames, C., Hepburn, S., Shah, D., & Williams, J. M. G. (2014). Comfort from suicidal cognition in recurrently depressed patients. *Journal of Affective Disorders, 155,* 241–246.

Hackmann, A., Bennett-Levy, J., & Holmes, E. A. (2011). *Oxford guide to imagery in cognitive therapy.* New York, NY: Oxford University Press.

Holmes, E. A., & Mathews, A. (2005). Mental imagery and emotion: A special relationship? *Emotion, 5*(4), 489–497.

Holmes, E. A., Arntz, A., & Smucker, M. R. (2007). Imagery rescripting in cognitive behaviour therapy: Images, treatment techniques and outcomes. *Journal of Behavior Therapy and Experimental Psychiatry, 38*(4), 297–305.

Shneidman, E. S. (1998). Further reflections on suicide and psychache. *Suicide and Life-Threatening Behavior, 28*(3), 245–250.

Wesslau, C., & Steil, R. (2014). Visual mental imagery in psychopathology: Implications for the maintenance and treatment of depression. *Clinical Psychology Review, 34*(4), 273–281.

Tip 71: Discourage Thought Suppression

"The paradoxical effect of thought suppression is that it produces a preoccupation with the suppressed thought."
Daniel Wegner and colleagues
(1987, p. 8)

Many suicidal individuals try to bury their suicidal thoughts, ignore them, or stop them – whatever they can do to keep them out of mind. However, considerable research shows that when people try to push away thoughts, they experience temporary relief but then the thoughts come back even more strongly, a tormenting "rebound effect" (Abramowitz et al., 2001). It is as if the thoughts fight back. And then, to make matters worse, individuals' failed efforts at suppressing thoughts can lead to feelings of frustration and helplessness.

Although the topic is not well studied, this rebound effect may apply to suppression of suicidal thoughts, too. In one study, the more that people tried to suppress their suicidal thoughts, the worse the suicidal thoughts became (Pettit et al., 2009). This finding underscores the importance of looking at whether the person tries to silence suicidal thoughts, and the consequences of such efforts:

- *"Do you try to stop yourself from thinking of suicide?"*
- *"What do you do to try to stop your suicidal thoughts?"*
- *"What do you think will happen if you do not try to push suicidal thoughts out of your mind?"*

If the person does report engaging in efforts to suppress their suicidal thoughts, examine the consequences of these efforts: *"Does it work? That is, are you able to get yourself to stop thinking of suicide?"* *"How long does it last, if so?"* In many cases, this line of questioning leads the person to realize that, for all their efforts to stop thinking of suicide, maybe they need to try something else. One approach to counter fruitless efforts at thought suppression is observation and acceptance of suicidal thoughts, which is discussed in the next tip.

"I Keep Telling Myself, 'Don't Go There.'"

"I'm trying really hard not to think of suicide," Janna, 47, told Miguel, a clinical social worker. "I don't like that I think this way. I want to stop."

"That makes sense," the social worker, Miguel, said. "It's distressing, isn't it, to have these thoughts keep coming to you?"

"Yes, completely," Janna said. "It really makes me think I'm crazy. And the more I have suicidal thoughts, the crazier I feel. And the crazier I feel, the more I have suicidal thoughts."

"Sounds like a vicious cycle," Miguel said. "What do you do to try to stop the suicidal thoughts when they do come?"

"I keep telling myself, 'Don't go there. Don't go there.' It's like a mantra."

"Does it work?" Miguel asked.

"I don't think so," Janna said. "Because I keep thinking of suicide even when I don't want to."

"That's not uncommon," Miguel said. "There's actually research that shows that the more we try to get ourselves to stop thinking of something, the more we end up thinking about it. It's sort of like someone on a diet who keeps telling themselves, 'Don't think of eating ice cream.' They have to keep thinking of ice cream in order to tell themselves not to."

"That makes sense," Janna said. "But what do I do instead?"

This poignant question provided a natural segue for Miguel to advocate for nonjudgmental observation and acceptance of suicidal thoughts, a technique described in *Tip 72*.

Works Cited

Abramowitz, J. S., Tolin, D. F., & Street, G. P. (2001). Paradoxical effects of thought suppression: A meta-analysis of controlled studies. *Clinical Psychology Review, 21(5)*, 683–703.

Pettit, J. W., Temple, S. R., Norton, P. J., Yaroslavsky, I., Grover, K. E., Morgan, S. T., & Schatte, D. J. (2009). Thought suppression and suicidal ideation: Preliminary evidence in support of a robust association. *Depression and Anxiety, 26(8)*, 758–763.

Wegner, D. M., Schneider, D. J., Carter, S. R., & White, T. L. (1987). Paradoxical effects of thought suppression. *Journal of Personality and Social Psychology, 53(1)*, 5–13.

Tip 72: Foster Acceptance of Suicidal Thoughts

"It's okay to have suicidal thoughts, just don't act on them. They are just thoughts."

Susan Rose Blauner

(2002, p. 5)

Many people strive to stop thinking of suicide altogether. Yet people cannot control what thoughts come to them, only what they do in response. And, as *Tip 71* explains, trying to suppress thoughts often fails and leads to yet more feelings of hopelessness. A healthy alternative to thought suppression is acceptance. Acceptance of suicidal thoughts does not mean the person accepts suicide as inevitable. Instead, acceptance calls for observing suicidal thoughts as they come and go, without condemning the thoughts, trying to control them, or giving them more power than they deserve.

Acceptance and observation of suicidal thoughts involves meta-cognitive awareness. This skill calls for observing one's thoughts as "passing events in the mind," rather than as true reflections of reality or fundamental parts of oneself (Teasdale et al., 2002, p. 285). These concepts are consistent with acceptance and commitment therapy's focus on cognitive defusion, which essentially emphasizes not taking the content of thoughts literally (Hayes et al., 2011).

The prospect of giving up efforts to control suicidal thoughts frightens many people. They fear that letting themselves think of suicide, without resistance, will lead to losing control and acting on the thoughts: *"The thoughts will take over."* In reality, thoughts are momentary phenomena that can come and go if the person does not become entangled with them. Thoughts *happen*. Thoughts may or may not be true. They do not define people or their actions.

You can draw from a cornucopia of rich metaphors to illustrate how to let thoughts flow without judgment, without control, and without avoidance. The psychologist Marsha Linehan offers an excellent metaphor of cars on a railroad train:

> Imagine you are sitting on a hill near train tracks, watching train cars go by.... Imagine that thoughts, images, sensations, and feelings are cars on the train.... Just watch the train cars go by.... Don't jump on the train.... Just watch the train cars go by.... If you find yourself riding the train, jump off and start observing again...
>
> (Linehan, 2015, p. 187)

Other metaphors abound. Entreat the person to watch their thoughts float by as if the thoughts were leaves in a stream. The person can choose not to reach into the water, grasp onto a thought, and hold on to it. Thoughts also can be compared to clouds floating in the sky, a storm passing through, and other ephemeral events that can always be observed but never controlled.

There are many other ways, too, for the person to adopt a stance of acceptance. *Mindfully observing suicidal thoughts* is one way. The person can simply observe, *"I'm having the image that _____"* or *"I'm noticing that I'm thinking that _____."* Consider the qualitative difference in these two statements: "I don't deserve to live" vs. "I am having the thought that I don't deserve to live." One is presented as a fact, the other as a fallible belief.

Acting as a commentator can further distance the person from the suicidal thoughts. Like a television reporter, the person can dispassionately note what they observe: "There go those thoughts again, telling me that I don't deserve to live. My thoughts do that a lot."

Remaining curious is another way to practice acceptance. When suicidal thoughts or imagery visit, the person can wonder what caused the thoughts, how long they will last, and what will come next. The person might pay attention to how much (or how little) they buy into these products of the mind, which emotions are triggered, and what physical sensations are experienced as a result. Consistent with meta-cognitive awareness, the process of thinking becomes more important than the content of the thoughts.

Counting suicidal thoughts also allows a person to observe the process of thinking. By keeping a count of how often suicidal thoughts occur (whether hourly, daily, or weekly), the person moves from actor to observer. In doing so, people can achieve some distance from the suicidal thoughts and also disarm them, at least a little, of their power.

Whatever approach the suicidal person takes to observing thoughts, the objectives are the same: The person will accept having the thoughts without trying to control them or overinflating their importance. Meanwhile, establishing distance from suicidal thoughts can strip them of their power. Naked, thoughts are revealed as momentary events of an unrelenting mind. The suicidal thoughts might persist, but they need not have the force of truth.

Newer cognitive therapies such as acceptance and commitment therapy and mindfulness-based cognitive therapy embrace nonjudgmental observation of thoughts as a necessary ingredient for healing. Though not specific to suicidal thoughts, helpful books to recommend to clients include *Get Out of Your Mind and Into Your Life: The New Acceptance and Commitment Therapy* (Hayes, 2005), and *The Mindful Way Workbook: An 8-Week Program to Free Yourself from Depression and Emotional Distress* (Teasdale et al., 2014).

"I Am Believing the Thought that I Should Kill Myself"

"I'm a loser and don't deserve to live." This thought and others like it ran through Neveah's mind constantly. She treated the thoughts as essential truths. She would think, "Because I am a loser and don't deserve to live, I need to kill myself." The thoughts were so upsetting that Neveah tried to

force herself to stop having them. And then, when the thoughts inevitably persisted, she felt worse about herself.

With psychotherapy, Neveah, 43, learned to respond in other ways. When a suicidal or self-deprecatory thought intruded, she would observe it and tell herself, "I just had the thought that I'm a loser and need to kill myself. That doesn't mean it's true." When she found herself buying into her suicidal thoughts, she began to tell herself, "I am believing the thought that I should kill myself." These subtle changes in wording highlighted that the suicidal thoughts could be observed without being believed, or acted on.

Works Cited

Blauner, S. R. (2002). *How I stayed alive when my brain was trying to kill me: One person's guide to suicide prevention.* New York, NY: William Morrow.

Hayes, S. C. (2005). *Get out of your mind and into your life: The new acceptance and commitment therapy.* Oakland, CA: New Harbinger Publications, Inc.

Hayes, S. C., Strosahl, K. D., & Wilson, K. G. (2011). *Acceptance and commitment therapy: The process and practice of mindful change.* New York, NY: Guilford Press.

Linehan, M. M. (2015). *DBT skills training manual* (2nd ed.). New York, NY: Guilford Press.

Teasdale, J. D., Moore, R. G., Hayhurst, H., Pope, M., Williams, S., & Segal, Z. V. (2002). Metacognitive awareness and prevention of relapse in depression: Empirical evidence. *Journal of Consulting and Clinical Psychology, 70*(2), 275–287.

Teasdale, J. D., Williams, J. M. G., & Segal, Z. V. (2014). *The mindful way workbook: An 8-week program to free yourself from depression and emotional distress.* New York, NY: Guilford Press.

thirteen
Improving
Quality of Life

Tip 73: Enhance Coping Skills

"The ability to tolerate and accept distress is an essential mental health goal..."

Marsha Linehan
(1993, p. 147)

Many people do not know how to cope constructively with their mental pain. Their suffering is excruciating, and they see suicide as the only way out of the pain. Or they try to cope in ways that worsen the situation they are already in, by resorting to substance use, isolation, cutting, or other destructive habits. These harmful behaviors and the consequences they bring can intensify urges to die by suicide.

Dialectical behavior therapy provides numerous pathways for teaching the suicidal person how to cope with distress. It is beyond the scope of this book to cover the many different skills that DBT imparts, and I recommend reading the *DBT Skills Training Manual* (Linehan, 2015b), along with its companion book *DBT Skills Training Handouts and Worksheets* (Linehan, 2015a). For the sake of illustration, two skill sets from DBT for tolerating painful emotions are described here: Changing body chemistry naturally, and distracting oneself from emotional pain.

First, a caveat: Although DBT has demonstrated effectiveness at reducing suicidal behavior (Linehan et al., 2015), the individual skills taught within the skills modules have not been studied for effectiveness in isolation of each other. With that in mind, as with other tips and techniques in this book, you should monitor which exercises are helpful to your clients.

Changing Body Chemistry Naturally

The idea behind changing one's body chemistry naturally is to induce a physiological calming response. The DBT manual proposes four means for achieving this during an emotional crisis:

Applying cold water to one's face. The person might hold their breath and put their face in a bowl of cold water, or they might hold a plastic bag full of cold water to the eyes and cheeks. The frigid water triggers a calming physiological response, called the "diving response," in which the heart slows down and blood flow is redirected from nonessential organs to the brain and heart (Gooden, 1994).

Exercising intensely, even if episodically. Physical exercise can improve mood and increase energy and wakefulness (Kanning & Schlicht, 2010). Moreover, exercise can serve as a distraction. Ideally, the person will have a regular exercise regimen, but when emotions prove overwhelming, intense exercise can help produce feelings of calm.

Slowing down one's breathing. The person takes deep belly breaths, while breathing out more slowly than breathing in. This can trigger the relaxation response (Benson & Proctor, 2010).

Practicing muscle relaxation. Working from the head to the toes, or vice versa, the person tenses up a set of muscles (e.g., arm muscles) while inhaling and then relaxes the muscles upon exhaling. The person tenses up each muscle group one at a time for 5–6 seconds before relaxing for 10–15 seconds. The DBT manual recommends pairing the releasing of tension with the word "relax," so that over time the person can achieve relaxation simply by saying the word.

Caution is needed with physical activities that increase heart rate (e.g., exercise) or decrease it (e.g., cold water immersion). As a result, the DBT manual recommends that people consult their physician before trying these exercises if they have a heart condition or other medical problem.

Distracting Oneself from Emotional Pain

DBT conceptualizes the human mind as having three parts: emotion mind, reasonable mind, and wise mind (Linehan, 2015b). Just as the names imply, emotion rules emotion mind, and logic governs reasonable mind. Wise mind is the marriage of both, where neither emotion nor reason operates unfettered by the other. The goal of DBT skills training is for people to access wise mind more often and easily.

In the skill set "Wise Mind ACCEPTS," the person calls on logic and emotions to temper emotional flooding. The acronym "ACCEPTS" stands for Activities, Contributing, Comparisons, Emotions, Pushing Away, Thoughts, and Sensations:

Activities. These activities might include getting tasks done, doing enjoyable things such as listening to music, getting together with friends, or whatever else can consume the person's attention.

Contributions to others. The person can help someone else, give someone a compliment via phone, text, or email, do volunteer work, or give a gift to another person.

Comparisons. So often, people compare themselves to those who have it better than them, which then makes them feel inadequate and aggrieved. Comparisons to people who are less fortunate or coping worse, or to oneself during a worse time, can help place things in perspective.

Emotions. The person actively tries to conjure emotions that are different from what they are currently experiencing. The person might watch a scary movie, read a funny book, or even read political material that riles them up.

Push away the pain. Although thought suppression generally is discouraged (*Tip 71*), DBT calls for pushing away negative thoughts, feelings, and memories temporarily, if possible. This can involve visualizing putting the problem in a box, telling oneself "no" while ruminating, and simply leaving the topic for a while.

Thoughts. The person becomes absorbed in a mental challenge, such as doing math problems, completing puzzles, or something else that requires logic, which then distracts the person from the emotional pain.

Sensations. Here, DBT calls for the person to experience other physical sensations as a means of distraction. This can include taking a very hot or cold shower, holding ice, running one's fingers along a particularly soft or scratchy texture, singing songs, or anything else that brings other sensations into the mix (see also *Tip 54*).

An Elaboration: Dialectical Behavior Therapy

Helping suicidal individuals to stay alive is not enough. They also need to suffer less and find meaning in living. DBT aims to improve people's quality of life through a blend of psychotherapy, skills training, and on-call availability for skills coaching (plus, for the DBT therapist, a consultation team to help navigate the complexities of working with oft-challenging clients). Among the many components of DBT, a focus on emotion dysregulation lies at its core (Linehan, 1993). Initially developed for people with borderline personality disorder and chronic suicidality, DBT now is commonly used across many different populations and problems.

Psychotherapy in DBT stresses dialectics – a synthesis of opposites, in contrast to rigid dichotomous thinking. As such, DBT calls for the therapist to balance efforts to help the person change problematic behaviors with simultaneous acceptance and validation of the person as they are in the present moment. Interventions use a blend of behavior therapy and mindfulness techniques drawn from Eastern contemplative practices. The DBT therapist works from a set of four priorities, privileging safety first.

Next, any behaviors of either the therapist or client impeding the therapy's success take precedence, followed by problems that interfere with the person's ability to thrive (e.g., depression, substance use, relationship problems). The fourth priority is improving skills in coping and functioning; these are largely covered in the skills-training component.

Skills training usually takes place in a group format concurrently with individual therapy. Skills are taught across four categories: distress tolerance, emotion regulation, mindfulness, and interpersonal effectiveness. The repertoire of skills is expansive, from the simple (e.g., half-smiling) to the complex (e.g., behavioral chain analysis).

Research consistently finds that DBT reduces suicidal behaviors (Panos et al., 2014; Linehan et al., 2015). Additionally, the skills training is effective even without the individual psychotherapy (Linehan et al., 2015). The effectiveness of DBT translates to untold thousands of improved lives. As one DBT veteran stated, "By empowering me to make the next minute or hour better than the one before it, in even the slightest, most incremental way, this therapy kindles hope. Better hours become better days, and several years on I've discovered my own resilience" (Lippincott, 2015).

Works Cited

Benson, H., & Proctor, W. (2010). *Relaxation revolution: The science and genetics of mind body healing.* New York, NY: Simon and Schuster.

Gooden, B. A. (1994). Mechanism of the human diving response. *Integrative Physiological and Behavioral Science, 29*(1), 6–16.

Kanning, M., & Schlicht, W. (2010). Be active and become happy: An ecological momentary assessment of physical activity and mood. *Journal of Sport & Exercise Psychology, 32*(2), 253–261.

Linehan, M. (1993). *Cognitive-behavioral treatment of borderline personality disorder.* New York, NY: Guilford Press.

Linehan, M. M. (2015a). *DBT skills training handouts and worksheets* (2nd ed.). New York, NY: Guilford Press.

Linehan, M. M. (2015b). *DBT skills training manual* (2nd ed.). New York, NY: Guilford Press.

Linehan, M. M., Korslund, K. E., Harned, M. S., Gallop, R. J., Lungu, A., Neacsiu, A. D., McDavid, J., Comtois, K. A., & Murray-Gregory, A. M. (2015). Dialectical behavior therapy for high suicide risk in individuals with borderline personality disorder: A randomized clinical trial and component analysis. *JAMA Psychiatry, 72*(5), 475–482.

Lippincott, W. (2015, May 16). No longer wanting to die. *New York Times.* Retrieved January 30, 2017, from http://opinionator.blogs.nytimes.com/2015/05/16/no-longer-wanting-to-die.

Panos, P. T., Jackson, J. W., Hasan, O., & Panos, A. (2014). Meta-analysis and systematic review assessing the efficacy of dialectical behavior therapy (DBT). *Research on Social Work Practice, 24*(2), 213–223.

Tip 74: Cultivate Mindfulness

"Through mindfulness, suicidal individuals are taught to observe the dark calculus of suicide with equanimity, cultivate kindness and self-compassion toward themselves, and to return to living each moment to its fullest."

Jason Luoma and Jennifer Villatte
(2012, p. 274)

Mindfulness involves paying attention to what we think, feel, and do in the present moment, without steeping in memories of the past or fears of the future. And when such departures do inevitably occur, mindfulness is about returning back to the present moment. This goal might seem counterintuitive. If the present moment involves suffering, then wouldn't focusing on the present moment intensify the experience of suffering? The reality is that acceptance of the here and now, without flight or avoidance, helps people distance themselves from their suffering. They are observing their pain rather than *being* their pain.

In general, the practice of mindfulness involves observing phenomena within one's mind, body, or environment as they occur without judgment, attachment, or reactivity to what is being observed. In the case of suicidal thoughts, mindful observation can help the suicidal person to recognize thoughts as just that – *thoughts*. Not facts. Not truth. Not a call to action. Mindfulness prompts people to recognize just how transitory thoughts, feelings, and other internal experiences are. They come and they go, like clouds in the sky.

Many books address mindfulness. A classic is *The Miracle of Mindfulness*, by Thich Nhat Hanh (1999). The author describes how mindfulness can saturate any act, no matter how mundane: washing dishes by hand, drinking a cup of hot tea, eating sections of a tangerine, walking along a dirt path. A common mindfulness exercise is to observe one's breath, taking note of the sensation in one's nose or mouth as the breath enters the body, feeling the rise of the belly, and then noticing how it feels for the breath to leave as the belly falls. Moment after moment, breath after breath, the process repeats. The objective is to remain mindful of the present moment and all that it entails, no matter what it entails.

Cultivation of mindfulness is at the heart of mindfulness-based stress reduction (Kabat-Zinn, 2011) and mindfulness-based cognitive therapy (Williams et al., 2015). Dialectical behavior therapy (DBT) and acceptance and commitment therapy (ACT) also emphasize mindfulness. These therapies offer abundant exercises for helping people strengthen their skills at mindfulness.

Encourage people to start small. They might try *mindfully eating* a piece of fruit, paying attention to the feel of its texture in the hand and on the lips, the sensation of the fruit against the teeth, the rush of saliva, and so on. Another small way to start is the *three-minute breathing* exercise used in mindfulness-based cognitive therapy (Williams et al., 2007). In this exercise, the person spends the first minute maintaining awareness overall of their thoughts, feelings, and physical sensations. Then, as if the three minutes are shaped like an hour glass, the person narrows their focus onto the act and physical sensations of breathing itself. And then the person expands their awareness again onto their body as a whole. Also useful is the *observe–describe–participate* exercise in DBT (Linehan, 2015). Individuals observe thoughts, sights, sounds, smells, touch, or physical sensations. Then they label and describe the sensations and experiences that they are observing, followed by immersing themselves in that experience.

In the context of the psychotherapies that incorporate mindfulness practice, relaxation and enlightenment are not the goals. Even so, feelings of calm and transcendence may occur as a byproduct of mindfulness. Increased mindfulness is linked to greater feelings of well-being, a reduction of psychological symptoms, and less reactivity and impulsivity (Keng et al., 2011). More specifically, research indicates that mindfulness-based cognitive therapy, which emphasizes a practice of mindful meditation, can reduce suicidal ideation (Williams et al., 2015).

Mindfulness has some risks. For some people, the practice can increase anxiety, exacerbate rumination, and open the floodgates to traumatic memories (Williams & Swales, 2004). To help alleviate these effects, teach grounding exercises (*Tip 54*) and other coping skills (*Tip 73*). Remind the person to observe and describe their thoughts and emotional experiences as if they are a phenomenon occurring outside of them (Linehan, 2015).

The practice of mindfulness has other risks, too. Especially when self-criticism is already rampant, people may experience a flood of self-punitive thoughts when they inevitably encounter difficulty remaining aware of the present moment. Without fail, distractions occur. The mind wanders. People get lost in their thoughts. They might then condemn themselves for not "doing it right" or for failing at mindfulness. Instead of simply viewing those condemnations as more thoughts to be observed, they believe them. If you use mindfulness as an intervention, try to prepare your clients for the self-blame and judgment that they might apply to their mindfulness practice. Emphasize the inevitability of distraction and the value of simply returning to the present moment when the mind wanders. Mindfulness is a practice specifically because it always requires practice. Perfection is unattainable.

It is recommended that clinicians who encourage mindfulness in their clients also practice mindfulness themselves (Williams et al., 2015). This practice can help you to understand the challenges your clients might experience, respond to clients with less reactivity, and model mindfulness to the people you encourage to live more mindfully. If you are not well-versed in mindfulness practice and have a client who would benefit from it, consider referring the person to a mindfulness instructor or group. People trained to teach mindfulness-based stress reduction or mindfulness-based cognitive therapy classes are especially good resources. The University of Massachusetts Medical School, which is where Jon Kabat-Zinn developed the mindfulness-based stress reduction program, maintains a listing of certified instructors and offers online courses; see https://umassmed.edu/cfm.

"Are You Like the Storm or the Sky Right Now?"

In the flash of a moment, everything in Mark's life changed. There was a car accident. His wife and two young children were in the car. None of them survived. In the months since, grief overwhelmed Mark so completely that he stopped going to work, tending to routine obligations such as paying bills, and taking care of himself. He felt convinced that the destructive machinations of his grief demonstrated his love for his family. In his mind, to find meaning in life without his wife and children would be to minimize their worth. Eventually, he attempted suicide by poisoning himself with carbon monoxide in his car, surviving only because a neighbor discovered him in time.

The psychologists Jason Luoma and Jennifer Villatte (2012) share this case history in their article on mindfulness and suicidality. They describe how, over a period of six months, the therapist taught Mark mindfulness skills in the service of helping him to experience his grief without reacting to it, and to disarm his belief that living a meaningful life insulted the meaning of his wife and children.

They started with brief, daily homework assignments that called for Mark to practice mindfulness during mundane activities, such as showering, walking, and eating. In time, he built up to practicing mindfulness for longer periods of time and observing, without judgment or interruption, his sensations, urges, and emotions.

Not surprisingly, Mark struggled with acceptance when flooded with feelings of grief and loss. His therapist guided him to observe his emotions without attachment as leaves floating by on a river. He also practiced observing his thoughts and feelings as storms that roll across the sky without ever touching it. His therapist would ask him sometimes, "Are you like the storm or the sky right now?" (Luoma & Villatte, 2012, p. 273). These experiences helped Mark learn how to "get out of his mind and into the present moment." It took a lot of work and practice, but eventually he learned to experience his pain without paralysis or being overwhelmed: "While his thoughts and memories still evoked powerful emotions," Luoma and Villatte write, "they exerted less control over his behavior and he was able to attend to other events as well."

Works Cited

Hanh, T. N. (1999). *The miracle of mindfulness: An introduction to the practice of meditation.* Boston, MA: Beacon Press.
Kabat-Zinn, J. (2011). Some clinical applications of mindfulness meditation in medicine and psychiatry: The case of mindfulness-based stress reduction (MBSR). In J. Kabat-Zinn &

R. Davidson (Eds.), *The mind's own physician: A scientific dialogue with the Dalai Lama on the healing power of meditation* (pp. 35–47). Oakland, CA: New Harbinger Publications, Inc.

Keng, S. L., Smoski, M. J., & Robins, C. J. (2011). Effects of mindfulness on psychological health: A review of empirical studies. *Clinical Psychology Review, 31*(6), 1041–1056.

Linehan, M. M. (2015). *DBT skills training handouts and worksheets* (2nd ed.). New York, NY: Guilford Press.

Luoma, J. B., & Villatte, J. L. (2012). Mindfulness in the treatment of suicidal individuals. *Cognitive and Behavioral Practice, 19*(2), 265–276.

Williams, J. M. G., & Swales, M. (2004). The use of mindfulness-based approaches for suicidal patients. *Archives of Suicide Research, 8*(4), 315–329.

Williams, J. M. G., Fennell, M., Barnhofer, T., Silverton, S., & Crane, R. (2015). *Mindfulness and the transformation of despair: Working with people at risk of suicide.* New York, NY: Guilford Press.

Williams, M., Teasdale, J., Segal, Z., & Kabat-Zinn, J. (2007). *The mindful way through depression: Freeing yourself from chronic unhappiness.* New York, NY: Guilford Press.

Tip 75: "Broaden and Build" Positive Emotions

"Little-by-little micromoments of positive emotional experience, although fleeting, reshape who people are by setting them on trajectories of growth and building their enduring resources for survival."

Barbara Fredrickson
(2013, p. 15)

Even brief moments of positive emotions can set into motion a chain reaction that leads to more creative and flexible ways of thinking and acting (Fredrickson, 2013). This broadened perspective then builds and improves on important aspects of coping, such as resilience, social motivation, and optimism. Fredrickson, who developed the "broaden and build" theory of positive emotions, calls this synergistic reaction an "upward spiral" (Fredrickson, 2001). It stands in stark contrast to the downward spiral so often triggered by despair.

There are 10 representative emotions that create positive momentum: joy, gratitude, serenity, interest, hope, pride, amusement, inspiration, awe, and love (Fredrickson, 2013). Each of these emotions can propel the person to take actions that lead to greater knowledge, skills, social connections, motivation, optimism, and awareness. It is an intuitive, even obvious, proposition: Positive emotions beget more positive emotions, along with healthier, more constructive ways of living. Yet when someone is at a point of distress so grave that they are considering suicide, positive emotions can be painfully hard to come by. A hallmark symptom of depression and other factors leading to suicidal thinking is a loss of interest in once pleasurable activities. To a suicidal individual, prescribing positive emotions can be akin to saying, "Don't worry, be happy." The challenge is to help people rediscover pleasure, even for mere moments at a time.

There are interventions designed specifically to help people generate positive emotions. Several activities that have demonstrated effectiveness at stimulating positive emotion are described below: lovingkindness meditation (Fredrickson et al., 2008), gratitude exercises (Seligman et al., 2005), identification and utilization of strengths (Seligman et al., 2005), and doing things that give pleasure (Berenbaum, 2002).

Lovingkindness Meditation

Lovingkindness meditation involves directing feelings of love and compassion toward oneself and others. While meditating, the person repeats various wishes for oneself and for others. Traditionally, these wishes are *"May I be free from danger," "May I have mental happiness," "May I have physical happiness," "May I have ease of well-being"* (Salzberg, 1995). The practice is flexible, and people can construct their own phrases. Lovingkindness meditation is described at length in the book *Lovingkindness: The Revolutionary Art of Happiness* (Salzberg, 1995).

Gratitude Exercises

Gratitude exercises shift the focus from what is missing or painful in one's life to what is present and good. One exercise calls for people to keep a journal every night in which they write three good things that happened that day. Another is to write a letter expressing thanks and gratitude to someone who has been helpful to the person. Generally speaking, these activities can lead to increases in happiness and decreases in depression (Seligman et al., 2005). When used with people hospitalized for suicidal thoughts, the exercises of counting one's blessings and writing a gratitude letter were associated with decreased hopelessness and increased optimism (Huffman et al., 2014).

Some caution is necessary with gratitude exercises. Although helpful for many people, they can actually make some people feel worse (Li et al., 2012). Gratitude can stimulate feelings of guilt, inadequacy, and even failure, along the lines of "I'm a bad person for thinking of suicide when I have so many good things in my life." Especially in collectivist cultures, the suicidal person might ruminate about their inability to reciprocate kindnesses to others (Li et al., 2012). If you use gratitude exercises, be on the lookout for both good *and* bad effects.

Identification of Strengths

Strengths-based interventions typically follow a similar format (Parks et al., 2013). First, the person completes a questionnaire that identifies their strengths; a good questionnaire to use is the Values in Action Survey, available for free at www.viacharacter.org. Next, you and the person can brainstorm ways the person can use their strengths more. These activities can generate feelings of appreciation, accomplishment, and pride. *Tip 65* goes into more detail about ways to incorporate the suicidal person's strengths.

Pleasurable Activities

"Pleasurable activities" is the clinical term for things that are fun, feel good, or at least distract people from their pain. Help the person come up with ideas of things to do: "*What can give you even just a few moments of pleasure, even if it is as simple as eating your favorite dessert or watching a funny TV show?*" If the person has trouble coming up with ideas, the Internet contains many lists of pleasurable activities that people can draw from, and the Pleasant Events List in the *DBT Skills Training Handouts and Worksheets* is also a good resource (Linehan, 2015). For people who lack motivation or interest in experiencing pleasure, behavioral activation can help jump-start the process (*Tip 76*). If the person finds that they are unable to feel pleasure when doing the activities, empathize with this difficulty and engage in problem-solving about what the person can try next.

Words of Caution

The pursuit of happiness and other positive emotions can backfire. People who focus too much on whether they feel good paradoxically can feel worse, because of unmet expectations, rumination about how one feels, and an inability to be in the present moment (Catalino et al., 2014). As with gratitude exercises, remain vigilant for negative effects of efforts to build positive emotions.

"I'm Just ... Blah"

Shanique, 52, had trouble seeing the value in getting out of bed, let alone getting up and doing something that might feel good. So when her social worker brought up the idea of doing some activities that would bring pleasure, it felt like a cruel joke. "If it were as simple as taking a bath or eating a hot fudge sundae," she told him, "I wouldn't be thinking of killing myself."

"I know that seems overly simplistic," he said. "And it's true that doing something for pleasure or distraction can't, by itself, heal the tremendous pain or anxiety that you feel. But even just a few minutes of positive emotions can help you to feel better in the long run. How about if you give it a try and see if it has any effect?"

Shanique agreed, but then she was at a loss as to what she could do. "I don't enjoy anything anymore. Even food doesn't taste good. I'm just ... blah," she said.

"What has given you pleasure in the past?" the social worker asked.

"Well, before all this happened, I liked to ride my bike around the lake."

"Could you try riding your bike sometime this week, even if just for a few minutes?"

Shanique agreed. The next session she reported to him that she rode her bike for 10 minutes around the park near her house. The first five minutes "sucked," she said. "I kept telling myself that this was stupid." But she kept at it. Even though the bicycle ride itself was not helping her mood, it gave her a small bit of relief to know that she was trying. The fact that she made it out of the house gave her hope that she could do so again. The relief and hope felt good.

Her newfound positive emotions did not instantly cure her of her suicidal thoughts or depressed mood. But over time, as she attempted more pleasurable activities, she found that they generated gratitude, joy, and more hope. Her efforts to reacquaint herself with positive experiences broadened not only her emotions, but also her world.

Works Cited

Berenbaum, H. (2002). Varieties of joy-related pleasurable activities and feelings. *Cognition & Emotion, 16*(4), 473–494.

Catalino, L. I., Algoe, S. B., & Fredrickson, B. L. (2014). Prioritizing positivity: An effective approach to pursuing happiness? *Emotion, 14*(6), 1155–1161.

Fredrickson, B. L. (2001). The role of positive emotions in positive psychology: The broaden-and-build theory of positive emotions. *American Psychologist, 56*(3), 218–226.

Fredrickson, B. L. (2013). Positive emotions broaden and build. *Advances in Experimental Social Psychology, 47*(1), 1–53.

Fredrickson, B. L., Cohn, M. A., Coffey, K. A., Pek, J., & Finkel, S. M. (2008). Open hearts build lives: Positive emotions, induced through loving-kindness meditation, build consequential personal resources. *Journal of Personality and Social Psychology, 95*(5), 1045–1062.

Huffman, J. C., DuBois, C. M., Healy, B. C., Boehm, J. K., Kashdan, T. B., Celano, C. M., ... & Lyubomirsky, S. (2014). Feasibility and utility of positive psychology exercises for suicidal inpatients. *General Hospital Psychiatry, 36*(1), 88–94.

Li, D., Zhang, W., Li, X., Li, N., & Ye, B. (2012). Gratitude and suicidal ideation and suicide attempts among Chinese adolescents: Direct, mediated, and moderated effects. *Journal of Adolescence, 35*(1), 55–66.

Linehan, M. M. (2015). *DBT skills training handouts and worksheets* (2nd ed.). New York, NY: Guilford Press.

Parks, A. C., & Biswas-Diener, R. (2013). Positive interventions: Past, present and future. In T. Kashdan & J. Ciarrochi (Eds.), *Mindfulness, acceptance, and positive psychology: The seven foundations of well-being* (pp. 140–165). Oakland, CA: New Harbinger Publications, Inc.

Salzberg, S. (1995). *Lovingkindness: The revolutionary art of happiness*. Boston, MA: Shambhala Publications.

Seligman, M. E. P., Steen, T. A., Park, N., & Peterson, C. (2005). Positive psychology progress: Empirical validation of interventions. *American Psychologist, 60*, 410–421.

Tip 76: Pair Behavioral Activation with Values

"Regaining old routines, or finding new ones, is often important in the healing process."

Neil Jacobson and colleagues
(2001, p. 259)

Often, people who consider suicide, especially those with depression or anxiety, experience a sense of paralysis. They stop doing things that might help them to feel better, and then they feel bad about themselves for not doing what might help them feel better. Behavioral activation can help break this pattern (Kanter et al., 2009). A component of cognitive behavior therapies, behavioral activation is a structured process that enables the suicidal person to reconnect with worthwhile, often fundamental, activities that can counter the forces of suicidality.

A key principle of behavioral activation is that people should not wait until they feel better to start doing the things that can help them feel better. Behavioral activation offers a series of concrete steps for the person to take (Kanter et al., 2009). First, the person monitors and writes down what they do each day, hour by hour, and their mood during those time periods. When reviewing the person's activities, look for counterproductive things (e.g., staying in bed) that the person does too much and constructive things (e.g., socializing) that the person does too little. Also identify activities that influence mood, one way or the other. This activity monitoring provides a springboard for identifying neglected activities that, if restarted, would improve the person's mood and quality of life.

Borrowing from acceptance and commitment therapy (Hayes et al., 1999), the clinician also assesses the person's values as a means to identify additional activities that would give the person's life purpose (Kanter et al., 2009). Values should be explored in the domains of work/school, relationships, religion and spirituality, service to others, self-care, pleasure, and other areas that are important to the person. Identification of values helps steer the person toward activities that are congruent with the life the person wants to live. The psychotherapist and coach Russ Harris (2009) offers these questions to help people home in on their values (p. 11):

- *"Deep in your heart, what do you want your life to be about?"*
- *"What do you want to stand for?"*
- *"What truly matters to you in the big picture?*

Some people's hopelessness or sense of futility is so severe that they are unable to come up with any values. In such cases, empathize with their state of hopelessness and focus only on activating behaviors.

Once daily activities and values are addressed, the clinician and person jointly create an activity hierarchy, ranking in order of complexity and difficulty the activities that the person identified as meaningful and necessary. Starting with the easiest activity, the person breaks it down into small units. A person who has stopped exercising, for example, might simply put her athletic shoes on the first day, walk to the end of the driveway a few days, then work her way up to walking to the end of the block a few days, then around the block, and so on. An "upward spiral" can ensue (*Tip 75*), wherein the activities help improve mood, making it easier to do the activities again. Meanwhile, the person continues to list their activities throughout the day and rate their mood before and after each activity. As the days increase, so do the amount and complexity of each activity.

Emphasize the value of accepting one's emotional state in the moment and moving forward regardless, with the understanding that the person need not feel well to act as if they do. This approach will help the person to attend to obligations of daily living while living in accord with their values. At the same time, be careful not to set the person up for feelings of failure if their immobilization persists. Frame the tasks that lie ahead as experimental – the person will discover what works well and what doesn't, examine the obstacles to engaging in activities, and modify accordingly.

Although behavioral activation has not been studied specifically in relation to suicidality, it has a rich evidence base to support its effectiveness in people with depression. A review of studies indicates that behavioral activation is even more effective than medication in helping people recover from a depressive episode (Ekers et al., 2014). The effect of behavioral activation is especially large when depression is severe (Ekers et al., 2014) The ease of applying behavioral activation, combined with its evidence base, supports its use with people who need help reconnecting with activities that increase feelings of mastery, competence, and reasons to stay alive.

"That's Easier Said than Done"

Like a bully taunting him at every turn, Wei's inner critic incessantly condemned him as worthless, a failure, and undeserving of life. These ruminations caused Wei, 37, to recoil from contact with his parents, his brother, and his friends. He only rarely returned emails and texts. He ignored phone calls altogether. And he left the house only to go to work and attend to essentials. If he stayed to himself, he could avoid confronting the gross evidence, in his mind, of his deficiencies and the anxiety that they provoked. Yet this self-imposed isolation deprived him of the connection, camaraderie, and love of others that could counter his mind's abuse.

Wei's psychologist needed to help him re-engage with others even though Wei felt incapable of doing so. The psychologist started with activity monitoring. She gave Wei a form with which to record his activities every day for a week, and to rate his mood on a scale of 0 (miserable) to 10 (joyful) during each activity. A pattern became evident: Every evening after returning from work, Wei retreated to his apartment and essentially parked himself in front of the TV until he fell asleep on the sofa, where he remained until the next morning. He did not eat dinner. He did not attend to things he needed to do. And he felt far worse about himself because of this neglect. On the weekend, this pattern reasserted itself for the entire stretch of a day. He did not shower or change his clothes. He simply hibernated.

The psychologist explored with Wei his values and goals. Despite his mind's ruthless torment, Wei wanted to live a life populated with friends and family, even a wife and children someday. He yearned to be a part of a world from which he felt exiled. Wei was able to see how his actions were antithetical to his values, but he felt unable to do anything about it.

Wei's psychologist challenged him on this. "The idea here isn't for you to feel less anxious when you're with others – not yet, anyway," she told him. "The goal is for you to connect with others even though you feel anxious."

"That's easier said than done," Wei replied.

"That's true," she said. "It is hard to do. That's why we'll start with very small steps."

The psychologist and Wei then brainstormed about ways to break down his re-entry into his social world. To start, they agreed that the next day after work, once ensconced on the sofa in his apartment, Wei would send a brief text to his parents: "Hi. Sorry I've been out of touch." Wei was worried that this would open the floodgates. If his parents' texts overwhelmed him, he would text back, "Not able to keep texting, just wanted to say hi for now." On his activity schedule, he would rate his mood before sending the text and afterward. Then the next day he would repeat the process with his best friend and with his brother. Another scheduled activity was for Wei to stop watching TV at 10 p.m. and move to his bed to sleep. With each day, his activation tasks increased. Over the weekend, he would shower one of the days and put on fresh clothes. The next weekend he would shower both days. Wei strove to complete these activities, but sometimes he felt too paralyzed. The psychologist sought to understand the obstacles and to empathize with his difficulties.

In time, as Wei texted his family and best friend more often and took better care of himself, he came to feel more connected, even a little hopeful. He still had relentlessly negative thoughts about himself. He still had thoughts of suicide. However, he did not let these thoughts stop him from doing what he needed to do to rebuild his life and rediscover hope.

Works Cited

Ekers, D., Webster, L., Van Straten, A., Cuijpers, P., Richards, D., & Gilbody, S. (2014). Behavioural activation for depression: An update of meta-analysis of effectiveness and sub group analysis. *PloS One, 9*(6), e100100.

Harris, R. (2009). *ACT made simple: An easy-to-read primer on acceptance and commitment therapy.* Oakland, CA: New Harbinger Publications, Inc.

Hayes, S. C., Strosahl, K. D., & Wilson, K. G. (1999). *Acceptance and commitment therapy: An experiential approach to behavior change.* New York, NY: Guilford Press.

Jacobson, N. S., Martell, C. R., & Dimidjian, S. (2001). Behavioral activation treatment for depression: Returning to contextual roots. *Clinical Psychology: Science and Practice, 8*(3), 255–270.

Kanter, J. W., Busch, A. M., & Rusch, L. C. (2009). *Behavioral activation: Distinctive features.* New York, NY: Routledge.

fourteen
Moving Forward After a Suicide Attempt

Tip 77: Differentiate Between Suicidal and Non-Suicidal Self-Injury

"In clinical settings, mistaking NSSI [non-suicidal self-injury] for attempted suicide can lead to unnecessary and potentially iatrogenic hospitalizations, inaccurate case conceptualization and treatment planning, and misallocation of valuable emergency resources."

E. David Klonsky and colleagues
(2013, p. 232)

Non-suicidal acts of self-injury can look like a suicide attempt. Indeed, many people who intentionally injure themselves call the act a suicide attempt, even while they acknowledge that they had no desire to die (Kessler et al., 2005). The key distinction between a suicide attempt and NSSI is the intent underlying the act. In a suicide attempt, the person has at least some intent to die, even if considerable ambivalence is present. In NSSI, the person's intent is to feel better in some way, making NSSI "a morbid form of self-help" (Favazza, 2006, p. 2284).

To assess whether the self-injury constituted NSSI or a suicide attempt, helpful questions include:

- *How much did you want to die when you hurt yourself?*
- *What did you want to happen when you hurt yourself?*
- *What did you expect to happen?*
- *How did hurting yourself help you, if at all?*

People who engage in self-harm often are confused about what their intentions were (Freedenthal, 2007). Look at both what the person says and what they did. Objective indicators of suicidal intent include taking precautions against discovery, not telling anyone after hurting oneself, making arrangements to wrap up one's affairs, and writing a suicide note (Beck et al., 1974). Don't give the absence of a suicide note too much weight, though; 60–85% of people who die by suicide do not leave a note (Callanan & Davis, 2009).

Non-suicidal and suicidal self-injury often overlap. Many people who hurt themselves without suicidal intent also have thought about or attempted suicide at some other time in their life (Muehlenkamp, 2014). Even in the absence of a suicidal history, NSSI increases suicide risk (Wilkinson, 2011). Regardless of whether the self-injury is suicidal in nature, frequent assessment of suicide risk is essential.

"It Calms Me Down"

In the privacy of his bathroom, standing over the sink, Alejandro, 15, prepared to cut his wrist. He knew it would hurt. He knew people would wonder why. But he didn't care. It did hurt the first few moments he started cutting, but soon he felt no pain. He felt only relief. Then he looked down at his wrist. The amount of blood in the bathroom sink shocked him. With his wrist wrapped in a towel, he went to the kitchen and told his mother. She took him immediately to the hospital, where the doctor stitched up his wound.

The ER social worker was concerned. She asked Alejandro, "When you cut your wrist, how much did you want to die?"

"I didn't want to die," Alejandro said. "I just wanted to feel better."

He explained that his girlfriend had broken up with him that day at school. "I couldn't stop crying," he said. "When I cut myself, it calms me down. I swear, I wasn't trying to kill myself."

The social worker believed him, but only after completing a suicide risk assessment and talking with Alejandro's mother for corroboration. Alejandro had not previously revealed any signs of suicidal thoughts or behaviors. There was no sign that he had undertaken preparations to end his life. And Alejandro did not appear to have depression or another mental disorder.

For safety planning (*Tip 38*), the social worker helped Alejandro come up with safer things he could do to relieve emotional pain, as well as places and people he could turn to for distraction and help. She also provided a referral for a psychotherapist. The ER discharged Alejandro, and he went home with his mother.

Works Cited

Beck, A. T., Schuyler, D., & Herman, I. (1974). Development of suicidal intent scales. In A. T. Beck, H. L. P. Resnik, & D. J. Lettieri (Eds.), *The prediction of suicide* (pp. 45–58). Bowie, MD: Charles Press.

Callanan, V. J., & Davis, M. S. (2009). A comparison of suicide note writers with suicides who did not leave notes. *Suicide and Life-Threatening Behavior, 39*(5), 558–568.

Favazza, A. R. (2006). Self-injurious behavior in college students. *Pediatrics, 117*(6), 2283–2284.

Freedenthal, S. (2007). Challenges in assessing intent to die: Can suicide attempters be trusted? *Omega: Journal of Death and Dying, 55*(1), 57–70.

Kessler, R. C., Berglund, P., Borges, G., Nock, M., & Wang, P. S. (2005). Trends in suicide ideation, plans, gestures, and attempts in the United States, 1990–1992 to 2001–2003. *JAMA, 293*(20), 2487–2495.

Klonsky, E. D., May, A. M., & Glenn, C. R. (2013). The relationship between nonsuicidal self-injury and attempted suicide: Converging evidence from four samples. *Journal of Abnormal Psychology, 122*(1), 231–237.

Muehlenkamp, J. J. (2014). Distinguishing between suicidal and nonsuicidal self-injury. In M. K. Nock (Ed.), *The Oxford handbook of suicide and self-injury* (pp. 23–46). Oxford: Oxford University Press.

Wilkinson, P. O. (2011). Nonsuicidal self-injury: A clear marker for suicide risk. *Journal of the American Academy of Child & Adolescent Psychiatry, 50*(8), 741–743.

Tip 78: Determine the Person's Reaction to Having Survived

"Clinical attention must be paid to the patient's perspectives on the continuation of life."

Marjan Ghahramanlou-Holloway and colleagues
(2012, p. 238)

Of all the questions to ask a person after a suicide attempt, one of the most important is, *"How do you feel about still being alive?"* This simple question has the power to identify people who are at higher risk of dying by suicide – or of making another nonfatal attempt – in the months and years following the attempt. People who attempt suicide and regret having survived are more likely to eventually die by suicide than those who are glad to be alive (Beautrais, 2004; Henriques et al., 2005). Ambivalence about survival also places someone at elevated risk for another suicide attempt (Bhaskaran et al., 2014).

Research indicates that most people who survive a suicide attempt are grateful, at least to some extent, for having survived. About 35% regret making the attempt in the first place, 43% are ambivalent, and the remaining 22% regret surviving (Henriques et al., 2005). It may seem puzzling that so many people who tried to die now appreciate life. Although evidence is mixed (Pompili et al., 2009), it is possible that a suicide attempt has some sort of cathartic effect, reconnecting the person with a desire to live. An alternative explanation is that a suicide attempt mobilizes social support (Walker et al., 2001). The expressions of caring by others can help ameliorate the suicidal person's feelings of isolation and sense of being a burden to others, enabling the person to move forward with renewed hope and resolve.

Whatever the reasons, some people regret having survived a suicide attempt, others are happy to still be alive, and still others fall between these two poles. It behooves you to learn which stance applies to your client.

"I Wish My Husband Never Found Me"

Juanita, 55, lay curled in a ball in her hospital bed, her eyes glassy as she stared at the psychiatrist in the chair next to her. The psychiatrist had all sorts of questions about her suicide attempt the night before. Lying in the intensive care unit, Juanita dispassionately answered all of his inquiries in a weak monotone – until he asked the next question.

"So, how do you feel about being alive?" he asked.

Juanita came alive. She sat up in bed and looked the psychiatrist in the eye. "To be honest, I'm furious. I took those pills because I wanted to die. And then I woke up in a hospital room with a tube down my throat. I wish my husband never found me."

"You're pretty clear that you still want to be dead," the psychiatrist said. "Is there also any part of you that's glad to be alive?"

She didn't hesitate. "No, there really isn't. If I could, I would kill myself right now. But they gave me a baby sitter." She pointed to the aide sitting in a chair by the door of her room. "He's watching everything I do. Besides, there's not really anything here I could use to kill myself."

Based on Juanita's recent attempt, continuing suicidal ideation, and regret about her survival, it was clear to the psychiatrist that Juanita was still a danger to herself. He told the attending physician, who agreed and recommended transfer to the inpatient psychiatric unit once Juanita was medically cleared.

Works Cited

Beautrais, A. L. (2004). Further suicidal behavior among medically serious suicide attempters. *Suicide and Life-Threatening Behavior, 34*(1), 1–11.

Bhaskaran, J., Wang, Y., Roos, L., Sareen, J., Skakum, K., & Bolton, J. M. (2014). Method of suicide attempt and reaction to survival as predictors of repeat suicide attempts: A longitudinal analysis. *Journal of Clinical Psychiatry, 75*(8), e802–e808.

Ghahramanlou-Holloway, M., Cox, D. W., & Greene, F. N. (2012). Post-admission cognitive therapy: A brief intervention for psychiatric inpatients admitted after a suicide attempt. *Cognitive and Behavioral Practice, 19*(2), 233–244.

Henriques, G., Wenzel, A., Brown, G. K., & Beck, A. T. (2005). Suicide attempters' reaction to survival as a risk factor for eventual suicide. *American Journal of Psychiatry, 162*(11), 2180–2182.

Pompili, M., Innamorati, M., Del Casale, A., Serafini, G., Forte, A., Lester, D., ... & Girardi, P. (2009). No cathartic effect in suicide attempters admitted to the emergency department. *Journal of Psychiatric Practice, 15*(6), 433–441.

Walker, R. L., Joiner, T. E., Jr., & Rudd, M. D. (2001). The course of post-crisis suicidal symptoms: How and for whom is suicide cathartic? *Suicide & Life-Threatening Behavior, 31*(2), 144–152.

Tip 79: Conduct a Chain Analysis

"The ability to analyze our own behavior allows us to determine what causes it and what maintains it."

Marsha Linehan
(2015b, p. 143)

A behavioral chain analysis breaks down any problem behavior into distinct, sequential parts that each represent links of a chain. In the context of suicidality, the clinician and client scrutinize in fine detail the thoughts, emotions, warning signs, and events leading up to a suicidal crisis. The chain analysis can reveal why the attempt occurred, by illuminating the triggers, functions, and reinforcements of suicidal behavior. The chain analysis also can reveal what the person needs to do differently to avoid another suicide attempt.

In its simplest form, a behavioral chain analysis involves asking the person to walk you through the exact sequence of events between the trigger for their suicidal behavior and then everything that ensued between that moment and the suicide attempt. If the person can't identify a trigger at first, ask them to go backwards from the suicide attempt, identifying every link in the chain until they are able to reach the point at which, during this acute episode, they first thought about attempting suicide.

You might choose to invoke the image of a show: *"Imagine that we're watching what happened to you as if it were a movie or play. Tell me everything that we would see happen, and what the character is thinking and feeling with each step."* Ask the person to get as specific as possible. Links in the chain can be any thought, emotion, behavior, physical feelings, or event in the environment (Linehan, 2015a). Key prompts and follow-up questions are those that will help the person identify every possible piece of the chain: *"What did you think, feel, or do after that? ... Then what happened? ... What next? ..."*

More formally, in dialectical behavior therapy (DBT), a chain analysis involves eight steps for the person to complete (Linehan, 2015a, pp. 21–22):

1.   The person specifies the problem behavior to analyze. (In this case, a suicide attempt.)
2.   The person identifies the event that prompted the chain of behaviors leading to the suicide attempt.
3.   The person explains what increased their vulnerability to attempting suicide. This can include physical illness, substance use, stressful external events, intense emotions, and so on.
4.   The person describes in highly specific detail each link in the chain between the prompting event and the suicide attempt.
5.   The person analyzes the consequences of the suicide attempt.
6.   The person identifies what they could have done differently at each link in the chain to avoid attempting suicide.

7. The person strategizes about ways to reduce their vulnerability to suicidal behavior.
8. Where applicable, the person attends to negative consequences of the problem behavior.

Whether you teach the person the informal or formal technique of behavioral chain analysis, the end results should be the same: A keen understanding of the events, thoughts, and feelings leading up to the suicide attempt; of the positive and negative consequences; of obstacles to healthier solutions; and of constructive ways for the person to respond in the future.

"I Started Thinking of the Vicodin I Have..."

Desiree, 44, often had suicidal thoughts in the previous two months, but she never came close to acting on them. Thursday night was different. Out of nowhere, it seemed, she suddenly felt stricken. She *had* to do it. *Tonight.* Within 15 minutes, she had downed a handful of pain killers.

"Walk me through that, OK?" her psychiatrist said three days later. "I want to understand the sequence of events that led to your taking those pills. First, what do you think happened that made you want to kill yourself that night?"

"I'm not really sure," Desiree told him. "It just came on suddenly."

"It can be hard to remember the details, can't it?" the psychiatrist said. "Well, what were you doing immediately before?"

"I was watching a movie," Desiree said.

"Where were you? What were you watching?"

"I was at home, on the sofa, watching *When Harry Met Sally.*" Desiree paused, then started crying. "I'd forgotten…. It was at the part where she said she's almost 40 … in 8 years. And she said something about it being a deadline. Like, oh my God, her life was over if she wasn't married by the time she's 40."

"Then what did you think?"

"I thought, well I'm 44, and I'm still single. So I'm a loser."

"You're doing a really good job remembering and painting a picture of what happened," the psychiatrist said. "So you're sitting on the sofa alone, having this really painful thought that you're a loser because you're single. Then what?"

"I just started crying. I felt so lonely. So unloved. And unlovable, really," Desiree said.

"You were really in a dark place. Then what happened?"

"I started thinking of the Vicodin I have left over from when I broke my ankle."

There was a missing link. The psychiatrist leaned forward in his chair. "What happened between feeling sad and lonely, and then thinking of getting the pills?"

"I don't know," Desiree said. "I guess I just had the thought that this is the way I'm going to be forever. Nobody will ever love me. I mean, no one has yet. And this is the way I'm always going to be. A lonely loser."

"And you decided you didn't want that for yourself?"

"Exactly," Desiree said. "I thought it would be better to end it."

"So then what happened?"

In time, as the psychiatrist continued prompting Desiree for specific details about what she thought, did, or felt next, Desiree described the different links in the chain. What she revealed provided the basis for her to consider the places where she could have soothed herself, challenged her self-talk, reached out for help, or otherwise reacted differently to her mind's indictments. The chain analysis also cast light on what made it difficult for Desiree to do those things, and what she could do in the future to avoid another suicide attempt.

Works Cited

Linehan, M. M. (2015a). *DBT skills training handouts and worksheets* (2nd ed.). New York, NY: Guilford Press.

Linehan, M. M. (2015b). *DBT skills training manual* (2nd ed.). New York, NY: Guilford Press.

Tip 80: Evaluate Where the Safety Plan Fell Short

"Remember, the recurrence of suicidal behavior is always labeled as an opportunity to investigate what worked and what did not work with a specific problem."

John Chiles and Kirk Strosahl
(2005, p. 113)

If the person who attempted suicide had a safety plan already (*Tip 38*), the plan obviously fell short. It either missed important actions to take or contained options that were difficult for the person to carry out. Potential obstacles include feelings of hopelessness, lack of motivation, or simply a desire to not be stopped from suicide. While being careful not to appear blaming, seek to understand what thwarted the person from following their plan to stay safe. Ideally, this exploration will reveal how the safety plan needs to be modified.

"I Was Too Far Gone"

After Malik, 20, wrote down his safety plan, he folded it into his wallet so that he always carried it around. It was a good plan. It included things he could do to distract himself, like go for a run or watch YouTube videos of his favorite comedian, as well as people he could call or spend time with. But a few weeks later, suicidal urges overwhelmed him, and he did none of the things on his safety plan. Instead, he attempted suicide.

A few days later, his counselor at the university counseling center wanted to understand why. "Is it that the safety plan missed something important, or was it hard for you to follow, or was it something else?" she asked Malik.

"Everything on the plan seemed so small compared to what I was going through," Malik said. "When you're having these super strong thoughts of killing yourself, watching Louis Black on YouTube just isn't going to cut it."

"I can see why you'd feel that way," the counselor said. "It might seem sort of like trying to put out a fire with a squirt gun. Yet you can't really know it won't help if you don't try it out, can you?"

"I guess not," Malik said.

"And let's play this out and assume that you tried out all of the things to distract yourself but they didn't help. What about the next steps, like calling someone or spending time with someone? One of the things on the plan was to call me. I want to be clear, I'm not angry or judging you. Really, I'm curious and want to understand."

"I know," Malik said. "Honestly, I thought nobody could help me. I was too far gone."

"That's important for us to know," the counselor said. "What would make it easier to call me or someone else when you feel so hopeless?"

Malik said he thought it would help him if he talked with his mother and girlfriend in advance about what they should say and do (and *not* say and do) if he called them in a suicidal crisis. As for his counselor, he told her he was scared she would try to hospitalize him against his will. She reiterated that hospitalization would be the last choice, something she wanted him to avoid as much as he did. Instead, she told him, she would problem-solve with him on the phone about additional ways he could resist suicidal urges and stay safe.

Malik ended up not changing his safety plan. It was a good plan. What changed, at least for now, was his resolve to follow the plan if suicidal thoughts came again.

Work Cited

Chiles, J. A., & Strosahl, K. D. (2005). *Clinical manual for assessment and treatment of suicidal patients.* Washington, DC: American Psychiatric Publishing.

Tip 81: Take Advantage of the "Teachable Moment"

"What more teachable moment exists in life than the one in which a suicidal person is trying to decide between life and death?"

Paul Quinnett

(2007, p. 24)

A "teachable moment" is the brief window of opportunity when a person's receptiveness to change is heightened (Lawson & Flocke, 2009). The immediate aftermath of a suicide attempt often is one of those times. The psychologist Stephen O'Connor and colleagues note that surviving a suicide attempt can "increase an individual's emotional state, sharpen perceptions regarding risks and positive outcomes associated with personal choices, and add clarity to social role and self-concept, such as 'I am a spouse, father, and/or son'" (O'Connor et al., 2015, p. 428). This heightened awareness, in turn, can increase the motivation to change.

To take advantage of this especially fertile time, O'Connor (2015) developed an intervention called the Teachable Moment Brief Intervention. While it emphasizes first building rapport and finishing with a crisis response plan, the core part of the intervention calls for examining in depth the person's suicide attempt and suicidality.

The clinician explores first what led the person to attempt suicide, then the motivations underlying the suicide attempt. When people attempt suicide, death is often only one of several objectives. Other reasons might include escaping unbearable pain in the moment, communicating distress or anger to others, taking control of the situation, and more. Examining the person's relationship with suicide illuminates how attached the person has become to fantasizing or planning their death.

Next, the intervention pays attention to the attempt survivor's view of the positive and negative consequences of their attempt. Often, professionals gravitate only toward the negative consequences without recognizing that the person might also gain something from a suicide attempt. Be careful not to focus excessively on the positives consequences, but do seek to understand them both because these gains could reinforce suicidal behavior, and because they point to the need to problem-solve around healthy ways to achieve the same results.

After helping the person to develop a crisis response plan (also called a safety plan; see *Tip 38*), the Teachable Moment Brief Intervention concludes with you providing a summary of key points and returning the focus to the present moment. Convey the importance of the choices that lie ahead and provide any relevant information and referrals. O'Connor (2015) writes: "Accentuate the patient's choice to view this situation as either a steppingstone or a gravestone" (p. 11).

Preliminary evidence for the Teachable Moment Brief Intervention is promising. In a randomized controlled trial, people who received the intervention experienced greater improvements in readiness to change and reasons for living than those in the control group (O'Connor et al., 2015). Whether one uses the formal intervention designed for a teachable moment or explores the aftermath of a suicide attempt in a less structured way, it is a time to seize the opportunity for lasting change.

"Has Anything Been Gained?"

To examine losses and gains following a suicide attempt, O'Connor (2015) gives the example of someone admitted to the hospital following an intentional overdose, who laments that they might lose their housing as a result of attempting suicide. The clinician empathizes and then probes for crucial information: "I'm wondering what else has been lost and gained from your perspective." The person describes damage to friendships as another loss, and the clinician asks, "Has anything been gained?" The person states that the suicide attempt offered a temporary respite from mental pain. On reflection, the person decides that far more was lost than gained, a realization that can awaken motivation to change.

Works Cited

Lawson, P. J., & Flocke, S. A. (2009). Teachable moments for health behavior change: A concept analysis. *Patient Education and Counseling, 76*(1), 25–30.

O'Connor, S. S. (2015). The teachable moment brief intervention. Unpublished manuscript. University of Louisville.

O'Connor, S. S., Comtois, K. A., Wang, J., Russo, J., Peterson, R., Lapping-Carr, L., & Zatzick, D. (2015). The development and implementation of a brief intervention for medically admitted suicide attempt survivors. *General Hospital Psychiatry, 37*(5), 427–433.

Quinnett, P. (2007). *QPR gatekeeper training for suicide prevention: The model, rationale and theory.* Spokane, WA: QPR Institute.

Tip 82: Attend to the Therapeutic Relationship

"Reestablishing the therapeutic alliance after a client's suicide attempt can be particularly challenging when the attempt brings on emotional reactions that strain the relationship."

Jenny Cureton and Elysia Clemens

(2015, p. 355)

The aftermath of a client's suicide attempt can unleash many emotions, for both you and the client. Common reactions among professionals include anger, disbelief, guilt, sadness, nervousness, helplessness, betrayal, and self-doubt (Scocco et al., 2012). The person who attempted suicide might harbor negative feelings about you, too. The person might blame you for failing to help them heal and thereby prevent the suicide attempt. Alternatively, they might be scared that you will express anger or disappointment.

These emotional responses on both sides of the helping relationship can threaten the therapeutic alliance. Explore the person's feelings toward you and the therapeutic alliance. If the person discloses negative reactions, then respond non-defensively and maintain a stance of curiosity.

Sometimes, mental health professionals' negative responses to a person's suicide attempt cause them to reject the person (Ramsay & Newman, 2005). For example, some clinicians believe that a suicide attempt shows that the treatment is not working, so they require the person to see someone else. These clinicians might have good intentions when arriving at this decision, but often, they simply are afraid. They do not want a suicide on their watch. If they end the watch, the problem is solved – for them, but not for their client.

A suicide attempt is not reason enough for the professional to unilaterally end treatment. The psychologists Russell Ramsay and Cory Newman (2005) identify three scenarios in which a clinician's termination of treatment following a person's suicide attempt is ethical and appropriate. (1) New clinical information indicates the person needs a different or more intensive type of treatment that the clinician cannot provide, such as substance use treatment. (2) The suicide attempt represents a pattern of behaviors that "maintain an unhealthy dependency on a given therapist" (p. 415) and the person is getting worse as a result. (3) The person has done something that threatens the clinician's safety. Even when a legitimate need to end treatment with the person exists, be sure to find a new provider or agency where the person can be seen soon, to avoid abandoning the client.

Fortunately, in most cases there is no need to end the therapeutic relationship after a suicide attempt (Ramsay & Newman, 2005). Still, to shore up trust in the process for both you and the suicidal person, the treatment plan and ground rules for therapy may require some revision. Setting forth new expectations might include, for example, requiring the person to allow you to talk with their significant other even though they previously refused, or insisting that the person attend therapy more reliably.

As your treatment with the person resumes, an important step toward managing your emotional responses is to be aware of them (*Tip 4*). Talk about your anger, fear, or other emotions with a colleague or consultant (*Tip 43*). Depending on the context and content, it would be appropriate to share your reactions with the client only if the purpose is to meet their needs, not your own (e.g., *"Your suicide attempt scares me. I care about you and want to see you get better, not dead. How much does your suicide attempt scare you?"*) A stance of compassion and acceptance can deepen the attempt survivor's trust in you and provide a model that they can extend to themselves.

"Do You Want Me to Not Come In Anymore?"

In the memoir *Waking Up*, Terry Wise (2012) poignantly recounts when she took a nearly fatal overdose of medication. Her psychologist, Betsy Glaser, describes her reaction when Terry told her of the suicide attempt:

> When Terry told me that she had tried to kill herself, the world went white. At the moment of impact, I was overwhelmed and bombarded by emotion. All of my feelings were intensified – rage, inadequacy, sadness, concern – and they continued to buzz in my ears long after Terry had left my office.
>
> (Glaser, cited in Wise, 2012, p. 233)

Meanwhile, Terry experienced fear of rejection and rebuke by her therapist. "Do you want me not to come in anymore?" she asked Dr. Glaser. She goes on to write:

> I braced myself, waiting for her to tell me that our trust had been irreparably destroyed and that she could no longer treat me.
> "Do you really think you are worth that little?"
> "Yes," I murmured, awestruck by her response. ... I would *never* forget the reassuring implication that I was still worth something to her.
>
> (p. 126)

This raw exchange, along with Dr. Glaser's description of her reaction, captures the turbulent emotions that can follow a suicide attempt, for both the professional and the attempt survivor. And it brings into sharp focus the need to respond to the suicide attempt survivor with acceptance and compassion.

Works Cited

Cureton, J. L., & Clemens, E. V. (2015). Affective constellations for countertransference awareness following a client's suicide attempt. *Journal of Counseling & Development, 93*(3), 352–360.

Ramsay, J. R., & Newman, C. F. (2005). After the attempt: Maintaining the therapeutic alliance following a patient's suicide attempt. *Suicide and Life-Threatening Behavior, 35*(4), 413–424.

Scocco, P., Toffol, E., Pilotto, E., & Pertile, R. (2012). Psychiatrists' emotional reactions to patient suicidal behavior. *Journal of Psychiatric Practice, 18*(2), 94–108.

Wise, T. L. (2012). *Waking up: Climbing through the darkness*. N.P: The Missing Peace, LLC.

Tip 83: Address the Trauma of the Suicide Attempt

"Bear in the mind that the person who survives a suicide attempt has escaped attempted murder."

John Maltsberger and colleagues
(2011, p. 672)

A suicide attempt is obviously a threat to one's life. To experience such violence against the self can lead to post-traumatic responses. Although little research has addressed the topic, one small study found that 46% of people who attempted suicide experienced post-traumatic stress disorder (PTSD) specifically as a result of the attempt (Bill et al., 2012). In addition to physical violence to one's body, the internal experiences leading up to the suicide attempt also can be traumatic.

To address this trauma, basic education about common responses to trauma can help an attempt survivor to make sense of their moods, emotions, and behaviors. Educate the person about the traumatic nature of their ordeal, the physical and emotional toll that trauma can take, and the previous trauma that it can revive. Going over the *DSM* (American Psychiatric Association, 2013) criteria for PTSD with the person shows how common such responses can be.

There are many evidence-based interventions for trauma to draw from, such as trauma-focused cognitive behavior therapy, prolonged exposure therapy, and EMDR (eye movement desensitization and reprocessing therapy). It is beyond the scope of this book to describe these strategies. First, in the context of a suicide attempt, it is necessary to recognize that trauma therapy might be needed at all.

"I Should Be Over It"

Almost every night, Fatima is subjected to the same horror. She stands at the top of a three-story parking garage, dreading the sensation of hitting the pavement below. Sometimes a stranger pushes her. Sometimes a vicious slice of wind knocks her over. And sometimes she jumps. Each time, she awakens from the nightmare before her body lands, but the terror leading up to it is itself excruciating.

These dreams embarrass Fatima. "I'm weak," she tells her counselor. "I should be over it." She is 20. It has been seven months since she jumped from the fourth story of the parking garage on her university campus and shattered both her legs, requiring repeated surgeries that left her with metal plates and screws in her bones.

Her counselor educates her about the nature of post-traumatic stress, emphasizing the fact that her body and mind's response to trauma is beyond her control. That is, the nightmares are not a matter of "weakness." They are not her fault. He assesses her symptoms based on DSM criteria and discovers that in addition to re-experiencing the trauma of her suicide attempt in nightmares, she is also experiencing symptoms of avoidance, hyperarousal, and cognitive and emotional changes related to the trauma. The counselor believes that Fatima would benefit from EMDR. He is not trained in this modality, so he refers her to a colleague for adjunctive therapy. He will continue to see Fatima for therapy, and he will stay in contact with the EMDR therapist about their sessions. He has hope that, soon, Fatima will be able to sleep through the night without reliving the day she almost died.

Works Cited

American Psychiatric Association. (2013). *Diagnostic and statistical manual of mental disorders (DSM-5)*. Washington, DC: American Psychiatric Publishing.

Bill, B., Ipsch, L., Lucae, S., Pfister, H., Maragkos, M., Ising, M., & Bronisch, T. (2012). Attempted suicide related posttraumatic stress disorder in depression: An exploratory study. *Suicidology Online, 3*, 138–144.

Maltsberger, J. T., Goldblatt, M. J., Ronningstam, E., Weinberg, I., & Schechter, M. (2011). Traumatic subjective experiences invite suicide. *The Journal of the American Academy of Psychoanalysis and Dynamic Psychiatry, 39*(4), 671–693.

Tip 84: Explore Shame and Stigma

"Informed by traditional socio-cultural understandings of suicide as indicative of deviance, insanity and overall questionable integrity, the moral discourse constructs suicidal acts as a signifier of personal failure."

Sara Bennett and colleagues
(2003, p. 294)

People who think of suicide often experience shame as a result (e.g., Ganzini et al., 2013). These feelings can become even more pronounced after a suicide attempt. It is not uncommon for people who have survived a suicide attempt to describe feelings of being a failure, both for attempting suicide and for having survived (Wiklander et al., 2012). Many also experience shame and guilt about having lost control. "You are a loser, indeed, if you try to commit suicide...," one suicide attempt survivor said (as quoted in Vatne & Nåden, 2012, p. 309).

The negative judgments that some suicide attempt survivors reserve for themselves can mirror the biases of others. For example, researchers asked undergraduates if they would date somebody who had attempted suicide in the previous year (Lester & Walker, 2006). Half the students said no. Many suicide attempt survivors who receive hospital care for their injuries encounter hostile, disdainful attitudes among physicians, nurses, and other hospital staff (Saunders et al., 2012). In one study, an attempt survivor recounted how he needed a blood transfusion after a suicide attempt, and the physician told him "that I was wasting blood that was meant for patients after they'd had operations or accident victims. He asked whether I was proud of what I'd done..." (Brophy, 2006, p. 50).

The shame experienced by suicide attempt survivors can create a vicious cycle. Even before a suicide attempt ever occurs, feelings of shame can catalyze a suicide attempt (Wiklander et al., 2012). The suicide attempt then generates more shame, which then can increase risk for another suicide attempt. This makes it especially important to probe for and address feelings of shame specific to the suicide attempt.

"I Was So Stupid"

In the days after he attempted suicide, Viktor hid. He called in sick to his job. He refused calls from his mother and his brothers. He almost skipped his appointment with his therapist, but instinct forced him to go. After exploring various aspects of his suicide attempt with him, the therapist, a clinical social worker, said, "Some people who attempt suicide then feel bad about themselves for attempting suicide. Does that fit for you, too?"

Viktor, 59, covered his face with his hands as sobs escaped him. "Yes, all it did was make things worse. I was so stupid," he said. "To be honest, this is hard to admit. But I'm so ashamed."

This opened the door to an exploration of Viktor's negative judgments stemming from his suicide attempt. His therapist listened reflectively, validated his emotions, and conveyed empathy. Once she truly understood, she challenged him to consider whether he blames people who get pneumonia, cancer, or other "physical" illnesses. He said no.

"Is there a reason you blame the suicide attempt on yourself instead of your illness?" she asked, alluding to his longstanding bipolar disorder.

"I hadn't thought of it that way," he said.

"Let me ask you another question. You love and care about your husband. If he had bipolar disorder and attempted suicide while he was depressed and hurting, would you blame him?"

"No," Viktor said. "I see what you're getting at. I would tell him it wasn't his fault."

It helped Viktor to blame his illness, instead of himself. He still felt a sense of shame, but he was able to talk back to it. The next week he told his therapist, "I tell myself, it's not my fault. Blame the bipolar disorder. And then, that's what I do."

Works Cited

Bennett, S., Coggan, C., & Adams, P. (2003). Problematising depression: Young people, mental health and suicidal behaviours. *Social Science & Medicine, 57*(2), 289–299.

Brophy, M. (2006). *Truth hurts: Report of the National Inquiry into Self-harm among young people: Fact or fiction?* London: Mental Health Foundation. Retrieved January 30, 2017, from www.mentalhealth.org.uk/sites/default/files/truth_hurts.pdf.

Ganzini, L., Denneson, L. M., Press, N., Bair, M. J., Helmer, D. A., Poat, J., & Dobscha, S. K. (2013). Trust is the basis for effective suicide risk screening and assessment in veterans. *Journal of General Internal Medicine, 28*(9), 1215–1221.

Lester, D., & Walker, R. L. (2006). The stigma for attempting suicide and the loss to suicide prevention efforts. *Crisis: The Journal of Crisis Intervention and Suicide Prevention, 27*(3), 147–148.

Saunders, K. E., Hawton, K., Fortune, S., & Farrell, S. (2012). Attitudes and knowledge of clinical staff regarding people who self-harm: A systematic review. *Journal of Affective Disorders, 139*(3), 205–216.

Vatne, M., & Nåden, D. (2012). Finally, it became too much: Experiences and reflections in the aftermath of attempted suicide. *Scandinavian Journal of Caring Sciences, 26*(2), 304–312.

Wiklander, M., Samuelsson, M., Jokinen, J., Nilsonne, Å., Wilczek, A., Rylander, G., & Åsberg, M. (2012). Shame-proneness in attempted suicide patients. *BMC Psychiatry, 12*(50), 1–9.

fifteen
Building
Resilience

Tip 85: Warn about the Possibility of Relapse

"Once suicidal thoughts have emerged as a feature of depression then they are likely to be reactivated whenever sad mood reappears."

Isaac Sakinofsky
(2010, p. 299)

For many people, suicidal thoughts come through a door that, once opened, never fully closes. Even after recovery, having thought about suicide makes a person vulnerable to suicidal thoughts trespassing again. For example, in a 20-year longitudinal study of boys and young men, only one-third of people who reported suicidal ideation in one year never reported it again (Kerr et al., 2008). Worse still, the more that door is opened, the easier it becomes for suicidal thoughts to re-emerge (Rudd, 2000; Lau et al., 2004).

To help the person prepare, gently let the person know that sometimes – though not always – suicidal thoughts recur. Warning the person about the possibility of relapse creates a natural segue for strategizing about what to do if suicidal thoughts do return. Such a discussion can also help inoculate the person against feelings of failure.

Even so, do not paint a grim picture. Not everyone who recovers from a suicidal crisis finds themselves there again. And people who do find themselves there again often have new knowledge and tools to help get them through the ordeal. This is one reason why it's important to help the person review lessons learned, consolidate gains, and think through what to do in the event of relapse, which are the topics of the next two tips.

"You Think I Will Fall Apart Again"

It took four months for Annabelle, 16, to want to live again. Those four months were hell, and now she is terrified of ever going to that awful place in her head again. So, Annabelle felt devastated when her psychiatrist said to her, "This might not happen to you, but suicidal thoughts do come back for some people if they get to a place again where they're sad or depressed."

"It better not happen to me," Annabelle said. "I don't ever want to feel that way again. Ever."

"Well let's talk about that," the psychiatrist said. "You're a lot stronger now than you were four months ago. You've learned a lot. What I'd like to do next is go over what you've learned and what you can do differently if suicidal thoughts do come again."

"But that makes it seem like you think I'm going to fall apart again," Annabelle said.

"That's not it," the psychiatrist said. He paused for a moment as he searched for his words. "Have you flown on a plane before?"

Annabelle nodded.

"You know how the flight attendants tell you how to use the oxygen mask and flotation device in case there's an accident? That doesn't mean the flight attendants think the plane will crash. But they want people to know what to do if it does. And that's what I want for you."

The analogy made sense to Annabelle and gave her some comfort. She understood that her plane wasn't destined to crash, but if it did, she should know what to do to survive.

Works Cited

Kerr, D. C., Owen, L. D., Pears, K. C., & Capaldi, D. M. (2008). Prevalence of suicidal ideation among boys and men assessed annually from ages 9 to 29 years. *Suicide and Life-Threatening Behavior, 38*(4), 390–402.

Lau, M. A., Segal, Z. V., & Williams, J. M. G. (2004). Teasdale's differential activation hypothesis: Implications for mechanisms of depressive relapse and suicidal behaviour. *Behaviour Research and Therapy, 42*(9), 1001–1017.

Rudd, M. D. (2000). The suicidal mode: A cognitive-behavioral model of suicidality. *Suicide and Life-Threatening Behavior, 30*(1), 18–33.

Sakinofsky, I. (2010). Evidence-based approaches for reducing suicide risk in major affective disorders. In M. Pompili & R. Tatarelli (Eds.), *Evidence-based practice in suicidology* (pp. 275–316). Göttingen: Hogrefe.

Tip 86: Review Lessons Learned

"A common theme in the experience of persons who have experienced major life challenges is an increased sense of their own capacities to survive and prevail."

Richard Tedeschi and colleagues
(2015, p. 503)

Life is often a cruel teacher, but there is value in the lessons learned. To help consolidate this new knowledge, the psychiatrist John Chiles and psychologist Kirk Strosahl (2005) recommend guiding the person to develop a "suicide prevention plan," in which the person reflects on various questions in case another crisis occurs (p. 126):

- *"What are my most important goals for the next year?"*
- *"What stresses do I anticipate in the next year, both ongoing and new, and how do I plan to cope with them?"*
- *"What are the most valuable ideas I have learned in treatment up to now, and how do I plan to remember them?"*
- *"What are the most valuable coping strategies I have learned in treatment, and how and when do I plan to use them?"*
- *"What hurdles might occur that would get in the way of using these coping strategies, and how would I overcome them (e.g., too tired to cope, get down on myself for having problems)?"*

Chiles and Strosahl's "suicide prevention plan" is essentially a reflection or informal dialogue. The next tip describes a relapse prevention protocol that takes more time and brings with it more depth and structure (Wenzel et al., 2009).

A Bumper Sticker's Words of Wisdom

If Gus, a 45-year-old construction worker, learned one thing from his recent struggle with suicidal thoughts, it was this: He could endure unfathomable suffering and come out on the other side. Five months earlier, he nearly died from his suicide attempt. Now, with newfound hope, stability, and coping skills, he was grateful to be alive. He looked forward to spending time with his three-year-old nephew, tending to his garden, and taking his Bernese mountain dog for long walks in his tree-lined neighborhood and in the nearby Blue Ridge Mountains. He knew that life would not magically be problem-free. He would need to remain vigilant for signs that his longtime nemesis, depression, was making a return. This meant watching out for the return of insomnia, irritability, and obsessive thoughts about his shortcomings. Should those occur, he would heed them as signs to take better care of himself: Go to his psychiatrist for a possible change in medication, exercise more, eat better, reach out to friends. If suicidal thoughts reasserted themselves, he would review his coping statements, go through his hope box, re-read his list of reasons to live, and pull out his safety plan, just in case. Most of all, he would remind himself of an important lesson he had learned, pithy words of advice he first had seen on a bumper sticker, of all places: "If you're going through hell, keep going."

Works Cited

Chiles, J. A., & Strosahl, K. D. (2005). *Clinical manual for assessment and treatment of suicidal patients.* Washington, DC: American Psychiatric Publishing.

Tedeschi, R. G., Calhoun, L. G., & Groleau, J. M. (2015). Clinical applications of posttraumatic growth. In S. Joseph (Ed.), *Positive psychology in practice: Promoting human flourishing in work, health, education, and everyday life* (2nd ed.; pp. 503–518). Hoboken, NJ: John Wiley & Sons.

Wenzel, A., Brown, G. K., & Beck, A. T. (2009). *Cognitive therapy for suicidal patients: Scientific and clinical applications.* Washington, DC: American Psychological Association.

Tip 87: Complete a Relapse Prevention Protocol

"The relapse prevention protocol was developed specifically for suicidal patients to demonstrate to their therapist and to themselves that they can successfully apply the skills they have acquired in treatment."

Amy Wenzel and Shari Jager-Hyman
(2012, p. 128)

The relapse prevention protocol involves a series of guided imagery exercises in which you guide the person to describe in minute detail three different situations (Wenzel et al., 2009):

1. The situation in which the person attempted suicide or felt most suicidal.
2. The same situation, with the person noting what they could have done differently, based on lessons learned subsequently.
3. A future situation in which suicidal thinking might recur, with the person envisioning how they will apply their new coping skills.

Revisiting the situation or internal state that prompted suicidal urges can understandably upset the individual. This is why, before the guided imagery exercises begin, you should describe the process to the person, provide the rationale, assure the person that you will help them get through it, and explicitly ask for their permission to move forward (Wenzel et al., 2009). Problem-solve together about what to do if the person deteriorates during the relapse prevention exercise. For example, one option is to take a break. Another option is to stop reviewing the prior crisis and look only at the hypothetical future crisis. Some people choose not to participate in the relapse prevention protocol. If your client rejects it, then informally review together the coping skills and knowledge that the person can apply to crises in the future (*Tip 86*).

To begin the first guided imagery, the suicidal person is asked to vividly recount the events, thoughts, and emotions leading up to the recent suicide attempt or suicidal crisis, using the present tense as if it were happening now. The psychologist Amy Wenzel and colleagues (2009) give this example with a person who attempted suicide:

> I would like you to close your eyes and think about the day that you made the suicide attempt. I would like you to imagine the point in time just before the event that seemed to trigger the sequence of events that led to the attempt. Picture in your mind what happened on that day, and describe these events and your reactions to these events to me as if you were watching a movie of yourself.

(Wenzel et al., 2009, p. 204)

Similar to a behavior chain analysis (*Tip 79*), the guided imagery exercises call for you to coax very specific and evocative memories from the person. Questions are asked in the present tense but they apply to the remembered event: *"Then what happens?" "What do you do next?" "What thoughts run through your mind?" "What emotions do you feel?"*

The second guided imagery exercise goes much like the first, except that this time the person mentally rehearses applying the skills and insights that they have learned. You can prompt the person to invoke these skills with various questions: *"Picture yourself thinking of other options right now. What might those be?" "Picture yourself using your safety plan right now. What does it say?" "How else might you solve the problem?"* (Wenzel et al., 2009, p. 207). Ask the person to anticipate obstacles to using their new skills and safety plan, and to describe how they would work around those obstacles.

Finally, in the third guided imagery exercise, the person identifies a stressful scenario coming up and describes how they will safely resist suicidal urges, should those emerge. Again, ask the person how likely it is that they will use their new coping skills and invite the person to brainstorm how to increase that likelihood.

After each guided imagery exercise, explore the person's emotions about their suicidal episode and the reliving of it, or about the prospect that they might fall into a suicidal crisis again. This is also a time to assess current suicidal ideation. If completing the relapse prevention protocol destabilizes the person significantly or exposes areas where more work is needed, the treatment plan should change accordingly. Otherwise, the person's ability to draw from coping skills can help you decide whether it is appropriate to shift the focus in therapy from suicide prevention to some other topic, or to conclude therapy altogether.

Old Pain, Fresh Realizations

Raj, 82, felt nervous. He did not particularly want to "go there" – to revisit the night in the nursing home when he retrieved his stash of sleeping pills from the black sock in his dresser drawer and swallowed all of them at once. But the hospital social worker said it could help him, and he trusted her, so he went along with it. His nervousness was well founded: It was indeed upsetting when he described his experience that night, moment by moment. He felt in his gut the same sense of desperation that had overwhelmed him then: The feeling of being trapped in this institution, of missing his wife of 49 years, of having nothing to look forward to. In the reliving of those feelings, he also saw holes in his thinking at the time. He recognized that his feelings were not necessarily facts, and where they were true, he could mindfully observe his pain, reach out to other residents or staff for help, and remind himself of his reasons for staying alive.

He thought he could be of use to others where he lived. Help them. Listen. Be there for those without regular visitors. Though he was nearing the end of his life, though he had lost his wife, his home, and his independence, he felt with conviction that his life still had meaning. His coping statements reflected this: *"There's a reason you're still here." "Life is meant to be lived." "Wait until your time comes."* By reminding himself of these essential truths, by asking staff for help, and by repeating his coping statements like a mantra, he could bear the desperation that he feared would return during late nights alone in his room, and he could stay alive.

Works Cited

Wenzel, A., & Jager-Hyman, S. (2012). Cognitive therapy for suicidal patients: Current status. *The Behavior Therapist, 35*(7), 121–130.

Wenzel, A., Brown, G. K., & Beck, A. T. (2009). *Cognitive therapy for suicidal patients: Scientific and clinical applications.* Washington, DC: American Psychological Association.

Tip 88: Propose a Letter to the Suicidal Self

"Compassionate letter writing can be an extremely powerful, emotional, and beneficial exercise."

Mary Welford
(2013, p. 197)

Wisdom hard-earned during a crisis is fluid. Often, people forget. Then, if a new crisis develops, they may find themselves locked again in darkness, unable to recall all the reasons they had for maintaining hope and rejecting suicide. A compassionate letter to their future self can help them remember (Overholser, 1998). Even if the person never looks at the letter again, the act of writing it can be a therapeutic exercise. If the person does read the letter again in a dark time, hopefully it reminds them of the light outside their view.

The content of the letter is up to the person's imagination, but if they need suggestions about what to include, here are a few ideas:

- truths the person learned the hard way about how to get through a suicidal crisis;
- reasons for hope, and for staying alive;
- the person's strengths and other good traits, which often become obscured in crisis;
- advice about how to make it through the crisis alive.

"I Am Still Here, Your Healthy Self"

Dear You,
You must be hurting awfully if you want to kill yourself again. You have been in this dark place before. Each time, you thought you would not get out. And you got out. Every time. And you were grateful.

This last time, you made important discoveries. You discovered that you do not need to be perfect; you can be "good enough." You discovered that you can watch your moods and thoughts like they are weather, always changing, without needing to control or get rid of them. You discovered that people do care about you, even when it seems like you are nothing but a burden.

You remembered that you have really cool, important reasons for living: You love traveling. You want to see the northern lights in Canada, the humpback whales off of Hawaii, the Inca ruins at Macchu Pichu. You love to read, and even if right now you can't read because it is hard to concentrate, you will read again. You love your family and friends. You might feel like they don't care about you right now, or they would be better off without you. Remember that your mind is a cruel liar when you are depressed.

You deserve to live. You are smart, funny, and loving. You help children through your work as a nurse. You are fundamentally a good person.

I am still here, your healthy self. The one that wants to live. Sometimes in the darkness, you cannot see me. But I am always present. Please remember that.

Although the above letter is fairly long and heartfelt, a letter to the suicidal self can take any shape. It can be short or long, funny or sad, poetic or pragmatic. Except in cases of verbal abuse of the self, there really is no right or wrong.

"Don't Believe It"

Hey, Jimmy. Don't do anything stupid, OK? You've been through this before and can get through it again. Just remember to pray, go to [AA] meetings, take your meds, see your doctors, take good care of yourself, and when your mind tells you it's hopeless, you'll never feel better, don't believe it. It's full of crap. When your mind tells you to keep going and never give up, believe it!

Works Cited

Overholser, J. C. (1998). Cognitive-behavioral treatment of depression, part X: Reducing the risk of relapse. *Journal of Contemporary Psychotherapy, 28*(4), 381–396.

Welford, M. (2013). *The power of self-compassion.* Oakland, CA: New Harbinger Publications.

Tip 89: Follow Up

"Systematic follow-up contacts gave the patient a feeling of being seen and heard by someone."

Alexandra Fleischmann and colleagues

(2008, p. 707)

The idea was remarkably simple: For five years, send brief "caring letters" every few months to people discharged from a psychiatric hospital, and see if these little missives can help prevent suicide. That is what Jerome Motto and Alan Bostrom (2001) did in a randomized controlled trial of 843 people who had been hospitalized for depression or suicidality. Half received the follow-up letters, and half did not. The study followed the two groups of discharged patients for 15 years and compared their suicide rates over time.

The results were most striking in the first two years following discharge. Almost twice the proportion of people (3.5%) in the no-contact group died by suicide, compared to those who received letters (1.8%). As the years went by, suicide rates among those who received letters remained lower, though not to a statistically significant degree, until finally in year 14 the rates of suicide became equal for both groups. The dramatic differences in the two years after discharge are impressive nonetheless, because that is an especially high-risk period for suicide.

Subsequent intervention studies have tried to achieve similar reductions in suicide or suicide attempts by maintaining some form of contact with people after their treatment has ended. In a review of 12 such studies, the suicide rate among those who received some communication was only 60% the rate of those who received no communication (Milner et al., 2015). These results were not statistically significant, so it is possible that the lower rates were coincidental.

At least for some people, the letters provided a sense of connection. Consider this feedback from a participant in Motto and Bostrom's study (2001, p. 832): "You will never know what your little notes mean to me. I always think someone cares about what happens to me, even if my family did kick me out. I am really grateful." Another participant wrote to the study team: "Your note gave me a warm, pleasant feeling. Just knowing someone cares means a lot."

Notably, one study looked at adverse effects of follow-up by email and postal letters and found none (Luxton et al., 2012). With some evidence that brief letters can help prevent suicide, and with no evidence that they do harm, there seems little reason for professionals to not at least extend an occasional show of concern after treatment ends.

If you choose to maintain some sort of follow-up contact, be sure that your client is on board with your plan. In your intake paperwork you can ask new clients to indicate whether it is okay for you to contact them after therapy ends. It is also important to ask them to check off which forms of communication are acceptable, including text, email, phone, or regular mail. Note on the intake form that the person can always opt-out of receiving contact from you.

A brief email might be as simple as, *"Hello [name], I am touching base to let you know I hope you are doing well. If you want to, please feel free to let me know how you are doing."* The best time and way to end communication remains to be determined. In one ongoing study, the final email will state:

> "This is officially our last email to you and we hope that you have enjoyed getting our little notes over this time. As we said in our last email, it has been a true joy for us to drop you a few lines here and there to let you know that we truly care about you and hope you are doing well. If you wish to write us and let us know how you have been doing over the years, we would be glad to hear from you."
>
> (Luxton et al., 2014, p. 257)

"Remember, I'm Here to Talk…"

In the months following her suicide attempt, Beatriz, 79, met with a pastoral counselor on a weekly basis. The counselor helped her to cope with feelings of devastation after her partner's death in a car accident. Medication helped, too. After 13 sessions, a sense of acceptance and even hopefulness had replaced the suicidal urges, so Beatriz finished therapy. A month later, Beatriz received a card from the counselor. *"Hello Beatriz,"* the counselor had hand-written. *"I wanted to touch base and see how you are doing. Remember, I'm here to talk if ever the need arises. No need to respond, but feel free to if you wish."* Beatriz was surprised. She had thought the counselor would be relieved to get her out of his hair. It felt good to know that he cared. She did not feel a need to respond, and six months later she received another such note. Thereafter, every year on her birthday, a card came from the counselor. She never did go back to see him, but it gave her comfort to know that he remembered her, and that he cared.

Works Cited

Fleischmann, A., Bertolote, J. M., Wasserman, D., De Leo, D., Bolhari, J., Botega, N. J., … & Schlebusch, L. (2008). Effectiveness of brief intervention and contact for suicide attempters: A randomized controlled trial in five countries. *Bulletin of the World Health Organization, 86*(9), 703–709.

Luxton, D. D., Kinn, J. T., June, J. D., Pierre, L. W., Reger, M. A., & Gahm, G. A. (2012). Caring letters project: A military suicide-prevention program. *Crisis, 33*(1), 5–12.

Luxton, D. D., Thomas, E. K., Chipps, J., Relova, R. M., Brown, D., McLay, R., … & Smolenski, D. J. (2014). Caring letters for suicide prevention: Implementation of a multisite randomized clinical trial in the U.S. military and veteran affairs healthcare systems. *Contemporary Clinical Trials, 37*(2), 252–260.

Milner, A. J., Carter, G., Pirkis, J., Robinson, J., & Spittal, M. J. (2015). Letters, green cards, telephone calls and postcards: Systematic and meta-analytic review of brief contact interventions for reducing self-harm, suicide attempts and suicide. *The British Journal of Psychiatry, 206*(3), 184–190.

Motto, J. A., & Bostrom, A. G. (2001). A randomized controlled trial of postcrisis suicide prevention. *Psychiatric Services, 52*(6), 828–833.

For More Information

To learn more about how to help the suicidal person, visit this book's companion website: www.helpingthesuicidalperson.com. The site contains information about books, trainings, online courses, webinars, educational websites, and other resources for enhancing your skills in suicide assessment and intervention.

Index

Attempted Suicide Short Intervention
Program *see* ASSIP
attorneys, consultation with 135
autobiographical memory 194
autonomy needs 159

Beck Hopelessness Scale 66, 68
Beck, Aaron 61, 66, 196, 202, 234
Beck, Judith 194, 196, 198, 203, 204, 209
behavioral activation 196, 225, 227; and
  values 229–31
behavioral chain analysis 33, 196, 220,
  238–40, 257
behavioral incident technique 31, 33
belongingness needs 141, 146, 162–3
Bennett, Sara 250
biases about suicide 3, 5–7, 250
bipolar disorder and chronic suicidality
  143
Black women: suicide risk 86, 88–9
Blauner, Susan Rose 168, 214
body chemistry, changing naturally 218
Bongar, Bruce 19, 108, 129, 132, 134,
  159–60
borderline personality disorder 47, 112,
  143, 144, 219
Bostrom, Alan 261
boundaries: 16, 19; and increased contact
  140–1
breathing exercises, 218, 221–2
Brent, David 128
Britton, Peter 125
broaden and build positive emotions 225–8
Brown, Gregory 66, 119, *121*, 184, 196
Bryan, Craig 28, 81, 95, 100
Burns, David 195, 198

C-SSRS (Columbia Suicide Severity Rating
  Scale) 66–7, 152
calming response 218
Campo-Engelstein, Lisa 131
CAMS (Collaborative Assessment and
  Management of Suicidality) 3, 46–8, 67,
  138, 173
CASE (Chronological Assessment of
  Suicide Events) approach 64–5
catastrophizing 163, 199, 204
"catch", the 175–6
CBT (cognitive behavior therapy) 3, 163,
  196; acceptance of suicidal thoughts
  214–16; acceptance-based cognitive
  behavior therapies 202; behavior chain
  analysis 33, 196; behavioral activation
  196, 225, 229–31; and belongingness
  163; cautions about 200, 204–5, 227;

challenging negative thoughts 196,
  202–6; cognitive constriction 194, 195,
  196; cognitive distortions 194, 195, 196,
  198–201; coping statements 186, 196,
  207–8, 209–10; and hope 186; and hope
  boxes 196; impact on suicide rates 196;
  for mental health professionals 14;
  overgeneral autobiographical memory
  194, 195; and perceived burdensomeness
  163; perfectionism 194, 195; poor
  problem-solving 194, 195; and positive
  thinking 204 relapse prevention protocol
  196; rescripting suicidal imagery 196,
  209–11; thought suppression 212–13;
  trauma-focused cognitive behavior
  therapy 248
chain analysis *see* behavioral chain analysis
child protection services 109, 128
children: access to firearms 72, 128;
  confidentiality rules 79; hospitalization
  108, 109, 112; safety plans 120, 153
Chiles, John 53, 112, 171, 179–80, 186, 241,
  254
chronic pain 148
chronic suicidal ideation or suicidality:
  134, 143–4, 219; and increased contact
  141; treatment planning 143–4
chronic suicide risk 99–100, 103, 104; 107,
  134; Chronological Assessment of
  Suicide Events *see* CASE
Chu, Joyce 86, 87
coercion 19, 46–7
cognitive behavior therapy *see* CBT
  cognitive behavior theory 194
cognitive constriction 181, 194, 195, 196
cognitive defusion 214
cognitive distortions 162–3, 194, 195,
  198–201, 204, 205
cognitive processing therapy 156
Cognitive Therapy for Suicidal Patients 196
cognitive therapy for suicide prevention
  189
cold water application 218
Cole-King, Alys 31
collaboration 46–8, 118, 125, 160, 163
Collaborative Assessment and
  Management of Suicidality *see* CAMS
  Columbia Suicide Severity Rating Scale
  see C-SSRS
command hallucinations 61, 76, 97, 108
competence: of mental health professionals
  1, 14; and hope 186; psychological need
  159
confidentiality: children and adolescents
  79; consultation 135; exceptions 79;

Taylor & Francis eBooks

Helping you to choose the right eBooks for your Library

Add Routledge titles to your library's digital collection today. Taylor and Francis ebooks contains over 50,000 titles in the Humanities, Social Sciences, Behavioural Sciences, Built Environment and Law.

Choose from a range of subject packages or create your own!

Benefits for you

» Free MARC records
» COUNTER-compliant usage statistics
» Flexible purchase and pricing options
» All titles DRM-free.

Benefits for your user

» Off-site, anytime access via Athens or referring URL
» Print or copy pages or chapters
» Full content search
» Bookmark, highlight and annotate text
» Access to thousands of pages of quality research at the click of a button.

REQUEST YOUR FREE INSTITUTIONAL TRIAL TODAY	**Free Trials Available** We offer free trials to qualifying academic, corporate and government customers.

eCollections – Choose from over 30 subject eCollections, including:

Archaeology	Language Learning
Architecture	Law
Asian Studies	Literature
Business & Management	Media & Communication
Classical Studies	Middle East Studies
Construction	Music
Creative & Media Arts	Philosophy
Criminology & Criminal Justice	Planning
Economics	Politics
Education	Psychology & Mental Health
Energy	Religion
Engineering	Security
English Language & Linguistics	Social Work
Environment & Sustainability	Sociology
Geography	Sport
Health Studies	Theatre & Performance
History	Tourism, Hospitality & Events

For more information, pricing enquiries or to order a free trial, please contact your local sales team:
www.tandfebooks.com/page/sales

Routledge
Taylor & Francis Group

The home of
Routledge books

www.tandfebooks.com